D0926652

CENTRAL

LOLLY SUSI

THE CENTRAL BOOK

ADDITIONAL RESEARCH BY

KEITH SKINNER

OBERON BOOKS
LONDON

First published in 2006 by Oberon Books
in association with the Central School of Speech and Drama
Oberon Books Ltd, 521 Caledonian Road, London N7 9RH
Tel: 020 7607 3637 / Fax: 020 7607 3629
e-mail: info@oberonbooks.com / www.oberonbooks.com
Central School of Speech and Drama, University of London
The Embassy Theatre, Eton Avenue, Swiss Cottage, London NW3 3HY
Text copyright © The Central School of Speech and Drama 2006
Photographs copyright © the copyright holders

A catalogue record for this book is available from the British Library.

ISBN: 1 84002 710 X / 978-1-84002-710-5

Printed in Great Britain by Antony Rowe Ltd, Chippenham.

CONTENTS

*Plate sections of photographs can be found
between pages 96 and 97 and between
pages 160 and 161.*

ACKNOWLEDGEMENTS

I WANT FIRST TO THANK Gary Crossley, who not only conceived of a book on Central's history, but also believed I could write it. I would also like to thank the many Central staff who gave of their time and their expertise, including Rose Faria, Meg Ryan, Tony O'Dowd, Peter Collett, Stephen Sageman, and a special thanks to Susan Emanuel, who responded graciously to endless requests and intrusions. My thanks also go to Keith Skinner for his helpful additional research, and to my editor, Linda Cookson, for her unfailing patience and support.

My special thanks go to my agents Simon Trewin and Nicky Stoddart at Peters, Fraser and Dunlop. Thank you, Rick Lipton, for so generously lending your library and sharing your knowledge, and Jacqueline Cowdrey, archivist at the Royal Albert Hall, for allowing me access to the Hall's archives and its backstairs. My gratitude goes to Martin Worth for sharing his mother's, Muriel Wigglesworth's, documents and personal memorabilia. Thanks to Christine Caldwell for her memories and photo collection of Central's Exeter evacuation years, and to Mark Jones, Robert Grange, Trevor Bentham, Colin Burnie and Jodi Myers for their additional material. I am most grateful to the many people who so generously gave of their time to share with me their Central memories, including: Bridget Davies, Patty Miller, Caroline Cornish, John Clotworthy, Birdie Valdez, Vera Sargent, George Hall, John Jones, Renee Hosking, Debbie Scully, Linda Cookson, Darren Lawrence, Graham Norton, Virginia Snyders, Bardy Thomas, George Kitson, Robert Fowler, Sally Grace, Alan Marston, Stephen Sageman, Simon Quarterman, Sally Mackey, Elaine Hodkinson, Joan Haines, Livvy Wilson-Dickson, Bill Hobbs, Adele Bailey, David Carey, Geoffrey Colman, Ross Brown, Nickolas Grace, Sara Kestelman and Lionel Guyett. My deep appreciation goes to all those who contributed their written reminiscences for this book.

Thank you to my brother, Peter, who made me laugh when I was overwhelmed, and deepest gratitude to my dear friends – Paris Jefferson, Adrienne Thomas, Francine Morgan, Kim Thomson, Carol Harvey, Douglas Moffat, Harriet Thorpe, Mike Yeaman, Tom Knight, George and Leah Newhouse, Michael Fendler and Mindy Loveitt – who for endless months not only put up with my anxieties about 'the book', but also gave me their continued support through phone calls, dinners and, of course, laughter.

Lolly Susi, 2006

1

1865–1906

ANY HISTORY of the Central School of Speech and Drama must begin with an overview of its extraordinary and far-sighted founder, Elsie Fogerty.

Her portrait, which hangs in the foyer of the Embassy Theatre, shows us a stern and elderly matron with a downwardly curved nose, intense eyes, and a distant, benevolent smile. Those who knew her said she never seemed to change. Short and stout, with hair that seemed always to have been grey, or going grey, or nearly grey, she was 41 years old when she started Central. Miss Fogerty must always have seemed old to her young students, but, in spite of her 'advanced age', she was active, agile and full of energy. She had a quick intelligence, a powerful personality, a rich, deep voice and an irascible, often terrifying, temper. Yet she could also be intensely feminine. She had graceful, expressive hands, and though plump and almost pigeon-shaped, she was compact and glided as though on rollers on her tiny, delicate feet. A former student remembered: 'She had a funny little trick of standing on one foot with the other tucked round the ankle, her hands together palms inward; head slightly on one side, she then peeped up at tall young men, laughing and teasing.' She may sometimes have played the coquette, but she did not always inspire affection. She did at all times, though, command respect. Elsie Fogerty was perhaps more Napoleonic than diminutive, and it's hard to imagine this imposing figure as a young girl.

• • •

In 1865, the electric light had not been invented, the American Civil War had just ended, and on 16 December Anna Elizabeth Fogerty was born in Sydenham, England. Unable to pronounce 'Elizabeth', she called herself Elsie. Later, students would call her Miss Fogerty to her face – and 'Fogie' behind her back – but her close friends and colleagues always called her 'Foge'.

Fogerty's parents were from Ireland. Joseph, a successful architect and civil engineer was often away working, and his wife, Hannah, a charming, intelligent woman, fourteen years younger than her husband, was an enthusiastic part-time student at the nearby Crystal Palace School of Art and Literature.

The Crystal Palace would figure greatly in Elsie's early life. It was originally built in 1851 in Hyde Park for the Exhibition of the Works and Industry of All Nations, but when the 'Great Exhibition' closed, the glass and iron building was bought by a consortium, then dismantled, enlarged and re-erected in a 200-acre park on a hill in Sydenham. Crystal Palace Park took its name from the building and consisted of lawns, lakes, mazes, grottoes and groves. The fountains gave gushing displays at appointed times, grand fireworks displays started the year Elsie was born, and on a six-acre island in a man-made lake stood, and still stand, life-size replicas of reptiles and dinosaurs. While the building provided a centre for education, art, music and exhibitions, the grounds hosted Crystal Palace Football Club and London County Cricket, providing Fogerty not only with a strong educational grounding in the arts but also an abiding interest in cricket.

An only child, Fogerty's early life was comfortable. Her mother was devoted to her, and although her father's work often took him abroad, it afforded the family a cook/domestic servant, and a housemaid. The nurse-governess was Swiss-French, and so at a very young age Elsie became fluent in both French and English. With her great 'ear' for languages, she would later easily learn German, Latin and Greek. Educated privately at a day school in Sydenham, Elsie took Highest Honours in her Junior and Senior University Certificates.

It was not a time when women were allowed to have careers, unless they needed to, so it is impossible to know what the Fogertys wanted for their intelligent daughter – other than marriage. Her mother encouraged Elsie's love of literature, music, poetry and Shakespeare, but although her father was happy to pay for music and elocution lessons, he strongly disapproved of any theatrical aspirations. His daughter, however, had strong ideas of her own, and she later wrote in her memoirs: '…I kept my plans to myself and hoped for the best.'

Drama schools did not yet exist, so Fogerty found training where she could, with a number of well-known specialist teachers. She took singing lessons from Alfred Blume and Henry Blower, music lessons from Alice Clinton, and drama lessons from a successful leading actor of the day – the American, Henri Vezin. As one of Fogerty's colleagues later recounted: 'Her teacher would stand on the hearthrug and say, "Hence home you idle Romans, get you home," and she at the other end of the room would say, "Hence home you idle Romans, get you home," and when you could no longer tell the difference between Henri Vezin at sixty and Elsie Fogerty at eighteen, you were doing very nicely.' [Elsie Fogerty Memorial Lecture, 1978]

Dramatic recitals given by enthusiastic amateurs were a very popular, even respectable, form of theatre in late-Victorian society, so when in 1884 Fogerty's vicar organised a series of Shakespeare 'evenings', there could be no question of parental censure. For the first public reading, the young vicar at Lower Sydenham, Russell Wakefield, was invited into the group to play Romeo to Fogerty's Juliet. She wrote many years later: 'My Romeo, from his boyhood, had been a pupil of Mrs Dallas-Glynn, the last of the Kemble tradition; he had a keen sense of humour; years of schooling in France and Germany had cleared away the pomposity of the old 'Elocution'; and a gift which could have placed him among the foremost of English actors made it a delight to work with him.' Fogerty remembered her first public presentation: '…That night I knew I could do it; that somehow – somewhere I must go on doing it for the rest of my life.'

The public readings continued throughout that winter, but when they were over, the group persuaded Wakefield to carry on teaching informal classes in dramatic and lyric speaking. For the next three years, he would provide Fogerty with her first tantalizing glimpse of what acting could be without the overpowering Victorian emphasis on grand gestures and over-coloured elocution. Along the way, Wakefield and Fogerty developed a deep and lasting friendship.

• • •

Elsie's father had spent a lot of time and a great deal of his own money designing an overhead electric railroad for the city of Vienna, and when in 1884 the Austrian Government cancelled the project, Joseph lost his entire investment. Very likely as a result, he suffered a severe stroke. His wife would care for him until his death in 1899, and his 19-year-old daughter was forced to become the family breadwinner. The Fogertys moved to humbler quarters, and with the help of friends, Elsie soon found work teaching the dramatic skills of which her father had so disapproved.

Her old music teacher, Alice Clinton, was the first to hire Fogerty – to teach diction to her adopted daughter, Muriel Elliot. Elliot would remain Elsie's lifelong friend, colleague and artistic collaborator, but in those early days of financial hardship, it was Alice Clinton's friendship that proved most valuable. When Alice's sister, Lucy Clinton, took over Hyde Park College, Fogerty was employed to give diction and elocution classes to the school's young ladies, and it soon became clear that Fogerty was a natural teacher. She gained experience and confidence, her reputation spread, and as more and more work came her way, she was soon able to move her family to more comfortable surroundings. In 1889, Vicar Russell Wakefield was hired to teach literature at the Crystal Palace School, and he recommended his young friend to teach elocution. Here, too, Fogerty's classes flourished. By the mid-1890s, she was teaching elocution at a number of institutions: Halliwick Manor and Levana (two of the first girls' finishing schools), Effingham House School, The Ivy in Wimbledon, The Elms in South London, and as far away as Kenton College in Folkestone. She would teach her classes at Crystal Palace, then rush north to Mill Hill, south to Wimbledon or Ascot, then travel 75 miles by train to Folkestone – visiting two or three schools while in each area. Considering how long it takes even now to cover these distances, it must then have been an exhausting schedule.

Fogerty had a hearty constitution, but she also possessed a quiet, deep faith, and no matter how busy she became earning a living, she always gave freely of her time and energy to good causes. In these early years, she offered free Elocution classes at Crystal Palace to the Church of England's Band of Hope – a Christian temperance league for children – and, asking only the most modest of personal expenses, she also began to provide diction and elocution lessons to the junior clergy, a practice that continued well into her old age.

Now, though, Fogerty was still young, and her great love remained the theatre. She had not dared risk the economic security of her family by becoming a full-time professional actress but, as her reputation as a teacher flourished, she occasionally indulged her passion. During the 1890s, she worked with a number of actors and directors (then called producers) who would influence her later voice and actor training, but perhaps the most significant of these was, as Fogerty described him, 'that strange, vague genius', the legendary producer, William Poel.

Born in London in 1852, Poel had spent his early years as an actor, but he truly made his mark when, in 1881, he famously produced the First Quarto of *Hamlet* – without scenery. In 1884, he formed the Elizabethan Stage Society, and his Society productions helped revolutionise the speaking and producing of Shakespeare. Victorian audiences had been used to seeing edited versions of Shakespeare's plays, but this did not always assure them of a short evening in the theatre. With every act (often every scene) set with sumptuous and cumbersome backgrounds, the action stopped as costumes and scenery were changed. Productions often went on for hours. Poel, on the other hand, insisted that speeches, scenes and acts continued without a break, and he wanted to refocus the audience's attention away from the visual and back to the auditory. His Elizabethan sets

ELOCUTION IN 1845

The following appeared in a 1933 *Viva Voce*, reprinted from an early book on Elocution, *The Principles of Elocution*, with a selection of pieces, by William Graham, teacher of elocution in the Naval and Military Academy, and the Scottish Institution for the Education of Ladies.

Elocution as a department of ornamental education is the art of speaking and reading according to a certain established standard of elegance...

In common conversation, our tone is light, and appears to come from the lip; in serious and impressive speaking, it appears to be formed farther back, and is accompanied by a greater tension of the muscles of the throat. This deeper formation of the voice is the secret of that peculiar tone which is found in actors and orators of celebrity. Some have this tone naturally, but the greater number must acquire it by assiduous practice. This peculiar voice, which is adapted to the expression of what is solemn, grand, and exciting, is formed in those parts of the mouth posterior to the palate, bounded below by the root of the tongue, above by the commencement of the palate, behind by the posterior part of the throat, and on the sides by the angles of the jaw. The tongue, in the meantime, is hollowed and drawn back, and the mouth is opened in such a manner as to favour the enlargement of the cavity described as much as possible.

The extract goes on to describe three kinds of reading:

Plain speaking, Ornamental reading, and Impassioned reading,

gives an example of gestures:

...in the suspension of a sentence, the hand may take an upward slide; while at the completion, the hand may sink in a line with the breast,

and includes exercises for the emotions, that use short extracts from poems and are headed by titles such as:

...Mournfulness – Despondency – Low, soft, middle tone, tremulous; Fear without guilt – Very low, slow, the whole tone sustained; Guilty Fear – Low, slow, harsh, the voice at times aspirated; Courage – High, loud, slow.

had two levels, which included an inner curtained area as well as a platform projecting into the audience, and there was little or no scenery. The actors wore Elizabethan dress. Whereas Victorian actors had alternated between a tragic, booming rant and an agreeable, comic chattiness, Poel encouraged rapid, musical speech, and urged his actors to stress for meaning and not just accommodate the accent of the line. However, there was a catch. This required a vocal strength and flexibility from Poel's actors that he was unable to impart within a limited rehearsal period, and so rehearsals often consisted of his teaching the fixed 'tunes' of the lines as he heard them. This was not a technique suited to everyone, but Fogerty was enthralled. In 1895, Fogerty played Viola to Lillah McCarthy's Olivia in Poel's production of *Twelfth Night*, and McCarthy – one of England's great beauties and in the early 20th century one of its most famous actresses – wrote of that experience: 'Elsie had a fine voice and spoke the exquisite poetry beautifully; even then her rhythm and diction were a fine example to us all. Later, when we had become great friends, she told me she had attended the rehearsals of all of Poel's productions, making notes on emphasis, speed, rhythm which he insisted on, and giving her excellent groundwork for her own teaching.' [1945 Memorial Issue, *Viva Voce*]

During this same period, Fogerty also worked with an actor who would figure greatly in her own future and that of her School. In 1900, while appearing as Josebeth in Racine's *Atalie* for the London-based American producer, Charles Fry, she met the young actor, Lewis Casson. Casson and his wife, Sybil Thorndike, became one of England's most famous acting couples, and throughout their lives they would support Fogerty and the Central School. Casson was one of Central's earliest Governors, Sybil Thorndike took private 'lessons' from Fogerty, and Sybil's sister, Eileen Thorndike, later taught at Central. Two of the Casson children trained at the School.

Though the date is reported differently in different sources, it was most likely during these busy years that Fogerty also studied for a short while at the Conservatoire de Musique et de Déclamation in Paris. The Conservatoire prepared young actors for entry to the Comedie Française, and only a limited number of foreign students were admitted to audit courses. It was an honour to be accepted, even if only as an observer. Conservatoire training fundamentally influenced Fogerty's later work – whether she incorporated it, developed it or actively rejected it. As she wrote later for the introduction to her own translation of Coquelin's *The Art of the Actor*: 'The defect of the Conservatoire method was to give the impression that there was a certain secret style and interpretation which was handed on by a teacher and impressed upon a pupil, and which consisted almost altogether of tricks: tricks of voice, tricks of movement, above all tricks of business – the most dangerous snare of the accomplished actor... One is conscious that the secret of the actor's success does not lie in any of these things, but rather in the development of that gift of supreme 'make believe', innate in the human mind, out of which grew myth and art...the faculty of projecting one's whole personality on to an imaginative plane where life is re-created to our will, as opposed to the real plane which dominates, cribs, cabins and confines our will... This is the emotional concentration by which imagination controls the whole field of actions, mental and physical.'

It seems obvious that Fogerty was devoted to the art of acting, but as much as she loved it, she rarely appeared professionally. She played Tilly in *One Summer's Day* at the Comedy Theatre in 1897, and in 1899, she appeared as Estrild (described in the programme as a 'meek slave with passion and unresisting affection') in Swinburn's *Locrine*. Lillah McCarthy played Guendolen in this production, later calling it one of Poel's greatest triumphs, but no matter how prestigious the work, Fogerty could not count on an occasional job to pay the bills. Besides, although she may have been a good actress, her reputation as a teacher was exceptional. A rare opportunity in this field now presented itself.

During the last years of the 19th century, a Mrs Fairfax taught one of the most successful voice and speech classes in England at the Royal Albert Hall. When Fairfax died in 1898, Fogerty applied to become tenant of the now vacant rooms. Permission was granted, and Fogerty began the first of her Albert Hall Saturday classes: 'There followed the sickening wait for two or three weeks with no pupils. Then, one little lady of about thirteen, brought by her mother, started with private lessons: never have I had a pupil with quite her concentration and industry! Her hair was a glory of copper, her eyes were green – though her name was Hazel – and she was destined to go far... Very soon several of the students from Sydenham came up for extra classes, and gradually London began to take notice.' [Fogerty, Fogie]

WILLIAM POEL FESTIVAL

In 1952 a number of successful actors who had known and worked with Poel organised the first commemorative matinée performance at the Old Vic Theatre. Out of this grew an annual competition that was originally held only for students from Central and RADA, with prizes given for the best speech or Shakespeare duologue. The Society for Theatre Research William Poel Festival of Elizabethan and Jacobean Drama eventually began to include other drama schools, and it is now also open to undergraduates in university drama departments. Winners of the Festival prize for 2004 (Joseph Kennedy) and 2005 (Emilie Patry) were both students in their final year of the Acting Course at Central.

This first young pupil, Hazel Thompson, enjoyed a successful career on the stage, but from 1920 to 1949 she would serve on the Central School staff as teacher, Registrar, and its first Director of Dramatics. In her early years as a student, Thompson and her voice teacher formed a friendship that would last a lifetime. Besides her ability as an actress and her genius for teaching, it seems Fogerty also had a great talent for friendship.

• • •

After Joseph Fogerty's death in 1899, Elsie and her mother moved to a small flat at 29, Queensbury Place, South Kensington, to be closer to the Albert Hall. While caring for her husband, Hannah Fogerty had also acted as Elsie's private secretary – typing her original recitations and correspondence, and organising her diary. Intelligent and personable, Hannah was the perfect assistant, and until her death in 1910, dedicated herself entirely to taking care of her daughter's increasingly busy life. In the spring of 1903, mother and daughter travelled to Stratford-upon-Avon to attend two weeks of plays staged by Frank Benson in commemoration of Shakespeare's birthday.

Sir Frank Benson (he was knighted in 1916) had been born in 1858. While at Oxford, he gained notoriety amongst the professional theatre community with his production of *Agamemnon*, which was performed in the original Greek, and after his graduation and a short engagement with Henry Irving at the Lyceum Theatre, he joined a Shakespearean touring company. In 1883, the manager left the company stranded and owing creditors, and Benson's well-to-do father sent money to buy the scenery and costumes. From this was formed the Frank Benson Company.

Benson's company presented innovative and short productions of Shakespeare's plays that, like Poel's, had minimum scenery and a continuity of action. At the height of Benson's popularity, he had as many as three companies on the road at once, and in 1901, he began his famous touring Shakespearean School for younger members of the company. This School continued until just before Benson's death in 1939, and many of the greatest actors of the early 20th century started on tour with Frank Benson, becoming what were known as 'Old Bensonians'.

Benson had initiated the annual Stratford Festivals in 1886, and was responsible for them almost every year until 1919, transforming them along the way from local to international and from two-week to three-monthly events. Though Fogerty had known of Benson, they did not meet until 1903: 'We stayed at the Shakespeare Inn that perfect spring; and somehow one got to know everybody, for the visit was a pilgrimage to us all…there we met Benson – to whom, more than to anyone else, we owe the revival of Shakespearean acting in this country… He had a delightful company – eager young actors, most of them new to the job; but the short season there was followed by a tour which gradually lengthened until it really became a year's engagement. Frank Benson kept his young players working as students, but was not satisfied with the standard they attained in the basic technique of speech and movement: and as the Tour grew longer and the Stratford season more exciting, he felt he needed more preliminary work. Sir Herbert Tree had just founded his Academy of Dramatic Art, with the intention of giving aspirants to the English stage a chance of technical training equal to that offered by the Paris Conservatoire. So Frank Benson determined to open a regular school in London, to give his people a preliminary grounding before he took them into the Tour.' [*Viva Voce*]

In 1904, Benson opened the London branch of his Shakespearean touring school, and Fogerty was engaged to teach speech and diction. Some of Fogerty's students from the Albert Hall attended classes in dramatic training at Benson's School in Hampstead. Within a year, however, it had become apparent not only that the London School was taking too much of Benson's attention away from his touring company, but also that many of the School's young students were only biding their time until they could join the company on tour. The School was not a success.

Meanwhile, Fogerty's Albert Hall classes were thriving. She had hired the daytime use of the little theatre over the West Porch, and the stage and theatre lighting had gradually been restored. '…I asked Sir Frank if I might take his remaining students to the Albert Hall, and suggested that – if he would become President – we could found a dramatic school with a full training course and examinations. To my great joy, he agreed, and

DRAMA SCHOOLS

Webber Douglas Academy began in 1906 as an opera training school in Paris, before moving to London in 1926. The London Academy of Music gave acting lessons in the first decade of the 20th century (and for a short while was a tenant of the Hampstead Conservatoire before the building was converted into the Embassy Theatre in 1927), only adding 'Dramatic Art' to its name in 1938, when William Foulis started a one-year full-time acting course. Some drama was taught at the Guildhall School of Music, and it added 'Drama' to its title in 1935. Sarah J Thorne, actress and manager of both the Theatre Royal Margate and her own touring company, taught drama at her School of Acting in Margate from 1879 until shortly before her death in 1899. Actor and producer Sir Phillip Ben Greet ran an Academy of Dramatic Art that accompanied his touring company; and Henry Irving and Ellen Terry both had schools attached to their companies.

promised to examine for us. So came into being the Central School of Speech-Training and Dramatic Art – in 1906. We chose our title to indicate the intention of finding a definite central body of principles for a stage training, avoiding extremes of theory of practice: and we held to our conviction that a proper training in Speech must come first. This first intention we have maintained – through expansion and development far beyond anything we had anticipated.'

2

1906–1913

WHEN ELSIE FOGERTY FOUNDED the Central School of Speech-Training and Dramatic Art at the Royal Albert Hall in 1906, she was 41 years old – only six years older than the building itself.

In 1850, Queen Victoria had established a Royal Commission – with Prince Albert as President – to plan the Exhibition of the Works and Industry of all Nations in Hyde Park. The Crystal Palace was built to house this 'Great Exhibition', and from 1 May to 11 October 1851 it had more than six million visitors and made a profit of over £186,000. Inspired by this success, Prince Albert began to imagine a further massive development entirely devoted to industry, education and the arts and sciences. With proceeds from the sale of Crystal Palace, as well as the Exhibition profits and some assistance from Parliament, the Royal Commission purchased Lord Gore's 87-acre estate in South Kensington for £327,500.

Henry Cole had worked closely with Prince Albert on other public projects, so when the Prince died of typhoid fever in 1861, it fell to Cole to promote the Royal Commission's plan to establish permanent institutions on the site. One of these, a great Central Hall of Arts and Sciences, was to be based architecturally on the Roman Coliseum and was designed to hold 30,000 people. When this plan was discarded as impractical, a final design by Colonel Henry Scott RE was accepted. Based on a Roman amphitheatre, it was designed to hold a mere 7,000.

In 1867, Queen Victoria laid the foundation stone for this Central Hall but, still grieving for her husband, at the last minute the Queen changed 'Central' to 'Royal Albert', and four years later, the Royal Albert Hall of Arts and Sciences – to give it its full title – opened to the public.

Throughout its early years, the Royal Albert Hall struggled to remain self-sufficient, and the letting of the Hall and its rooms covered the costs of maintaining the building and the payment of its staff. It hosted amateur boxing matches, bazaars, films, exhibitions, balls, baptisms and sporting events, as well as concerts, ballets, symphonies and the Proms. It may have been a beneficial financial arrangement for the Albert Hall to provide premises for Fogerty and her School, but it could also be said that the contract fulfilled part of the Hall's original remit: to support the development of the Arts 'for productive industry'.

Located on Kensington Gore in South Kensington, the Royal Albert Hall is oval-shaped, with a dome and four major entrances – North, South, East and West. A Royal Horticultural Society Conservatory was originally attached to the South Porch, but it fell into disrepair and was finally torn down in 1899. (A new South Entrance opened in 2004.) The North Porch faces Hyde Park and the Prince Albert Memorial, and was originally the Royal Entrance. Like the West and East Porches, the arches over the entranceways were built wide and fifty feet high to admit carriages and allow patrons to alight under cover. Once inside, they could take any of a number of hydraulic lifts, each large enough to take twenty members of the public to any tier. Later these lifts were stabilised, with only one remaining operational to move food and beverages to the upper tier bars, and when the Central School had important (even Royal) visitors, they were unceremoniously brought up to the Balcony level via the remaining 'goods lift'.

From 1951, students were asked to use the West entrance, but in the early days Central School staff, students

1906	The first theatrical union formed as Variety Artistes' Federation
	The Baker Street and Waterloo (Bakerloo) Line, a line from Hammersmith to Finsbury Park via Piccadilly, part of the new Victoria Station and the New Vauxhall Bridge open
	San Francisco's Great Earthquake
	Theatre includes Mrs Patrick Campbell in *The Bondman* by Hall Caine at Drury Lane; Herbert Beerbohm Tree and Constance Collier in *Antony and Cleopatra* at Her Majesty's Theatre; Ellen Terry in *Captain Brassbound's Conversion* at the Court Theatre in Sloane Square.
	Popular songs include 'It's the Motorcar', 'In the Shade of the Old Apple Tree' and 'The Flying Machine'
	Greta Garbo and Samuel Beckett are born; Henrik Ibsen dies
	Notices on beaches read: 'Bathing dresses must extend from the neck to the knees'
1907	The Actors' Union is formed
1908	Miss Annie Hornimann, the tea heiress, takes over the Gaiety Theatre and establishes the first modern repertory theatre in Manchester
1909	Diaghilev Russian Ballet season starring Nijinsky in Paris
	Victoria and Albert Museum is completed
	State old age pensions are first paid out
	Kenneth Barnes becomes Principal of RADA
1910	Edward VII dies
	Robert Baden Powell starts the Boy Scouts
1911	Mona Lisa stolen from the Louvre
1912	Invention of the translucent stage curtain called scrim
	SS Titanic sinks
1913	Actors' Equity Association formed in USA

and visitors entered via the main North Porch entrance, which was manned by a commissionaire. Vera Sargent, known to all but students as Sarge, was Fogerty's secretary from 1930 and Central's longest serving Registrar and Company Secretary from 1939 to 1967. She recalled the early days at the Hall: 'Normally one could go in the front entrance, and Captain Hook was there – with his false hand. He was the doorman, not just for us but for the entire Hall. You'd go in, and up these circling stairs. On one side there was the King's Room, where we had Governors' Meetings and other important events, and on the other side you went up to the School, which had rooms on every floor. We had a Common

Room, and there were two large rooms, one that went right behind the organ, which you occasionally heard being played.'

Looking at the building from Hyde Park, to the right of the dome is the West Porch entrance, and the windows directly above the arches were located backstage of what became Central's Theatre. In 1901, it was advertised in an Albert Hall Prospectus: 'The Theatre, situated over the West Porch, suitably fitted and decorated, and supplied with electric light, may be hired for Dramatic and Operatic Performances, Private Theatricals, Tableaux Vivants, Concerts, Lectures, Meetings, and other Entertainments; and, with the spacious and lofty Crush Rooms adjoining as Retiring and Supper Rooms, for Balls, Cinderellas, Conversaziones, Wedding Breakfasts, Receptions, & c.'

The West Porch/Central Theatre is now the Elgar Restaurant. During 2003 renovations, the ceiling was taken down above what used to be the stage, and parts of Central's lighting gantry still remained. In the early years of the School, the theatre was used in the daytime by the Central School, but hired out by Hall management in the evenings, by which time students were expected to have removed their personal belongings from the cloakrooms. As the School grew in the 1930s, Central hired sole use of the little theatre, and the dressing rooms below the stage were fitted with student lockers.

As one entered the Central Theatre from the Albert Hall Balcony (now called the Circle) corridor, the fan-shaped room backing onto the corridor was the auditorium. The raised section, directly over the West Porch, was the stage – 40' 2" wide, 18' 4" deep, with a Proscenium of 21' 16". The 1901 Prospectus notes: 'When required to be used as a Ball Room the whole or part of the stage floor can be lowered to the level of the auditorium.' By the time Central took over the theatre, the stage was permanent, and an entrance through the stage floor provided access via a staircase to the space below, which now houses the Albert Hall archive offices. Called the Porch Room, this cramped space was used variously as a library/classroom combined and as a dressing room for School productions. With no similar space under any of the other Porches, a curious Albert Hall Manager once decided to investigate the creation of this unusual space. All he could find out was that 'Miss Fogerty had once taken the architect out to lunch'. [Elsie Fogerty Memorial Lecture, 1978]

The small room next to the auditorium, House Right, was the first home to the Central canteen, but this canteen was also, at one point, beneath the stage. In the 1920s and 1930s, May – a middle-aged Irish lady in pink overalls – prepared student and staff refreshments, and looked after the cloakrooms.

Back along the corridor from the theatre towards the West stairs was the Upper Crush (now the North Circle Bar). When enrolment was at its height, Central had nine classrooms on three floors, as well as the Theatre, the dressing rooms beneath the stage, and daytime use of two public cloakrooms.

Fogerty taught most of her classes either in the Lower Crush (now the Concert Café) on the Grand Tier, or in the King's Room (Royal Retiring Room) across the corridor behind the Royal Box. Most other classes took place on the Balcony Level, in classrooms that could be accessed either through communicating doors or from the corridor. In the early years, the corridor doors were painted like the walls and therefore difficult for new students to locate in the dim light, and in the 2003 renovation, this paintwork was restored. Occasionally, students were allowed on the stage of the Hall itself, and it seems

LIVVY WILSON-DICKSON

" In Elsie Fogerty's verse speaking classes, we always hoped that the piece she had chosen for us to be assessed by her in the class would come after May had brought her tea, which consisted of a toasted, buttered bun and a cup of tea without milk or sugar. The butter on the bun was very lavishly spread, and Fogerty would have a little butter dribbling down her chin. This always put her in a better humour, and so you hoped you would be heard 'after the bun'. **"**

this was one of the more memorable events of student life. In preparation for Diction examinations, each student was sent to the conductor's rostrum, and Fogerty would sit in the Royal Box to take them through their paces. Livvy Wilson-Dickson (Stage '32) recalled: 'I remember doing my sonnet, and it sounded like a bat squeak. The voice from the Royal Box boomed down, "Speak along the floor, dear!" She meant, pitch your voice down, not up to the dome. If we spoke along the floor – "Shall I compare thee to a summer's day" – it would go right, and Elsie Fogerty could hear you.'

During her training, Livvy Wilson-Dickson (then Olive Rudder – stage name, Olivia Traverse) lived in a flat in Westbourne Terrace and walked across Hyde Park to get to the Hall. However, an integral part of the Central School for many female students was Queen Alexandra's House – to the right, and slightly behind the West Porch. Built by Sir Francis Cook in 1884 with the help of the Royal Commission, its purpose was to house female students of the Royal College of Art and the Royal College of Music – there were a number of pianos in practice rooms at the top of the house – as well as students in Needlework or the Sciences. Over the years, it was also home to a number of Central students and was remembered by a group of teacher-students from the early 1950s as 'The Virgins' Retreat'. The residence provided meals, a hand wash laundry (later washing machines), and a shop to buy cigarettes and sweets. The rooms were either single occupancy or, if you had to share, included a communal living space. Queen Alexandra's House still provides rooms for students studying at the Royal College of Art, and opens its doors to paying guests during the summer months.

• • •

When Central was founded in 1906, London theatre was changing. From the last decade of the 19th century, Fogerty had experimented to find a more natural approach to speech than the traditional Victorian, intoned elocution, but the theatre, too, was looking for a simpler, less declamatory style. Actor-dramatist Harley Granville-Barker and manager J E Vedrenne were at the forefront of this emerging theatrical movement. From 1904, four Vedrenne-Barker seasons at the (Royal) Court Theatre in Sloane Square gave nearly 1,000 performances of plays by dramatists such as George Bernard Shaw, John Masefield and Harley Granville-Barker. These productions were innovative for their naturalism, and from the early years of the 20th century, the Court began to provide some of the most cutting-edge theatre of its day.

It is unlikely that Fogerty would have missed these famous Court seasons. Her friend, Lillah McCarthy, was a leading actress in the company; and her first Albert Hall student, Hazel Thompson, was playing leading, as well as smaller, roles. Thompson recalled many years later:

> I was engaged as a regular member of the Vedrenne-Barker Repertory Company at the Court Theatre. Between 1904 and 1907, I played in eleven of the Shaw plays, most of them original productions, and understudied Ellen Terry in *Captain Brassbound's Conversion*. This was a fearsome job, though one felt it to be a great honour, as she had a way of not coming into the theatre till the five minutes had been called and one was feverishly beginning to dress. We did three of the Euripides tragedies, two plays by Ibsen, *Prunella* by Barker and Housman, two plays by Maurice Hewlett, two by St John Hankin, and plays by Yeats, Hauptmann, Masefield, and two by Granville Barker himself.

Shaw not only wrote plays for the company, but he also directed his and others' work, and for the first time devoted himself almost entirely to the theatre. During this productive and inspirational period, Shaw and Granville-Barker found another idea taking shape – an idea they shared with William Poel, Frank Benson and Elsie Fogerty – the desire for a National Theatre with a permanent home. Fogerty would continue to work towards this goal for the rest of her life, but in 1906 she had a more pressing project.

• • •

That spring and summer, Fogerty began to interview students for her new School, but more importantly – for this would shape Central's future – she also began to hire staff to share the increased teaching load. The first of these was Dr H Hulbert.

Dr Hulbert had always had a great love for the theatre, a passion he passed on to his two sons, Jack and Claude, who would both become well-known actors. Dr Hulbert had given numerous lectures in London on voice production, and Fogerty knew the focus of his work was the search for a method of controlled relaxation and effortless breathing.

As Fogerty recalled: 'About this time, scientists of many types were studying aspects of utterance, for it had become clear that the speech-mechanism was most intricate and vulnerable, and the analysis of speech was necessary. Also, the medical profession (Dr William Pasteur among the first) were considering the relief of brain-trouble resulting from the effects of accident or disease on speech. And our own Dr Hulbert – concerned in the universal struggle to discover some physical training to combat malformation of the chest before the incidence of consumption, and very interested in athletics – established a perfectly simple system of breathing exercises, quite different from the pernicious chest-stiffening arm movements of Swedish drill which actually restricted normal chest-expansion. Soon the medical profession recognised that this offered one of the best means of securing good rhythmic breathing in ordinary life, thus combating every form of chest trouble.' [*History of Central*, 21st Birthday Programme, 1927]

Fogerty always insisted the early years of Central were highly experimental, and she and Hulbert worked closely to find new methods of movement and voice training for actors. Dr Hulbert's work focused first on the physical, using exercises to strengthen and stretch. He next connected voice production to physical movement, and only then did he concentrate on the voice. Fogerty now combined her early work with Russell Wakefield and William Poel on text and her now quite extensive personal experience in voice with Hulbert's complementary system of movement and voice training. It may seem obvious to us today, but what she came up with was the revolutionary conclusion that movement and speech are inseparable. She would be often quoted as saying that speech is merely audible movement.

With Dr Hulbert in place, there were still a number of other subjects to be covered. Fogerty hired Ethel Radmar to teach Deportment, carrying on for Central what Elsie called 'the great d'Egville Michau tradition'. (Madame d'Egville Michau had been a 'professor' of dancing in Hove. Her treatise on the physical education of young ladies, published in 1861, was well known for its instruction in deportment, dancing and the social graces.) Theodore Filmer taught ballet, and a French fencing master was engaged to give fencing lessons. The first 'rehearsal masters', or directors, joined Central from the Benson School, and included a Mr Moss and Paul Berton. However, Fogerty also believed it was important for her students to train with actors and directors who had recently, or were currently, working in the professional theatre. She coerced and cajoled guest directors to work with her students in 'Rehearsal Classes', and was adept at getting others to work for very little pay – occasionally, even for free.

One might expect a certain amount of sacrifice in those early years of a new and exciting venture – a training school for actors – but for as long as she was Principal, Fogerty was never known for 'overpaying' her staff or her guest lecturers. She herself took no salary from the School for nearly twenty years, instead supporting herself and her mother by teaching privately. She continued to travel almost daily to give voice and

speech classes at schools and institutes in and around London, and in 1908, she started
giving fortnightly Friday classes at Roedean, near Brighton, which would continue for the
next 29 years. She also taught privately, and her private 'students' included many leading
actors of the day, as well successful as barristers, politicians and high-ranking members of
the clergy.

In addition to taking no salary from Central, Fogerty often contributed her own
money to hire specialists in anatomy and phonetics or to provide costumes and scenery
for productions. She also gave scholarships to students she felt demonstrated a special
talent, although the term 'scholarship' was used loosely and really only meant there would
be less money for the other things her School desperately needed.

• • •

In June 1906, before Central came into being, Fogerty produced a shortened version
of Swinburne's *Atalanta in Calydon* at Crystal Palace. Muriel Elliot was by that time an
accomplished musician, and Fogerty worked with her and the actors to find the rhythm
of the lines. Elliot composed the accompaniment, and the Chorus danced and sang the
lines on stage – aided in volume by a quartet of actors hidden out of sight in the orchestra
pit. Fogerty played Althea, Lewis Casson appeared as the Messenger; one of Fogerty's
private students from Crystal Palace, Ruby Ginner, led the chorus; Hazel Thompson
played Atalanta.

As a fundraiser for the English Society for Waifs and Strays, the production was a
tremendous success and played two performances at Crystal Palace and one matinée at the
Scala Theatre in London. Audiences were struck by what was then groundbreaking work
in speech and movement. By today's standards it would perhaps be considered corny – yet
it combined two of the most innovative theatrical trends of the time: the simplification of
design (as in the work of the revolutionary designer, Edward Gordon Craig) and the focus
on text (as with the work of William Poel). This reaction against Victorian scenic display,
and the adoption of the primacy of speech and acting, proved a great advertisement for
Fogerty's teaching and her new Central School. The production would be remounted in
Croydon five years later and play three matinées at the Lyceum Theatre in London.

For both productions of *Atalanta in Calydon*, the entire cast wore classical Athenian
dress. The lead actors were on a different level to the 15-woman Chorus, and at the
centre of this Chorus was the Altar of Dionysius. An unattributed review from the Central
archives of the 1911 production gives us an idea both of this production and the 1906
original. 'The Chorus was composed of a group of beautiful girls, who moved as we imagine
the Greek maidens moved of old – whose every action illustrated the emotion of the
moment, whose faces portrayed each shade of meaning given by the words, whose dancing
was the quintessence of grace, and whose singing was full of melody, clear and deep. There
was nothing mechanical or stereotyped in anything they did: each was individual – the

movements were different with each one. Some of them stood out even from the rest – where all were good – by their grace of their power of expression in face and limbs.'

Muriel Elliot had orchestrated her original music for string instruments, but, before one of the 1911 shows, Fogerty was informed that for some reason there could be no music at that performance. She called a rehearsal and drilled the Chorus to give their speeches to the metric beat previously laid down by Elliot's music. Fogerty remembered the resulting success as groundbreaking: 'Modern Choral Speaking had been born. We achieved a cadence to which it was possible to move – a veritable dance of words.' [*Fogie*] Central students would continue to excel in the art of choral speaking for another fifty years, but it was with this critically successful 1906 production that Central's unifying work in movement and speech first became known to the public, and it led to ever-increasing requests for Fogerty's teaching. However, even though her work in the theatre may have attracted young actors to her new School, from the outset the Central School of Speech-Training and Dramatic Art would develop in a way that set it apart from the few other theatrical training institutions then in existence.

When Fogerty taught at other schools, she often took her Central students to help, getting them to demonstrate exercises in breathing and elocution. She quickly realised that some of these earnest young actors were also very gifted teachers, and she heartily encouraged anyone with the interest and the talent. Central's teaching section gradually came into being. As early as 1912, an announcement in *The Times* of the forthcoming autumn term stressed: 'A special feature of the school is the training course for teachers in vocal and general physiology and the theory of voice production.'

That same year, Fogerty was asked to give weekly evening classes to 120 London County Council teachers at the Southampton Row Evening Institute. Billed as 'Dramatic Literature' and 'Elocution', these classes provided Central teacher-students with their first paid work, and out of these classes grew the 'Dramatic Circle Competition' that was mounted and run by Central's student organisation, the Pivot Club: 'These Competitions, which went on for years, are believed to be the first ever held for amateurs... When in 1918, the British Drama League was founded very largely through Elsie Fogerty's inspiration, their National Drama Festivals were started on the lines of the Pivot Competitions.' [*Fogie*]

· · ·

This brings us to the Pivot Club. At a 1939 Central Annual General Meeting, Ruby Ginner – one of Fogerty's earliest students at both the Crystal Palace and the Albert Hall, and long-time staff member at Central – spoke of the Pivot Club:

It was born in the autumn of 1906 and, like all great things, its beginnings came about in a very simple way. Two of Miss Fogerty's most devoted and enthusiastic students were sitting on the floor by the fire in a house in Norwood...talking about our great teacher and leader, and we decided that there must be an Old Girls' Club to keep us all in touch with Miss Fogerty and with one another. We did not do anything much that afternoon except get very excited about it all and decide there and then that as Miss Fogerty was the pivot round whom we all revolved, the Club should be called the 'Pivot Club'. That afternoon we also decided upon a motto which was: 'I prithee, sweet my Fog, be merry'...

After Becky [Amy Nankivell] and I had conceived the great idea we gathered a few more of the 'Chosen' to discuss the matter. Hazel Thompson was one of the first... Our next move was to ask Miss Fogerty to centralise operations by being 'The Pivot' and President. I remember so well her saying that it was lovely of us all to want to revolve round her, but that that sort of enthusiasm alone would not hold a thing together. She told us that if we wanted to form a club that would live, we must have some definite object to work for, and she suggested that we should form a fund to give training to those who had talent but no means to develop it – in fact a Scholarship Fund for the Central School. The idea was taken up with enthusiasm and the fund has...been responsible for producing some of Miss Fogerty's best people.

To fund their Scholarship, the Pivot Club put on a variety of plays and entertainments for a range of different audiences, at the same time providing the students with experience in both producing and performing. One of the Club's major tenets was to give 'pleasure, beauty and laughter to those poor and sick who have but little opportunity of such things in their lives,' so to fulfil this remit, Pivots would give an annual entertainment for children at a Mission in Notting Dale, which became known as a 'Slum Party'. The Club also published a regular newsletter, *Viva Voce*, which included news of its members, as well as a letter from their Principal and Pivot.

•   •   •

In 1906, Fogerty was a leading voice specialist in England, and she used her classes at Central to explore her emerging theories on voice and vocal naturalism. By 1912, she was willing to put the reputation of her School and her own teaching on the line, by inviting such eminent poets as Laurence Binyon, Gordon Bottomley and William Butler Yeats to adjudicate Central's annual Diction Examinations – the final presentations by Fogerty's verse speaking class. Having spent the Easter term teaching her young students not only to honour the metre and give balance to the music of the verse, but also to speak simply and convey its meaning, Fogerty had laid out for her students one of her most memorable tenets – the *matter* not the *manner*.

As well as simplicity in verse speaking, Fogerty sought for her students a more natural form of acting. Her observations at the Conservatoire de Musique et de Déclamation in Paris were of young actors mimicking their teacher's presentation of a part – much like art students being asked to reproduce the paintings of their masters and not dissimilar to her own early training with Henri Vezin. In her introduction to *The Art of the Actor*, Fogerty wrote: 'From the very beginning, a student was more or less fixed in a certain line of parts; the conventional types of the theatre of the day. ...This was not strictly type casting, rather a practical anticipation of the possibilities of the student's future career, based on his physical characteristics, vocal quality, height, mental affinities, etc.'

Almost everything taught at the Conservatoire was based around the student's study of a part and implied that a teacher could impart the 'secret' of a character through dictating sounds, movement and business. Fogerty believed that the true secret an actor must learn is his or her own imagination – an imagination so concentrated as to transform both mental and physical actions. 'What seems directly required is a more exact selection and an infinitely more searching training...which in the selected group shall give a perfect automatic control of mind and body, and enable the artist to concentrate freely on the mental conception of a part, secure that limbs, face, voice, diction, bearing and stage rhythm will adapt themselves to the intention of the mind as a skater's body does to his swing, or a dancer's to his musical pattern... An exhaustive vocal training which sets the voice in tune and leaves it safe from all mischance in any type of delivery; a physical training which will guarantee health, discipline and beauty throughout all the course of an artist's career; diction which can translate speech rhythm with the same accuracy as a singer can translate a musical line; style based on a knowledge of

PIVOT CLUB

The Pivot Club's aims, objectives and rules were formalised as the following:

1. To Pivot round the President. (Elsie Fogerty)
2. To maintain a fund for the 'Pivoting' of a student.
3. To organise entertainments for charitable purposes.
4. To provide a means by which all Pivots can keep in touch with each other, and thereby maintain a mutual interest in their dramatic and artistic pursuits.
5. Members must be past or present students or staff of the Central School.
6. That there be an Annual subscription of 3s 6d payable in January to the Honorary Treasurer.
7. Life membership, £3 3s 0d.
8. That there be an annual entertainment in aid of the Scholarship Funds.

The Pivot Club also awarded a three-year Pivot Scholarship to a worthy young student who had been previously taught by a Pivot. Candidates auditioned for a panel of Pivots, and the successful student was given either all or part of their Central fees. Money for this scholarship fund was raised through social events, but profits from these events were often not enough to keep the Club out of the red, much less provide a scholarship. Occasionally a generous ex-student would make a donation, but when things got particularly desperate, Elsie Fogerty would give a public recital, with all proceeds going to the Fund.

period, in drama, and with technical production; all this acquired early under conditions of deliberate experimental study, not by the accident of long runs which breed lethargy, and single week runs, which mean racked nerves and economic disaster.'

Fogerty believed that the actor must be at least a dual personality – the one who conceives the character and the one who realises the character – yet also somehow be able to watch, analyse and note at the moment of creation that which can be used in future creations. 'The really perfect technique becomes unconscious during rehearsal study, and…the actor is free to let himself go emotionally, if that method calls out his greatest gifts.'

Fogerty wrote all of this in 1932, post-Stanislavski, and these tenets may very well have come about with the benefit of hindsight. Nevertheless, whether or not one is prepared to believe that Fogerty was forming new concepts of actor training during the early years at the Central School, there can be no doubt she was a pioneer in another, more embryonic, subject.

● ● ●

At the centre of all Central actor and teacher training was Fogerty's abiding interest in voice and speech training. From her earliest years as a teacher, she had had students come to her with speech defects and, as a result, Fogerty began to forge links with medical specialists. She visited hospitals to consult with plastic surgeons and to observe their patients: accident victims, stammerers and those with congenital or degenerative diseases. She became, therefore, one of the first speech teachers to understand that disorders often came with certain neurological, as well as psychological, disorders. In the early years of the 20th century, she worked with the well-known phonetician, Daniel Jones, at University College London, to understand the analysis of phonetics. She became interested in breathing and in pacing the voice, and the effect that these might have on treatment. She became an expert in all facets of speech and voice production and used her range of vision to pull all of this disparate information together. In her search for information, she cast her net wide, and it was not long before the experts were coming to her for advice.

Fogerty was by no means the first British specialist to become involved with those suffering from speech defects. As early as 1906, the Local Education Authority in Manchester ran classes for people who stammered; and in the history of the Royal College of Speech and Language Therapists there is mention of work in the late 19th century in other parts of Great Britain for stammerers and deaf children. For the most part, however, remedial teachers and medical professionals worked in isolation, with no suitable forum to share their discoveries, classifications and methods. This isolation became increasingly obvious to Fogerty.

Often invited by doctors at St Thomas's Hospital to 'give lessons' to their patients, the more involved Fogerty became with the patients, the more she identified the profound confusion between the theoretical science and the practical application of speech training. Having recognised that professionals needed a forum not only to exchange ideas but also to encourage their enthusiasm and share their experiences, in 1910 she helped establish a Committee of Investigation at London University to look into the physiology of breathing. She and Dr Hulbert consulted University anatomists and physiologists, and one of these participants, Dr Charles Sherrington (and his work on the integrated action of the nervous system) forever influenced Fogerty's understanding of movement and voice. Two years later, Fogerty, Central and Bedford College for Women organised the first International Conference on Speech ever to be held in England. Out of this Conference came an invitation for Fogerty to read her paper 'The Faculty of Speech' at the 1913 Congress of the International School of Hygiene in Buffalo, New York. Her reputation was growing.

3

1913–1918

FOGERTY'S UNDERSTANDING of the voice was no longer solely practical, but it now also encompassed a wide-ranging medical knowledge of anatomy, physiology and psychology. Realising that speech problems could be caused by defects in any or all of a number of different areas, she formulated that a new kind of 'practical professional' must be created: 'From the beginning of the century, I was constantly being asked to take individual cases of serious speech-defect. Two London hospitals constantly appealed to us in cases of stammering children: it seemed almost impossible to get any guidance from the medical profession, yet I felt we did not know enough to be able to do real justice to these problems. Those of our students who had decided to become teachers were keenly interested; but there seemed a serious risk that we might slip into the kind of quackery which had had such ghastly results on the reputation of speech-training.' [Fogerty, *Viva Voce*]

Fogerty approached St Thomas's Hospital, and in 1914 they agreed to open a regular clinic on two afternoons a week. These clinics would allow Fogerty and her Central students to work out a scientific classification of speech defects and define a set of principles to underlie treatment.

The Royal College of Speech and Language Therapists note in their history that the clinic at St Thomas's Hospital started in the Lady Almoner's Department in 1909. An unofficial Central history later gave 1912 as the date for the first clinic. Fogerty herself once cited 1911. This conflict of dates perhaps merely reflects the less formalised nature of Fogerty's early work with patients. The Clinic at St Thomas's officially opened in 1914, but the less formal foundation, in the shape of private 'lessons' at the hospital, had long been laid.

No matter the exact date it began, this new clinic provided Central students with practical, supervised work in remedial speech. Problems of classification would remain for many years, but more importantly, from the earliest days in the clinic Fogerty and her 'remedial speech' students from Central not only adapted and developed established methods of treatment but also invented new ones. They gathered information into a cohesive system, recorded it, and carried it forward into what would become known as 'Speech Therapy'.

Daisy Harries, who had trained under Fogerty and was a founder member of the College of Speech Therapists, contributed the following to the Memorial Issue of the *Viva Voce* in 1945: 'It may be said that, even more than her writings on the subject, or her own work in the treatment of defects of speech, Elsie Fogerty's great contribution to Speech Therapy has been that she knew how to recognise special gifts for this work and to help those who might later become outstanding figures in their profession, to set their foot on the ladder and guide their first steps up. The seed she planted has grown into a sturdy sapling, and as it grows to full dimensions will be a permanent memorial.'

• • •

As Harries says, Fogerty was an inspiring teacher, and this talent was not limited to Central's 'remedial speech' students. Dame Sybil Thorndike contributed to the same 1945 *Viva Voce*: 'I don't believe she ever encouraged anyone to work on the stage unless she believed in them utterly. I have only heard her urge a very few to become actors, and this in itself is refreshing, for one seldom meets a teacher of voice or acting who does not try to push pupils into the professional theatre. I know it was Elsie's great disappointment that she herself wasn't on the stage, and a lesser person would have worked her stifled ambitions on pupils and enjoyed the profession vicariously – not so Elsie.'

Fogerty didn't need to live vicariously, for her own life was packed full of creative projects, and they usually included her Central students. In June 1914, only three months after she opened the St Thomas's Clinic, Fogerty directed *The Electra of Sophocles* at the Scala Theatre. She and her cousin, Armstrong Cochrane, had adapted the text, and Granville Bantock wrote the music. Central students past and present were in the cast: Philip Merivale played Orestes; Dion Titheradge was Aegisthus; Ruby Ginner headed the

1914 Archduke Franz Ferdinand is shot in Sarajevo; World War One begins
Majority of West End theatres close; most reopen with musical revues

1915 A German Zeppelin crosses the Norfolk coast and bombs Great Yarmouth, King's Lynn and Sandringham
Register of Women for War Service instituted
Rupert Brooke dies of blood poisoning from a mosquito bite
Sarah Bernhardt returns to the stage after amputation of her right leg

1916 Daylight Saving Time is instituted
First Battle of the Somme
Captain T E Lawrence backs Arab revolt against the Ottoman Empire
Rasputin is murdered in St Petersburg

1917 Russian Czar Nicholas II abdicates
The USA enters the War on 6 April
First aeroplane bombing raid on the East End of London kills more than 100 and injures more than 400 people. Until this, aeroplanes had only been used for reconnaissance.
Britain's first woman doctor, Elizabeth Garrett Anderson, dies

1918 Standard Actors' Equity Contracts are established
The Red Baron, Manfred von Richthofen, is shot down and killed during Second Battle of the Somme
Pop-up toaster invented in the USA by Charles Strite
Spanish Flu pandemic kills millions
By the time the Armistice is signed on 11 November, over ten million people have died in the First World War

Chorus. According to Fogerty's memoirs, Aileen Wyse's performance of Electra was one of the finest ever given by a student at Central. Wyse would remain significantly connected to the School for the next fifty years, and she will be mentioned again later.

As well as running the speech therapy clinic at St Thomas's and producing *Electra*, that summer Fogerty also interviewed prospective students for the 1914 autumn term. One of these young girls was Irene Mawer, who would later teach at Central for over a quarter of a century: 'Only gradually, during my student days, did Miss Fogerty let fall her deep interest in, and knowledge of French Mime, as taught in the Paris Conservatoire. Her own hands bore testimony to the natural genius and technical skill in that most difficult art. …Elsie Fogerty never taught mime as such; but if some student found difficulty in a particular piece of stage movement, she would say, "Irene, take her away and teach her!" So I came to feel that there must be some basic theory on which to teach the things which I appeared to do naturally. Through my dance classes with Ruby Ginner…I learned much of the theory of rhythmic movement and of muscular and nervous development, which – together with the co-ordination of the rhythms of speech and movement that we learned in Miss Fogerty's Greek Chorus classes – set me on to the lines which led to the establishment of a technical basis for the teaching of mime. This was later tried out and tested in the curriculum of the Central School, and finally became the accepted syllabus for the examinations of the Institute of Mime.' [*Fogie*]

On 3 August 1914 in that same busy summer, Central independently presented the first of its own Speech Conferences. Held in Stratford-upon-Avon at Shakespeare's old school, the King Edward VI Grammar, Fogerty arranged a number of speakers, including two of Britain's foremost poets, Lascelles Abercrombie and John Drinkwater. A group of American delegates travelled to England with Dr Edward Wheeler Scripture, an American pioneer in remedial speech and speech defects who had met Fogerty when she gave her speech in Buffalo, New York, the year before.

Forty Central-trained teachers also attended this Speech Conference, and it was from this group that the Association of Teachers of Speech-Training and Dramatic Art (ATST) was officially formed. Initially open only to those who held the full Central School Certificate, membership in the ATST provided proof of successfully completing the two-year training as performers and teachers. Membership in the ATST became an official acknowledgment and qualification for this new profession: teachers of speech and drama.

The Stratford Speech Conference was a great success, but it was overshadowed by tragic international events. In Sarajevo on 28 June 1914, a Serbian terrorist from a secret nationalist organisation, the Black Hand, assassinated Archduke Franz Ferdinand, the heir to the Austro-Hungarian throne. For the next five weeks, international alliances caused political mayhem in Europe. Austria-Hungary declared war on Serbia. Russia came to the defence of its ally, Serbia; Germany came to the defence of its ally, Austria-

Hungary. Bound by a treaty with Russia, France found itself at war with Germany, and Germany invaded Belgium to get to Paris. Britain had a longstanding treaty obligation to its ally, Belgium, and so declared war on Germany on 4 August.

• • •

Central struggled to keep its doors open for the next four years. Enrolment of male students was limited to those too young to serve in the military, and many young women chose to work for the war effort instead of attending school. The successful West End actor, Athole Stewart, had been working as a Central 'rehearsal master'. He enlisted and would become the first actor to receive an OBE, for his work in the Foreign Office. Dr Hulbert was called up for service, bringing his work at the School to an end – a deep loss to both Central and Fogerty. For eight years, Hulbert and Fogerty had developed an inseparable movement and speech training, and their experimental work in movement, speech and voice had challenged the accepted methods of physical and vocal training. Finding a replacement to carry on this work, especially during a time of war, seemed impossible.

As usual, Fogerty found only the very best for her School, and Dr William Aikin was invited to take over Dr Hulbert's classes. Author of *The Voice – Its Physiology and its Cultivation*, Aikin had long been interested in a scientific analysis of the human voice. A musician as well as a doctor, he had investigated the physical and physiological laws that govern the voice in both speech and song, and he firmly believed that the training of both should be based on scientific principles. (He was, however, reportedly uninterested in methods of teaching.) His daily voice classes focused only on understanding the living organ of the voice and anticipated later investigations into the nature of sound. Typical of the Central 'spirit' of the day, Dr Aikin not only worked for free, he also paid the rent for his own classroom at the Albert Hall.

From early on, Aikin insisted that all of his students be taught 'Anatomy, as Applied to Voice Production', and his influence is still evident today. Sally Grace (Teacher '58), who taught voice at Central for 13 years, recalls: 'When I was a student, we had lessons in Physics of Sound from Aikin's book, and a lot of lessons in anatomy. This underpinned everything one was doing with the voice. I tried to keep it going in some form or other at Central. When Margot Braund developed the one-year postgraduate voice course, I was there as an advisor, and we deliberately wrote in some of those Aikin elements.'

• • •

Inevitably, autumn 1914 found a reduced number of staff and students back at the Hall for the start of the term. Classes continued, but except for performances given for War Service, dramatic presentations were suspended. The war years were undoubtedly hard, but life for Central and its students by no means stood still.

In the spring of 1915, Fogerty and her students attended the annual Shakespeare Festival in Stratford-upon-Avon, and in August of that same year returned to Stratford to open Central's Summer School. This was the first of many, and over the next 23 years, Central Summer Schools grew in popularity and in length. A number of Dr Scripture's American delegates to the 1914 Speech Conference returned for the 1915 two-week Summer School, and they attended every year until the (by then) six-week Summer Schools were discontinued in 1939 – at the start of World War Two.

When Central was not in session, whether during the academic year or during the Summer School, everyone was also expected to contribute to the war effort. Students worked in all areas – industrial, agricultural, clerical – but then so did the staff. Fogerty worked one summer as a nurse for the Red Cross in France. Another summer, she went to Glasgow for what she referred to in her memoirs as helping 'with street-corner speaking in Glasgow, where production was not meeting requirements'. She would refer to the same event years later at the beginning of World War Two as fighting 'the enemy propaganda in the shipyards'. [*Viva Voce*]

In spite of the war, Fogerty continued to promote her Central School. In 1916, a 'Licentiate of the Royal Academy of Music (Elocution)' was instituted, which was seen as an invaluable development for those seeking employment in places that only valued those teachers who had some proof of their education. Fogerty was of the firm opinion that this qualification did nothing to prove her scope of knowledge or teaching ability, but she was one of the very first to gain these 'letters' – seeing them as validation that could be easily recognised by the world at large. She recognised the difficulty in trying to quantify practical abilities in her students, but she also recognised the need for acknowledgement in their highly specialised and completely undervalued field.

This would start Fogerty on the path towards gaining legitimacy for her students, but to reach this goal she must first achieve Central's own legitimacy – not only by providing great training, but also by providing proof that Central provided great training. In 1917, Frank Benson retired as President of Central, and Fogerty's old friend, the Vicar Russell Wakefield, by this time the Bishop of Birmingham, headed the first meeting dedicated to formally incorporating the Central School into a registered charitable company. This process would continue, to a greater or lesser degree, for the next eight years.

•   •   •

In the last year of the war, Central also started another Speech Clinic, specifically for those patients not being treated for their stammers at the successful clinic at St Thomas's Hospital. The London County Council Schools' Medical Officer in 1917, Dr E J Boome, and Mrs Boome (Honor Baines, an early Central student and a founding member of the College of Speech Therapists) wrote of this accomplishment:

Miss Fogerty's object was to bring to the notice of the Educational authorities the prevalence of this distressing affliction among children and the fact that definite and scientific means were available to combat it. The experiment was completely successful and, in 1918, the London County Council opened its first four Centres for Stammerers. There were undoubtedly many others becoming deeply interested in the study of remedial speech, but we venture to think that the subsequent formation of speech clinics throughout the country (the majority based on the methods used in London) would not have materialised so steadily if the Westminster Clinic had not opened its doors to a few children. The seed planted in those days has now grown into a mighty tree with many outspreading branches.

HONOR BAINES IN *FOGIE*

" Elsie Fogerty appeared to be, at times, a mass of contradictions, but always there was something alive and stimulating. Her argumentative powers often caused the temperature to rise and acrimony could flow round a council table: however, in spite of difference of opinion and outlook, her opponents held her in great affection and respect. Often they would disagree violently with her, for the ideas she expressed were very definite and frequently revolutionary; but nothing would divert her from her convictions: they often thought she was wrong, but the passing of time has proved how often she was right. Vague she could be; in fact the personification of vagueness – but it was never safe to trust it – for without any warning she could emerge from this state and express herself clearly and concisely, leaving her listeners aghast and/or full of admiration. **"**

Disorders of speech had opened up a new field of research, and the early pioneers, of which Elsie Fogerty was one, had perforce to invent their own terminology; unfortunately these pioneers did not always consult each other, so that the classification and terminology might be described as 'confusion worse confounded'. Elsie Fogerty, however, did much in the clarification of this confusion. She drew up a classification, which formed the basis for later research both for herself and for other students of speech therapy. She was one of the first people to study the problems of word-blindness and word-deafness (as they were then called) and her work on the treatment of these disorders is one of the many contributions that she made to speech therapy. Above all she realised the misery that can be felt by those who suffer from even a mild form of speech or voice disorder…' [*Fogie*]

• • •

During these difficult war years, Fogerty not only ran a successful school for actors, teachers and 'remedial speech teachers', she also visited both the St Thomas's and the Westminster Speech Clinics weekly, organised conferences, wrote papers, spoke at conferences, and regularly consulted with doctors and professionals on voice and voice defects. She also continued to teach outside of Central, although with the unreliable wartime public transportation she had to give up classes at any great distance from London – her fortnightly visits to Roedean in Brighton being the one exception. Since her mother's death in 1910, Fogerty had lived alone in her small South Kensington flat. With less outside teaching, she had a much-decreased income, and in spite of her simple lifestyle, for the first time she found it necessary to keep all of the fees for her private work, instead of using them to support Central. With reduced enrolment, Central was struggling financially, so when in 1916 two of Fogerty's ex-students, Ruby Ginner and Irene Mawer, created their School for Movement and Mime, Fogerty invited them to share the rooms, and the rent, at the Hall.

The wartime hardships culminated at the beginning of November 1918 when it was announced that the Albert Hall would be commandeered in a week's time, and both Central and the Ginner-Mawer School had to find alternative space if they wanted to continue classes. The Ginner-Mawer School immediately secured a studio space in Kensington, but Fogerty was less successful. It seemed likely Central would have to move in with Ginner and Mawer. It's hard to imagine what this would have ultimately meant to Central, but in a sudden reprieve, the Armistice was declared, the war was over, and the Albert Hall remained open. The Ginner-Mawer School moved to its new studio, establishing itself as a completely separate entity, and Central remained in its rooms at the Hall.

In 1939, Fogerty wrote of those World War One years: 'We believed then, as we believe now, that the younger generation needed the chance of accomplishing something in the way of fitting themselves for the world of after-war activities, along the lines in which they themselves are fitted to excel. As one looks back on the students of that generation there is no question but that that faith was justified. I look over some of the old *Viva Voces* and remember...Dion Titheradge throwing up the brilliant hopes of a great stage career to fight, and never recovering from the terrible strain; Lovat Fraser, the greatest loss the theatre sustained, dying a few years later with his work unforgettable to survive him; Basil Hallam's name on the Roll of Honour; an air raid over Queen Alexandra's House in full daylight and the senior student caught in the act of sneaking out of the front door – going to see the fun! A dark morning in the old Clinic rooms at St Thomas's when departing students suddenly waved and vanished, and a strange silence fell. People on the housetops waved to us as we came out, and on Westminster Bridge newsboys flung us their sheets in which we read only two words: 'ARMISTICE SIGNED.' On the other side of the bridge...opposite the Houses of Parliament, Sybil Thorndike and Lewis Casson rushed to embrace us as Muriel Bousfield [Wigglesworth] and I breathlessly caught at them. Then the hour outside the Palace; the crowd from the Victoria Monument to Charing Cross, and from Hyde Park Corner to the Embankment, shouting for the King whose nerve and utter loyalty had stood unshaken all through.' [*Viva Voce*]

• • •

With the war over, Central performances began once again, and life at the School quickly picked up pace. Fogerty directed and acted in *The Sumidajawa* (*Sumida River*), a Japanese Noh Play, translated by Marie Stopes and presented at the (Royal) Court Theatre in an Elsie Fogerty and Ruby Ginner Season. It was the first Noh play ever to be produced in Britain, and it also starred Henry Oscar and Fogerty's old student, Hazel Thompson, who had just returned from Japan with her husband.

The Pivot Club again presented fundraisers, entertainments, 'Slum Parties', and what was considered the gala event of the year, the formal 'Pivot Club Dance'. Before the war, the Pivot Club had celebrated Elsie Fogerty's birthday, 16 December, in a small hall in South Kensington, with all proceeds of this annual event going to the Pivot Club Scholarship Fund. After the war, the Birthday Dance began to be held in a ballroom at the Knightsbridge Hotel, making it a much larger, grander, and far more profitable, evening. However, an even larger informal occasion was the annual free 'Get-Together Party' that was held in the Upper Crush Room at the Hall. As many as two hundred Pivots, guests, and students past and present would come from all over the country and abroad to see old friends, tutors, and their favourite teacher, Elsie Fogerty. When 'Get-Togethers' were discontinued at the start of World War Two, the first official event to bring together past Central students from all courses and all years would be the 2003 Alumni Reunion at the Embassy Theatre.

4

1918–1927

BY THE END OF WORLD WAR ONE, Elsie Fogerty had a reputation as one of England's foremost specialists in voice, and her Central School was a leader in both actor and teacher training. Early in Fogerty's career, she had achieved a degree of success in the theatre as an actress. Now, actors she had trained were performing in touring and repertory companies, as well as in the West End. For over three decades, Fogerty had taught in schools in and around London. Now, teachers she had trained were taking important positions in schools throughout Great Britain and abroad, and those teacher-students who had decided to specialise in 'remedial speech' were working both privately and in clinics. Moreover, Central teachers helped not only those who wanted a more 'pleasing' voice or those with difficulty in creating speech, but in the days before sound equipment and microphones, the clergy, politicians and others in public life often came to learn to breathe properly and speak audibly without straining their voices. More glamorously, many famous West End actors suffering from voice strain, inaudibility or diction problems came to Fogerty for private tutorials, and for a while, her most prestigious student, Princess Louise, the Duchess of Argyle, never gave a speech in public without first consulting Elsie Fogerty. (In a 2005 interview, Martin Worth, son of Fogerty's lifelong friend, Muriel (Bousfield) Wigglesworth, remembered that when King George VI took the throne, Fogerty was convinced that the palace would call 'anytime now' to ask for her help with his stammer.)

Fogerty had many successes, and these were due not only to her innate talents, but more importantly, to her dedication and hard work. She taught mornings, afternoons or evenings at the Albert Hall, and then travelled by taxis and trains to teach at schools around London, both near and far. She reserved Sunday mornings for church, but on Sunday afternoons she would return to her modest South Kensington flat that overflowed with mementos, books and the upright piano from her childhood home, and there give private tutorials.

In the evenings, Fogerty wrote articles, lectures, recitations, personal letters, business letters, books and memoirs. She went to the theatre to see friends and ex-students, or to check up on a private student's progress. She visited Central's various remedial speech clinics at least once a week, and attended committee, staff and Governors' meetings.

ELSIE FOGERTY'S WEEKLY TIMETABLE, 1919

Monday	Morning	St Thomas's Hospital Speech Clinic
	Afternoon	Central School
	Evening	St George's School, Ascot
Tuesday	Morning	St George's School, Ascot
	Afternoon	Central School
	Evening	Wentworth Hill, Mill Hill
Wednesday	Morning	Central School
	Afternoon	Levana School, Wimbledon
	Evening	LCC Teachers' Classes
Thursday	Morning	Roland Houses and Glendower Schools, Kensington
	Afternoon	Central School
	Evening	Central School and Travel to Brighton
Friday	Morning	Roedean School, Brighton
	Afternoon	St Thomas's Hospital Speech Clinic
	Evening	Ivy House School, Wimbledon
Saturday	Morning	Central School, University Extension Lectures
	Afternoon	School Plays, Extra Rehearsals, Private Lessons
Sunday	Morning	Church
	Afternoon	Private Lessons

She also gave recitals that included not only poetry but often even some of her own original comic and tragic recitations. In spite of this arduous schedule, Fogerty was forever finding other pressing projects that demanded her attention. Lewis Casson once wrote: 'She had that same completely unselfish devotion to any work she took in hand, the same immense driving power to pull it through and, above all, the faculty of compelling all of us comparatively lazy people to throw our whole energies – even against our wills – into any enterprise in which she was interested; so that, however much we admired and loved her, there was always present a secret fear of our comfort being disturbed by her tireless energy.' [*Fogie*]

Now that the Great War was over, there were new projects to get under way; and Fogerty threw some of her 'tireless energy' in fresh directions.

• • •

In June 1919, less than a year after the Armistice, the British Drama League was inaugurated, with Harley Granville-Barker as Chairman and Fogerty as Organising Secretary. Fogerty immediately 'organised' the British Drama League's First English Theatre Conference to be held that August during the last weeks of the annual Stratford

1920	Prohibition of alcohol in the United States
1921	Sheffield Repertory Theatre founded
	Unemployment in Britain tops one million
1922	First broadcast from the newly founded British Broadcasting Company
	Michael Collins shot dead in Cork
1923	Paul Robeson appears in *All God's Chillun Got Wings* at the Embassy Theatre
	Sarah Bernhardt dies in Paris, aged 78
1924	Stage Guild formed
	Britain's first national airline created – Imperial Airways
1925	Tennessee jury rejects Darwinism in Scopes Trial
	First traffic lights tested at Piccadilly Circus
1926	Stratford Memorial Theatre burns down
	Princess Elizabeth born to Duchess of York
1927	The first travelling birth control clinic is set up in a horse-drawn caravan
	First Spotlight book published
	Arts Theatre Club opens

Festival. Attended by some of the most influential leaders in English Theatre, the Conference passed a resolution urging '... the importance of establishing a National Theatre policy adequate to the needs of the people, and a Faculty of the Theatre at the universities of the country, with the necessary colleges.' Neither resolution was new, but now that the war was over, each could be more forcefully advanced. Fogerty wouldn't live to see either come to fruition, but for the rest of her life she was dedicated to both.

• • •

Fogerty was forever finding ways to promote Central and its students, so it was no accident that the dates and venue of the League's Theatre Conference coincided not only with the Stratford Shakespeare Festival, but also with Central's Summer School.

Since 1915, the Summer School had been held annually during the final two weeks of the Stratford Festival, and it offered an active and demanding curriculum. There were classes in Poetics, Speech-training, Mime, and the History of Drama; and in the evenings students could attend any number of social events, relax by the river, or see a Festival show. The School culminated in a public matinee of one-act plays given by the students in the Shakespeare Memorial Theatre. John Laurie remembered 11 end-of-summer productions in that first post-war summer of 1919. Always on the lookout for talent, Fogerty saw promise in the young Laurie – then an architecture student from Scotland and later one of England's most renowned stage, film and television actors – and invited him to train at the Albert Hall. Fogerty seemed adept at collecting supporters, and Laurie became one of the Central School's greatest. Both he and his wife, Oona Todd-Naylor (Stage '23), a successful actress in her own right, would teach and direct at the School for many years, and Laurie became one of Central's earliest Governors.

During that same summer of 1919, Fogerty also first met Herbert Norris, who was then supervising costumes at the Stratford Memorial Theatre. She was about to produce her own religious drama, *The Mystery of the Rose*, which was set during the reign of Richard II, and she invited Norris to give an 'informal talk' to some of her students on the costumes of the period. The next year, Fogerty offered him a permanent appointment as Lecturer on Historical Costume, and he would remain at Central until 1939, instructing students on costumes, how to wear them, and the customs, manners and heraldry of period drama. These lectures on the History of Costumes from 600 BC to 1800 AD would later serve as the basis of the syllabus for the Costume Section for the first Diploma in Dramatic Art.

In the autumn of 1919, Fogerty's *The Mystery of the Rose* (also known as *The Miracle of the Rose*) was performed on the steps outside St Paul's Church in Covent Garden. Lewis Casson presented the Prologue, and the cast included James Dale as the King and Iris Baker as Lady Laura. Mary Casson, daughter of Lewis Casson and Sybil Thorndike, played the young child. Central students played the crowd.

• • •

Immediately after World War One, Central applications increased considerably. Full-time enrolment in 1919 was still only 30 students, but over the next three years registration more than doubled, with an equal number of part-time university extension, debate and private students. Yet in 1922–3, with full-time tuition at 15 guineas per year, the total income for the School was only £4,461 4s 0d. This hardly made for abundance, and Central's very existence depended on the willingness of Fogerty and her staff to accept little or no pay. An increase in enrolment, and therefore fee income, was imperative, but increased enrolment also meant adding new staff. Central had always been unified solely by the ideas and insights of Fogerty, so input from new staff could not help but affect Central training.

Athole Stewart was one of the most famous, and influential, of these early tutors. In 1918,

BRITISH DRAMA LEAGUE AND LIBRARY

In 1919, with Fogerty's help, Geoffrey Whitworth started the British Drama League, which would later become known as the British Theatre Association (BTA). By the mid-1980s, the BTA was struggling financially, and it sought a home for its 250,000 books and plays. Its incomparable reference library and over 25,000 play titles were available to BTA members and non-members alike. Anthony Cornish, a professional director with a long connection to the BTA as member, educator, adjudicator and Executive, contacted the Central Principal, George Kitson (Principal, 1978–87). Together with Kitson and BTA Director Jane Hackworth-Young, Cornish worked long and hard to bring the BTA collection to Central and enhance the prestige of the School's library. When the ILEA refused Central the money needed to house this valuable asset, negotiations foundered. Then, in 1988, the BTA faced final closure. Again Cornish began talks with Central so that they might acquire the collection, and for a while, it seemed certain that the library and all the BTA services would be transferred to the School. At the last minute, Robert Holmes à Court, through his family charitable foundation, stepped in and guaranteed the money to keep the BTA library and the BTA identity intact. In the spring of 1989, a few months short of its 70th Birthday, the BTA was dissolved and its valuable reference collection was passed to the Theatre Museum. The play sets now belong to the Drama Association of Wales.

aged 40, he had returned from war to a successful career as a West End actor. Though he had worked with Central students before the war, Fogerty now wanted to give him a more formal position within the School, and so officially engaged him as 'Director of Rehearsals'. His eagerness to take the position suggests the high status and outstanding reputation of the School, as no doubt the money offered was appalling. Hired to coordinate the dramatic work across both the Teacher and the Stage Courses, Stewart was another of Fogerty's inspired choices.

Early 20th century actor training in England was casual and experiential, mainly 'taught' on an ad hoc basis by directors or 'rehearsal masters'. Stewart recognised that acting could be studied not just through voice, movement and the rehearsals of scenes, but that it was a craft that could, and should, be examined and analysed. He looked for a means to approach a character, and his 'experimental' work at Central introduced radical questions such as 'What do we mean by character?' and 'What is acting?' Ultimately, Stewart's influence on actor training at Central was curtailed by circumstances. With increasing professional demands on his time, he left Central within the decade in order to devote himself to his career. Following his departure, Central actor training would remain pretty much unchanged until after World War Two.

There were other veterans like Stewart, who came to work at Central after World War One, and although they may have done little to transform the training, they at the very least added a male influence to what had been virtually a girls' school during the war. Herbert Marshall had been a successful actor pre-war, but having lost a leg in combat was unable to find stage work upon his return. In 1921 Fogerty hired him to take 'rehearsal classes'. Henry Craine, a student with Frank Benson before the war and a successful West End actor after, also assisted with 'rehearsals', as did Leslie Faber and Henry Oscar, also both working actors. Visiting actors, producers and teachers gave lectures and adjudicated performances, with perhaps the most historically significant to the actor training being the legendary French actor-producer and visionary, Jacques Copeau, who lectured at Central during the 1924–5 school year.

In addition to the more famous of her staff, Fogerty often hired ex-students to teach at Central, not only providing employment for those in whom she saw a special talent for such work, but also giving her Central training a constancy and through-line. There were many ex-students who remained loyal guest lecturers and directors, but there were also a number who would devote their lives to Central and its students. Hazel Thompson, Fogerty's first student at the Albert Hall in 1898, had upon her marriage retired from a successful acting career. By 1920, Fogerty had persuaded Thompson to join the Central staff, and it was not long before she was at the centre of the School: teaching, directing, and providing technical support in the form of costumes and stage management. In 1922, Thompson also became Registrar.

Irene Mawer had started teaching Mime classes immediately after she graduated in 1916. Mime, as taught by Irene Mawer, should not be construed to mean men with white faces massaging an invisible wall. There may have been elements of classical mime, but at its simplest, Mawer's Mime was closer to the over-acting that can be seen in old silent movies. Livvy Wilson-Dickson (Stage '32) spoke of these classes: 'I remember we used to do: "Terror in front" – that was advancing – arms in front. Then, "Terror

> ## JACQUES COPEAU
>
> In 1924, Jacques Copeau retired from the Parisian stage and took a company of 30 young actors to Pernand-Verglasses in Burgundy to found a theatre school. A member of this company, Copeau's nephew, Michel Saint-Denis, would later have a profound influence not only on the actor training at Central, but also on most of the drama schools in the English-speaking world.

behind" – swing your arms – and try not to give your neighbour a smart clip.' The following fragment was recorded by the American Mary (Beard) Brady in her 1936 Summer School notes on an 'Old Mystery Play in Mime'. It may also give a hint as to how Fogerty's flowery drama, *The Mystery of the Rose*, might have been staged a few years earlier:

> Women walk in two groups, bringing bowls and separating to talk. Girls run in with apple blossom branches up high, to centre. They all walk about together showing bowls and flowers…mixing up and stopping towards centre again. (Feet and shoulders at right angles to the person next to them.) Lonely woman comes in slowly – arms out to people, then around, looks at empty arms, cries out, turns to church door, kneels, wrings hands and falls across steps.

Ruby Ginner had begun teaching movement at Central, if not in the very first year of the School, surely very soon after. She taught basic movement classes, as well as Folk and Greek dancing, with the latter enhanced by Ginner's extensive background knowledge of Ancient Greek civilisation, its myths and legends. Ginner's classes were supposedly based on the balance of mind, body and spirit, and these tenets twinned perfectly with Fogerty's, Dr Hulbert's and Dr Aikin's requirements: that students gain a relaxed control to allow movement and speech to become one.

Post-war voice work at Central continued much as it had since 1914. Dr Hulbert did not return to Central, but Dr Aikin remained. Aikin had incorporated Hulbert's earlier discoveries into his own important work, and Aikin's students would in turn take what they had learned, develop it, and pass it on from generation to generation. One early fundamental of Central voice training is the concept of 'rib reserve', which Aikin describes in his 1923 address to the Association of Teachers of Speech-Training and Dramatic Art (ATST): 'Breathing, to be efficient in speaking or singing on a large scale, must be both capacious and under control, for we may have only a few opportunities of breathing in a minute, and must never be short of oxygen. At the same time control is needed to follow closely the accents and emphasis to denote the meaning of words and phrases. Our aim is therefore, to make the action of breathing-out not deliberately mechanical, but to leave it every possible freedom, while we maintain an expanded position of the lower ribs as an attitude of body conducive to good resonation. This is generally called "Rib Reserve".'

By the end of the 20th century, rib reserve breathing had ceased to be an acceptable constituent of good vocal training, but Aikin's other work, his 'Resonator Scale', lives on. Resonators are the hollow spaces in the neck, mouth and nose, which give both the general and particular qualities of sound and language, and the Resonator Scale is the arrangement of the vowel positions in the order of their resonant pitches. Even without access to the sophisticated modern instruments of measure, Aikin somehow created a Resonator Scale that has proved remarkably accurate even today.

Aikin's innovative and experimental voice work was not necessarily typical of all classes given at Central after World War One. Ethel Radmar still taught Deportment, as she had since 1906, and although it may not have been cutting-edge actor training, it remained an attraction for many. Central and the Academy of Dramatic Art were still seen by doting parents as the perfect way to 'finish' their daughters – giving them grace, style and etiquette, as well as a beautiful and well-modulated voice. There were some students who would never work in the theatre after graduation, but many would, to great effect, use their curtsy when later presented at Court.

In 1919–20, Fogerty taught Diction, Verse Speaking, Debating, Recitation, Prosody and Poetics, and the History of Drama. Miss K Salmon taught 'ear-training' classes. Dr Hogarth gave lectures on anatomy to teacher-students, who were also required to study elementary psychology in preparation for their practical remedial speech work sessions with patients at the St Thomas and the Westminster Clinics. All students were given instruction in make-up, stage management and the construction of costumes and props. Monsieur Tassart taught Fencing to the actors, and Herbert Norris lectured on the History of Costume and Crafts to all students. Walter Ripman taught French and Phonetics.

Walter Ripman had produced a phonetics textbook, *The Sound of Spoken English*, in 1906, and a reader, *Specimens of English*, in 1908.

DANIEL JONES

In 1907, when phonetics was still considered more closely aligned to speech training and elocution, Daniel Jones became a part-time lecturer in phonetics in the Faculty of Arts at University College London. By 1912, he had established his own department and, in 1921, he became the first Professor of Phonetics at a British University. One of the leading lights of this emerging subject, Jones is even now venerated for his concept of 'cardinal vowels' – reference vowels for phonetic description and transcription – and the International Phonetic Association still uses his model for phonetic analysis.

MURIEL (BOUSFIELD) WIGGLESWORTH

At the age of 12, Muriel Bousfield was brought to Fogerty for lessons to cure her stammer. At 18 she became Fogerty's private secretary, and soon after that, the first Registrar of the Central School. When Fogerty opened the remedial speech clinic at St Thomas's in 1914, Muriel began as a therapist, and later became clinic administrator. In 1917, she and ex-student Phyllis Reid opened the experimental Westminster Clinic for stammerers, and in 1918, she and Mabel Oswald (one of the original Fellows enrolled in the College of Speech Therapists upon its formation in 1945) were the first teachers hired for the London County Council's four Stammerers' Centres. Upon her marriage in 1922 to Harold Wigglesworth, Muriel passed on her clinic work to Central graduate, Belle Kennedy, and her work as Registrar to Hazel Thompson. After the birth of her children, Muriel Wigglesworth returned to therapy work at clinics in both Windsor and Reading. Fogerty was a close personal and family friend, became godmother to Muriel's first child, Ann, and spent almost every Christmas with the family until her death in 1945. It is largely due to Muriel (Bousfield) Wigglesworth's research, her collection of reminiscences, and her early (lost) manuscript that Marion Cole was able to produce her book on Fogerty's life, *Fogie*.

His arduous two- and later three-year phonetics course took students from the easiest transcriptions of standard English in their first term to the more advanced transcriptions of dictated German, Italian and Spanish, and of Chaucerian, Shakespearean and dialect English in the last term. From 1921, students could acquire a qualification in Phonetics from the International Phonetics Association. Examinations, given by Professor Daniel Jones, consisted of theory, pronunciation, reading from ordinary and phonetic script, phonetic dictation and transcription of both English and meaningless 'nonsense' words.

Classes at Central, or 'the Hall' as it was generally referred to, didn't start before 10 am. On Mondays at noon the entire School attended Fogerty's Lectures, where she made announcements and spoke on any number of subjects – theatre history, acting and characterisation, English language and literature, verse speaking – all under the general heading of 'Theory'. These lectures were unpredictable, spellbinding and inspirational, and they often provided the great lady a means to pull together her own ideas and theories into a cohesive whole. In the early 1920s, Fogerty's series of lectures, 'Thought in Action', formed the basis of her first major book, *The Speaking of English Verse* (1927).

Gwynneth Thurburn was a student at Central from 1919 to 1922. She would go on to teach voice under Dr Aikin and later become responsible for all voice work at the School. Even later, she would become Vice Principal and then the second longest-serving Principal after Fogerty. There will be much more of her later, but here she recalls with some amusement her own role as a student in penning Fogerty's first book:

> …Knowing that I had taken a secretarial course she sent for me and requested that I should take down the lectures verbatim. Anyone who knew her would recognise that this request was in the nature of a royal command. Obediently I agreed and for weeks

I spent long hours transcribing my shorthand into longhand. After a time I found that I could not keep it up and as she never mentioned the subject I took a chance, and though I continued to take down the lectures I did not transcribe them. I did my own revision from other people's notes which were far easier to follow and it seemed as if the whole affair had been forgotten. Two years later, however, I was politely requested to produce the lectures in terms that did not brook refusal or even explanation. There was nothing for it but to tackle the notes. Shorthand of the day before yesterday is bad enough but shorthand that is two years old is almost indecipherable. Somehow I achieved something and I shall always feel that a large part of *The Speaking of English Verse* was written in my blood. ['The Elsie Fogerty I Knew']

There is no mention of Thurburn in the book's acknowledgements, but Fogerty thanks Dr Aikin for a diagram of his Resonator Scale; Dr William Pasteur, for proofing her section on breathing; Dr Hulbert for his notes on position and movement; Dr Rouse and Professor Daniel Jones for phonetic transcriptions and an experiment in the notation of tonic accent; and Walter Ripman for phonetic notations and transcriptions.

In *The Speaking of English Verse*, Fogerty defines prose as 'setting forth our meaning as simply and clearly as possible' – a free rhythm. On the other hand, verse is used to 'express ourselves, our feeling and emotion as well as our logical meaning, through a metric pattern of words' – a fixed rhythmic pattern. Seeing rhythm as inseparable from the voice, Fogerty's first book foreshadows her last and most extraordinary work, *Rhythm* (1937) with this pronouncement: 'When space, time and force are all rightly measured under the exact guidance of intention the action which results is said to be rhythmical.'

Besides her legendary Monday Lectures, on Thursday afternoons Fogerty gave three-hour classes in Diction in the King's Room (now the Royal Retiring Room). Compulsory for second-year Central students, part-timers were also allowed to attend, and this increased attendance to sometimes as many as forty. The class culminated in a Diction Examination at the end of the Easter term, and these exams provide one of the oddest anecdotes of Central's history.

Ishbel MacGlashan Fox (Stage '31), long-time supporter and staff member at Central, wrote: 'The actual occasion took place on the stage of the little theatre, set with a large carved chair, in front of a screen draped with an embroidered shawl. We numbered students sat in rows in the auditorium and, five numbers before one's performance one was required to slip out under the stage to re-emerge in the wings, just three contestants before one's own turn. Facing you in the auditorium sat the rest of the school in serried ranks, and totally concealed behind another large screen – the adjudicators: probably a couple of poets and Miss F (or our particular Calvary, John Drinkwater and Clifford Bax).'

Poet Clifford Bax said of these exams: '...There was once a judge who was a famous poet, but one of austere morality. Against the name of a competitor he scribbled 'Very pretty legs' – no doubt a note intended to help him to identify her when they all came on stage to hear his summing up. But the result of it was that for several years afterwards we had a screen interposed between us and any pretty legs that might appear on the stage.' [Fogie] Although that might have been the intention, MacGlashon adds, 'Naturally in a state of total tremulous panic, one was still able to observe, while performing, the sly peeps of the adjudicators round their enforced blindfold.'

As the years passed, Central students grew to accept this strange custom as a tribute to the seriousness of their work, most never questioning its origin or its eccentricity.

• • •

Two of Central's most famous alumni trained with Fogerty in the decade after World War One. Both left the School in 1925, though one had trained for only one year (as was often the custom for men), while the other attended the Hall for two years.

Peggy Ashcroft's mother, Violet Bernheim Edward, knew Elsie Fogerty, having trained under her when a schoolgirl in Folkestone. Violet had been a keen amateur actress but, like Fogerty, her Victorian parents had discouraged a professional life on the stage. When her own daughter admitted a passion for the theatre, Violet insisted Peggy instead enrol at the Central School to become a drama teacher. Within a very short time, it was apparent that the young woman had a special and rare talent. Fogerty persuaded Violet, Violet conceded, and the 19-year-old Peggy was allowed to transfer to the Stage Course. There were 90 Stage students in Peggy's 1924–5 final year, and only five of these were boys. One of them was George Coulouris, who became a successful character actor on stage and in film in both the United States and Great Britain. Another was Laurence Olivier.

Laurence Olivier's older sister, Sybill, had trained as an actress at Central in 1920, and Laurence auditioned for Fogerty in the summer of 1924 with Jaques' speech, The Seven Ages of Man, from Shakespeare's As You Like It. When the flailing 17 year old finished, Fogerty fixed him with her dark eyes and placed a finger on the young man's forehead, drawing it down and over the bridge of his nose: 'You have a weakness, here.' Olivier later attributed his years of wearing fake noses to that one unguarded statement from the formidable Miss Fogerty.

Olivier's frugal father was well aware that Central might provide financial help for male students, and even though he had agreed his son should become an actor, he wouldn't go so far as to pay for it. As instructed by his father, after his audition Laurence Olivier told Miss Fogerty that he could not come to Central without both a scholarship and a bursary. Nasal weakness aside, Fogerty immediately agreed, and the young Olivier was notified on 24 September 1924 of a one-year scholarship to the Stage Course and a bursary of £50 for the year. Peggy Ashcroft remembered the young Olivier as shy, nervous – and broke. He lived in a cheap room in Paddington and walked to the Hall across Hyde Park – the School rumour being that he walked barefoot to save shoe leather. During his year at Central, rehearsal master Henry Oscar found Olivier his first paid work, as a walk-on – humble beginnings for a young man who would become one of the country's, and the world's, most celebrated actors.

Ashcroft later claimed that even as students both she and Olivier found Fogerty's training old-fashioned, but perhaps that shouldn't be surprising. Constantin Stanislavski's *My Life in Art* was first published in Great Britain in 1924, and it brought exciting new ideas on what acting and actor training might be. Besides, in 1925 Fogerty was already 60 years old. Her young students would no doubt have seen this old woman, with her focus on the 'voice beautiful', as behind the times. Nevertheless, Central trained voices that could fill theatres, and this was a skill that would prove invaluable to both Dame Peggy Ashcroft and Lord Olivier throughout their long and very successful careers.

At the end of the 1925 summer term, Ashcroft and Olivier left the School with Central Certificates and shared a Gold Medal for their performances as Portia and Shylock. Their careers would span over sixty years of 20th century theatre, but although they remained lifelong friends, they seldom worked together after they graduated – one rare exception the famous 1935 New Theatre *Romeo and Juliet*, directed by John Gielgud, in which Gielgud and Olivier alternated Romeos to Ashcroft's Juliet.

Initially, Ashcroft was less well known internationally than Olivier, who early in his career became successful in American films. However, in addition to her vast resumé of classical and modern roles for the Royal Shakespeare Company and the Royal National Theatre, in her later years she earned the respect and love of the general public for a number of acclaimed appearances on both television and film.

The success of these two extraordinary actors has lent glamour to Central over the years, but Fogerty delighted in their talents from their earliest student days. Livvy Wilson-Dickson (Stage '32) recalled: 'When I was there, Larry Olivier and Peggy Ashcroft had just left. At the end of each year, we would be given good parts in a play, suited to our type; and professional people would be invited to come and look at us. When we were introduced to them, Elsie would present us as "another of our dear little Peggys or Larrys".'

● ● ●

There is no record of exactly when the University of London first began accrediting Central's University Extension Lectures, but this arrangement was certainly in place by the end of World War One. Fogerty gave Extension students a special Diction class on Saturday mornings, but in some cases University students merely joined her regular classes on Thursday afternoons, an arrangement that suggests the standard at which Central classes were taught. Nevertheless, when Central applied to the University for affiliated status in the summer of 1921, the application was turned down.

That very autumn the Government Departmental Committee on English came out with a report, 'The Teaching of English in England', that recommended that a Diploma similar to that given in the Humanities should be awarded to anyone who completed a course in drama approved by them. As a result, to look into the *possibility* of a formal qualification in Drama, the Senate of London University appointed a Committee that consisted of the Principals of RADA and Central, leading actors, playwrights, theatre professionals, and representatives from the world of education. Fogerty noted in particular the support of RADA's Principal: 'The meetings of the Committee, which for fifteen months thrashed out the details of the Diploma, were delightful for many things: most of all for the close sympathy and co-operation of Sir Kenneth Barnes in all we were trying to do, though much of it – the teacher side – was not of direct advantage to the Royal Academy of Dramatic Art; always I had detested the foolish contention which kept apart our two Institutions, both working along the different, but harmonious lines to train people for the theatre.' [*Fogie*]

ASHCROFT AND OLIVIER

Dame Peggy Ashcroft and Lord Olivier remained loyal to Elsie Fogerty and Central for the rest of their lives, even though they were not always in agreement with the School and its policies and decisions. Both served as Central Governors, and later as Vice Presidents and successive Presidents; and both generously gave their time, energy and support to the School throughout their successful and demanding careers. In the last year of her life, Dame Peggy was in serious disagreement with the direction Central was taking towards Higher Education, and it has been said that, before her final illness she had intended to resign her Presidency in protest. In spite of this, or perhaps as passionate proof of it, until her final days, Ashcroft never stopped caring about the School or its future.

As a result of the work of this Committee, in 1923 Central, RADA and the Speech-Training Department of the Regent Street Polytechnic started two-year courses for any full-time student wishing to attain a Diploma in Drama. The Polytechnic later dropped out.

This was the first time anyone could attain a Diploma in Dramatic Art in the United Kingdom and, until Bristol University opened the first drama department in 1947, the Diploma was the only formal qualification available to any student interested in the theatre. A student could still choose to receive a Central Certificate for performing or for teaching – but they could only achieve the prized Diploma in Dramatic Art from London University by taking the required courses and sitting the arduous examinations. In 1925, the 28 Diploma students (only 18 would pass, three with distinction) sat examinations in English Poetics; the History of Drama, Shakespeare and Selected Plays; French; History of Theatrical Art, with Special Reference to Social Life, Manners, Customs and Costume; and Music Appreciation. In 1926, at Central only, a third year was instituted that would provide teaching practice and a teaching qualification. Exams were set in Phonetics; Theory and Practice of Voice Training; Elementary Anatomy and Physiology as Applied to Movement, Voice and Speech; and Elementary Psychology as Applied to Movement, Voice and Speech.

When in 1923 Central's syllabus was amended to satisfy the syllabus for the forthcoming Diploma, it became necessary for Central tutors to adhere to a more formal course structure. This was not Fogerty's style, and even though she had been a driving force towards acquiring recognised qualifications for her students, she personally found the changes difficult. Marion Cole, who trained on the Teacher Course in the 1930s and was author of the Fogerty biography, *Fogie*, wrote of this time: 'She always implied – probably believed – that we knew much more than most young people acquire at School. She certainly filled us with a desire for knowledge, and sometimes gave the whole hour to the facts that would meet university demands, and would present them in such way that they would never be forgotten, so that even notes were unnecessary. But too often Fogie wandered down delightful sidetracks, turned off into others, and the whole Lecture was sheer enjoyment – but our note-books were blank, though our lives were richer... Later generations demanded more helpful lectures, ever with an eye on those examiners. But Fogie confined to a syllabus could never be the real Fogie.' [*Fogie*]

Gwynneth Thurburn believed that, besides offering an education to her students, Fogerty was also instrumental in shaping their young lives: 'Elsie Fogerty taught me how to think, she taught me to question, not to take things for granted; and implanted somehow – I don't quite know how – an idea of service into my mind. Now I never remember if we were taught anything about service; but I think that implicit in our training was some idea that we were working not just for our own ends, but that we could be of service in a community; and I at all events was impressed by this, and it took root in me.' [Elsie Fogerty Memorial Lecture, 1978]

• • •

The same year Central began its new Diploma Course, Fogerty began another project, this time roping in a regular adjudicator for the Central Diction Exams.

In 1923, John Masefield was not yet Poet Laureate – King George V would bestow that honour in 1930 – but he was a thriving poet and an even more successful playwright. His 1908 West End play, *The Tragedy of Nan*, had starred Lillah McCarthy – now Lady Keeble and one of his neighbours in Boars Hill near Oxford. Poet Laureate Robert Bridges, the playwright, scholar and poet, Gilbert Murray, and the poet and novelist Robert Graves also lived nearby.

When the Scottish Association invited John Masefield to Edinburgh for a Verse Speaking Recital, the press reported that he 'doubted if any such beautiful verse-speaking could be heard in the South'. Fogerty not only disputed Masefield's assertion, but also challenged him to a verse speaking 'duel'. Masefield graciously, and grandly, accepted, and the first Oxford Recitations took place in the summer of 1923 at the Oxford University Examination Hall. The three-day competition attracted competitors from Scotland, Ireland, Wales, England and abroad, and the judges, Mr and Mrs John Masefield, Laurence

Binyon, Gilbert Murray and Sir Herbert Warren, awarded the top prize of a Silver Medal to Winifred Mattingley – a Central student from South Africa who had done no verse speaking until her training began at the Central School less than three years before. The runners-up, too, were all from Central.

Two requirements for the competition had been laid down, and both were in accordance with Fogerty's position on verse speaking. The first dealt with her most basic tenet, 'the matter not the manner', and to this end, gesture was not allowed. The second requirement was that the poems must be spoken from memory and not read. Fogerty had always asserted that the mental process of translating the printed word into sound, then emotion, and finally speech, blurred interpretation. As early as 1913, she had explained this theory to a clerical training course at Queen's College, Birmingham. Her speech was reported in *The Times*: 'The first essential of good reading was to give the eye time to report to the mind; to speak only when the meaning of what is to be spoken has consciously come to us. By practice this could be done with incredible speed, but at first it must be slow. Even later one must not forget that the process had to be carried out inversely in the minds of the hearers.' Seventy-seven years later, Fogerty's instincts seem to have been confirmed. At a Speech Conference organised by the Performance Department at the Central School in 2000, Professor Sally Grace (Teacher '58) was one of the speakers: 'A couple of days ago, I was talking to a director about a play that I am working on. He pointed something out to me that I had not known before... As I am talking to you now, the part of my brain which is involved in saying what I am saying is apparently scientifically a completely different part of the brain from if I now start reading my speech to you. So, an actor, when he or she is engaged with text, is in fact using a completely different cerebral system.'

Fogerty's theories certainly proved themselves effective in practice when Central students swept the board at the Recitation prizes. There had been few male entries to the first competition, but by the second year over eighty men applied, and it became necessary to separate the men's and the women's competitions. One of these competitors stood out, and Fogerty immediately offered Clifford Turner a scholarship to the Central School. Again Fogerty's instincts were impeccable: Turner would go on to teach voice at both Central and RADA, becoming one of Britain's foremost voice experts. His book *Voice and Speech in the Theatre* (1950) is still in use today.

• • •

Fogerty saw the Oxford Recitations as an excellent opportunity to extend Central's successful Summer School in Stratford by adding two weeks in Oxford to take in the Recitations. Central was gaining an international reputation for its Summer Schools, and it was already highly respected all over the world for the quality of its graduates. Nevertheless, its key competitor, the Academy of Dramatic Art, received its Royal Charter in 1920, while the Central School's business affairs were still in disarray. The process of

Central's incorporation had been initiated in 1917, but it was still incomplete, so in 1924, Jane Gavin was appointed Company Secretary to help Registrar Hazel Thompson. The two women went to work, and due largely to their enthusiasm and abilities – a particularly valuable combination in a time of over-work and reorganisation – in 1925 the School was finally officially registered as a charitable company: The Central School of Speech-Training and Dramatic Art (Inc). The Board of Governors took financial responsibility for the institution, and for the first time accounts were submitted to the Members at an Annual General Meeting.

Lee Matthews, Vice President of the Board, became Chairman of the newly formed Finance Committee and was made directly responsible for reorganising the business side of the institution. Matthews' first two edicts were pretty simple: 1, Miss Fogerty was not allowed to give any more 'scholarships' without first consulting the Board; and 2, for the first time, she was required to take a salary. The Governors also took steps to provide a pension for Elsie Fogerty's retirement – should that unlikely day ever arrive.

• • •

Central was no longer the free-form 'one man band' that Fogerty had started in 1906, and official incorporation finally gave the School some structure and stability. Central's reputation was impressive, enrolment was increasing, and it offered a prized Diploma in Dramatic Art from the University of London. In 1927, the School turned twenty-one. It had come of age.

Events were organised for Central's 21st Birthday Week. The Pivot Club provided an Entertainment for the Albert Hall 'At Home' party, and the students presented a 'Rag'. However, the culminating celebrity event was a matinée given at the Scala Theatre, and it was presented both as a celebration and as a fund-raiser. Central's Royal Patron Princess Louise, Duchess of Argyll, attended the Gala, which included contributions by ex-students such as Peggy Ashcroft, Mabel Constanduros, John Laurie, Alison Leggatt, Campbell Logan, George More O'Ferrall, Gwynneth Thurburn, Irene Mawer, Aileen Wyse, Ann Todd and Clifford Turner. Some of Fogerty's private students and colleagues also took part: Lewis Casson, Sybil Thorndike, Edith Evans, Reginald Dance, Leslie Faber and Henry Oscar. To honour Central's founder, Fogerty's friends and students bought her a ticket for a 1928 spring Hellenic Cruise.

The day after the Scala Matinée, with the week-long party over and Fogerty's cruise months away, Central and the Association of Teachers of Speech-Training

LEE MATTHEWS

One of Central's first Governors, Lee Matthews remained on the Board until his death in 1931. Matthews had a keen interest in the theatre, and had held Central's first verse speaking competition at his own home, adjudicating for many years and often helping in the selection of other judges.

and Dramatic Art opened the Second Conference on Speech at the Royal Society of Arts in Duke Street. The three-day international conference included a number of presentations and speeches, and perhaps most importantly, included a public statement on modern methods of treating stammering. Fogerty's own methods were difficult to describe, but her passion to research and record – and to share – her knowledge and techniques, had contributed to her growing international reputation as the accepted expert on speech defects in England.

•   •   •

ADDITIONAL CENTRAL FACTS

1925   • Elsie Fogerty interviewed for BBC Radio, followed by programmes on Ben Greet, Bridge Adams, Allardyce Nicoll, Nigel Playfair, John Drinkwater and Geoffrey Whitworth.

5

1927–1938

IN SPITE OF CENTRAL'S MANY SUCCESSES in the 1920s, financially the School had veered from red to black to red again. When in 1927–8 it looked as though there would be a profit, a new lighting system and a new curtain were purchased for the little theatre over the West Porch. Fogerty later explained to the Governors that that year's shortfall was caused by 'an outbreak of matrimony among the students; the fact that a number of teacher-students had gone over to the Stage side, and a marked decrease in the Summer School profits due to the enormous multiplication of Summer Schools all over the country.'

No matter the explanation, Lee Matthews and the Finance Committee decided that the only way to make up for a decrease in revenue was to cut staff salaries and increase staff duties. The Association of Teachers of Speech-Training and Dramatic Art (ATST) had recently asked that Central come into line with other teacher training colleges by sending a supervisor to observe students in their practice teaching, so Clifford Turner and Gwynneth Thurburn undertook this responsibility in addition to their regular obligations. To add to both the workload and the year's expenses, 1927–8 ended with the School's first public matinée in the West End. Potential employers, as well as family and friends, were invited to the Arts Theatre to mark the end of the students' training.

• • •

Elsie Fogerty returned from her Hellenic cruise in time for the 1928 Central Summer School, which by now included two weeks in London, two weeks in Stratford and two weeks in Oxford for the sixth, and final, Oxford Recitations. With each year proving more popular than the last, the Oxford competition had finally become too unwieldy to sustain, and after 1928 it was discontinued. Central graduate Eve Turner (Stage '27) was its final winner. To replace the Recitations, in the summer of 1929 a non-competitive Oxford Verse Speaking Festival was begun at John Masefield's home in Boars Hill. There, Masefield had his own private theatre, The Music Room, where he had often produced amateur theatrical productions of the work of Laurence Binyon, Thomas Hardy, and Gordon Bottomley, as well as recitations and recitals of his own and others' poetry. The new Festival was organised with Fogerty's help, of course, to take place during the Central Summer

School's residency. Presentations of poems or short plays were by invitation only, and performers at the first Oxford Festival included past winners of Oxford Recitation prizes – the majority of whom, of course, were Central graduates.

In that same 1929 summer as the new Oxford Festival, and for the only time, Central's two-week Summer School in Stratford was cancelled so that it might instead take up two weeks' residency at the first of Sir Barry Jackson's Malvern Festivals. The Malvern Festival was devoted to modern plays, particularly those of its patron, George Bernard Shaw, and the Festival Company included two recent Central graduates, Eve Turner and Yvette Pienne (Stage '28). Fogerty saw the Festival as yet another opportunity to promote Central and expand its ever-growing circle of influential friends, and it seems she was right. Shaw himself gave Central's first Malvern Summer School Inaugural Address. Fogerty wrote later of that first Festival summer:

IPHIGENIA AT TAURUS

Gilbert Murray was an internationally renowned scholar and Chair of Greek at Oxford until the late 1930s. In 1931, Fogerty used the Oxford Verse-Speaking Festival to indulge her own passion for Greek theatre by mounting a production of his translation of *Iphigenia at Taurus*. Set in the grounds of Blenheim House, the play starred Lillah McCarthy as Iphigenia, with Clifford Turner as Orestes. There are few personal accounts of any of Fogerty's productions, but Turner's review of *Iphigenia* from *Fogie* said: 'If the truth be told, some of her productions inclined to be grandiose in conceptions, or artistically vague. But she excelled in manoeuvring Greek Choruses…'. Turner's 'faint-praise'-opinion aside, the show was remounted in December 1932 for one sold-out matinée at the Haymarket Theatre in London, and McCarthy performed speeches from the play for many years to come.

> Every night, sometimes beginning as early as six o'clock, Festival plays took place in the beautiful theatre. Sir Barry Jackson himself with Mr Gordon Bottomley and several other friends attended the first of Mr Norris' two splendid costume lectures, and expressed his keen interest in the work of the School. A number of the actors came in to the tea and reception. Most of the younger members of the School disported themselves daily in the Swimming Pool and at the Festival Ball in the splendid dancing hall of the Pump Rooms, while the gardens were all beautifully illuminated. An exhibition of photographs, books and models and a certain number of original designs illustrating the English, American and Continental Theatre in relation to Mr Shaw's work was open in the Malvern Public Library during the Festival. Sir Barry Jackson received us all in the gardens of Lawnside for a wonderful tea-party, while many of us had the privilege of personal interviews with Mr Shaw and of invitations to meet many of the other distinguished visitors at Sir Barry Jackson's daily tea-parties. [*Viva Voce*, 1929]

The Summer School returned to Stratford the following year, but continued to use an extra week of Summer School to attend the Malvern Festival.

1930	British Actors' Equity registers as a trade union
1931	Lillian Bayliss reopens Sadler's Wells with Ninette de Valois' company (later the Royal Ballet) as first resident company
1932	Hunger Marchers arrive in London
	BBC opens new headquarters in Portland Place
	Shakespeare Memorial Theatre re-opens
1933	Hitler takes over as Chancellor of German Reich
1934	Mussolini welcomes Hitler to Italy
1935	Equity establishes a West End agreement and closed shop
	Severe dust storms sweep over half of the USA
1936	Spanish Civil War
	King George V dies, Edward VIII renounces throne for Mrs Simpson. Prince Albert becomes King George VI
	Crystal Palace burns down
1937	Guernica, cultural and spiritual home of the Basques, is destroyed by German bombs
	Coronation of George VI
1938	George Gershwin dies of brain tumour at age 38
1938	Disney produces first feature-length cartoon, Snow White and the Seven Dwarves
	Hitler annexes Austria
1939	Sikorsky flies his first helicopter, the VS39
	World War Two begins

Elsie Fogerty's reputation enabled her to surround her Central students with the most influential and forward thinking theatre practitioners of the day. Every year at Jehangir Hall, Imperial Institute, an Inaugural Lecture was given to all Diploma students from Central, RADA and the Regent Street Polytechnic. There is no record of who presented the first of these lectures in 1926 or 1927, but in 1928, Central Governor Ashley Dukes was the official speaker. Edith Evans also addressed the 36 students, as did the soon-to-be-appointed President of Central's Council of Governors, the Right Honourable 2nd Earl of Lytton.

When Sir Barry Jackson gave the Inaugural Lecture in 1930, he was Director of the Memorial Theatre at Stratford, Vice President of the British Drama League, and founder of both the Birmingham Repertory Company (1913) and the Malvern Festival (1929). A 1930 *Viva Voce* reported: 'Sir Barry, in his extremely interesting address, traced the history of the Birmingham Repertory Company from its earliest beginnings in a barn, up through its many vicissitudes among tables and gas brackets, to its present well-established popularity. He then said that to his mind the ideal theatre for "intelligent" drama was one in which the auditorium should be one large "pit" stretching right to the footlights, with the stalls and dress circle non-existent.'

Jackson was not just an 'interesting' speaker. He had been hiring Central graduates to join his Birmingham Company since its inception, and now that he was the Director of the Memorial Theatre in Stratford, the tradition of graduates performing there – as they had for Sir Frank Benson – would also continue. By the end of the 1920s, with an increasing number of repertory companies across Britain, actors were no longer limited to touring with large companies, doing smaller fit-up tours of one or two performances (in buildings 'fit-up' to be theatres) or, if they were lucky enough to suit the style of the day, playing the lighter fare of the West End. By this time, actors were also regularly taken into companies like Stratford or the Birmingham Repertory Company for a year or two at a time, and

Fogerty's and Central's contacts and reputation made this possible.

Central actors were not the only students to benefit from Central connections. There was still no separate speech therapy course, and students interested in specialising in this emerging field merely took 'remedial speech' classes in their final year on the teachers' course. By the end of the 1920s, Central helped its new graduates find positions in clinics and hospitals – that were run and staffed by Central alumni.

In addition, Central regularly played a part in its teacher-students' employment, serving almost as an employment agency. The School regularly placed graduates in positions throughout Great Britain, South Africa, America and Canada. They asked only that if a teacher decided to leave a post, he or she should contact

DR LEONARD COURTNEY

When Sir Frank Benson retired as President of the School in 1917, Dr Leonard Courtney became both President of the School and President of what, in 1917, was called the Provisional Council. The Provisional Council presided over the first steps toward Central's incorporation as a company. When Central incorporated, the Provisional Council became the Council (or Board) of Governors. The President of the School was up until this point also the President of the Council/Board. Later the two positions would be divided into two: President of the School and Chairman of the Board. After Dr Courtney's death early in 1928, the (Second) Earl of Lytton became President of the School and President of the Council (Board) of Governors, a position he would hold until 1948, when Lord Esher succeeded him.

Central first, thereby allowing the position to be filled by another suitable graduate. There had grown up a custom amongst teachers of selling these 'connections', and a number of school Principals wrote to Central in protest, maintaining that they were in no way bound by such an agreement. In 1931, Fogerty laid out guidelines for the transference of posts originally found by the School and issued instructions to teachers that they contact Central when such a position became vacant – before notice of resignation was given and before a successor was approached. She suggested that the letter of resignation not only include a list of Central-sanctioned possible successors, but also that it express the hope that the work would be carried on along the same lines as those established by the current teacher. It should in no way suggest that the sale of a connection had occurred. '...In regard to the sale of connections, we can only point out to our members that such transactions have no legal value whatever. ...The Central School never makes any charge for work found, or for any negotiations undertaken in transfer, and has, of course, to maintain the level of general employment and the excellence of the work done by our teachers throughout the world. ' [Fogerty, *Viva Voce*]

• • •

In spite of Central's support in seeking employment for its teacher-students, if a graduate wanted to work (and not all did), the first step became membership in the Association of Teachers of Speech-Training and Dramatic Art (ATST). The only early requirement for ATST membership was the two-year qualification from Central. As a result of Central's reputation, employers therefore saw the ATST as a reliable resource for skilled teachers of speech and drama. Employers knew Central graduates understood both the practical and theoretical elements of their work and could provide not only training in 'correct accents' for speaking, but also good reading skills, an appreciation of literature and the speaking of verse. Central graduates – and therefore ATST members – could also address problems or defects in speech and help improve the general quality of the voice, and they could direct school plays from a dramatic, as well as an educational, point of view. 'All that they do is intimately connected with the work of the Literature, Music, Dancing and Physical Education Classes; careful and scientific training in good respiratory movement, and in the accurate use of the whole Apparatus of Speech, produces a very marked improvement in the pupils' general health, bearing, and manner.' [Fogerty, Address to ATST, 1923]

There was a growing demand for teachers of speech and drama, but in 1928, teacher-training colleges also formally identified a need for a course to ensure that teachers should themselves speak 'good, clear English, in voices giving confidence and pleasure, without mumbling, mannerisms or shoddy grammar'. Central immediately responded by adding a new one-year course for those who already had a qualification in their chosen subject, and in 1929 the University of London awarded the first Certificate of Proficiency in Diction and Dramatic Art (CDA), a qualification only obtainable by taking this particular course at Central. Holding this new CDA also meant the teacher was allowed automatic entry into the ATST.

Since its formation in 1914, the ATST had only been open to Central graduates, but in 1934, it began to recognise teaching diplomas from the Royal College of Music and the Royal Music Academy. From that time, the ATST re-formed to become the Incorporated Association of Teachers of Speech and Drama (IATSD). In 1951, the IATSD became the Society of Teachers of Speech and Drama, which is still active today.

• • •

Leaving the Oxford Festival and the Summer School in the hands of her dedicated staff, in 1930 Fogerty embarked on an eleven-week lecture tour of universities in North America to raise Central's profile and promote its Summer School. Her first engagement was at Northwestern University in Chicago, Illinois, where Central teacher-graduate, Belle Kennedy, supervised 'speech re-education' at the University's newly formed speech clinic. Fogerty later gave lectures and presented verse recitals at a Teacher-Training College in Evanston, Illinois, the University of Michigan at Ann Arbor, the University of Wisconsin, Normal Schools (American teacher-training colleges) in Oregon, at the University of

California at Berkeley, and Carnegie Tech in Pittsburgh, Pennsylvania.

Fogerty's recruitment drive in the United States had mixed success. Many Americans made initial arrangements to come to England for the Summer School, but owing to the Depression that had begun with the Wall Street Crash, many then had to cancel. In spite of this, there was an increase in the number of Americans who attended the next year, and the Summer School actually made a profit of £200. The summer programme now ran for six weeks, with two weeks in London at the Albert Hall from mid-July, one week each to take in the Festivals at Oxford and Malvern, and a final two weeks in Stratford. It was possible to join the Summer School for only a fortnight, but a number of those Americans sponsored by the American Drama League regularly stayed throughout the full six weeks. After Fogerty's tour, American universities began to give academic credits for the Central courses, and groups of American university and high school lecturers, as well as British students, teachers and lecturers, also attended.

The Summer Schools attracted a high calibre of staff as well, and E Martin Browne – playwright, director and teacher of modern and medieval drama – wrote: 'As a teaching job it was not one of the easiest; one could not achieve, in the make-shift conditions, a finished production; and the students tended, understandably, to regard the

FOGERTY IN CALIFORNIA WITH MRS PATRICK CAMPBELL

Fogerty's 1930 trip was by no means all work, and when she arrived in Los Angeles, California, she met up with the famous English actress, Mrs Patrick Campbell. Fogerty remembered this colourful visit:

> Los Angeles is only a shadow of its lovely self, spoilt by the oil boom which has covered its beautiful beach with gleaming canisters spaced like a row of bathing boxes to gather and control the riches of the seeping oil wells. I hurried on to Hollywood, but not before I had got into touch with Mrs Patrick Campbell, who gave me a glorious day driving about with her through all the beautiful country round Hollywood, up to Santa Barbara, and to the lovely little Mission Inn which looks out over the whole bay and away to the South. I had brought many introductions, and spent a couple of days in the appalling experience of watching the commercial film being produced. It seems now like a sort of nightmare, in which a lady trying to dance a Spanish dance in a flower bed, under the instruction of a camera man who had never seen one – the endless and infuriating ejaculation of 'Oh Kay, Oh Kay, Oh Kay' made every human soul in the place – thirty-two people trying to act a scene without a scene plot – eighty-two performers banging at the door before it was ready, a noise like all the parrots in the Zoo fighting their last fight for freedom, which was supposed to represent human speech – and a complete moral and mental incompetence of *human* factors compared with the faultless precision of the machines, combined to bewilder one. This is the sort of impression left on my mind. [*Viva Voce*]

BELLE KENNEDY

Fogerty said of Belle Kennedy in 1931: 'She has done perhaps the greatest work in relation to speech defects of anyone connected with the Central School, and at present her work at Northwestern University in conjunction with Dr. Clarence T. Simon is attracting the attention of all America.' Kennedy graduated from the Teachers Course, and gained clinical experience when she took over the running of the London County Council's Clinics from Muriel (Bousfield) Wigglesworth in 1922. Northwestern had long had a School of Speech that offered a great number of courses in speech and the theatre arts, but when Belle Kennedy joined the University in the mid-1920s, she contributed to the establishment of a strong department of remedial speech as well. She was also instrumental in instituting the first National Poetry Speaking Festival ever to be held in the United States, thus encouraging the organisation of verse speaking contests and festivals in colleges and secondary schools throughout the country. Kennedy later became the Director of the Department of Voice and Speech Education at the College of Arts, Pasadena Playhouse, Pasadena, California.

School as really a holiday – though the Americans got 'credits' for attendances. But the compensations were more than adequate: two of England's beauty-spots, the Festival plays to see, and – not least – the chance to watch Miss Fogerty teach and to exchange views with her on a wide range of subjects.' [*Fogie*]

The organisation of this annual event was monumental, and Central's already overworked administrative staff accomplished it largely during the academic year, at the same time as running the School and organising Diploma examinations. When asked what she remembered most of her years at Central, Vera Sargent replied: 'Hard work!'

• • •

In 1933, Dr Russell Wakefield, CBE, passed away. Fogerty quietly mourned the loss of her friend, her Romeo and her teacher. A loyal supporter of Central for nearly fifty years, Dr Wakefield had provided Fogerty with help, advice, support, knowledge and friendship, and he had had an enormous influence on his young student. His early classes in dramatic and lyric speaking had instilled in Fogerty a strong reaction against the Victorian's artificial and vulgar Elocution. He had recommended Fogerty for her first major teaching post at the Crystal Palace School of Art. He had escorted Swinburne's sister to Fogerty's first production of *Atalanta in Calydon* in 1906. He had been on Central's Council of Governors since its inception, and was later described by Fogerty as a co-founder of the School. Although Wakefield's consecration as Bishop of Birmingham in 1911 had allowed him less time in London, he nevertheless served on the Provisional Council and in 1917 was the first to sign the minutes declaring the School's intention to incorporate. He was instrumental in securing the Earl of Lytton as President of the Council, and in 1927, he had attended Central's 21st Birthday Celebration at the Scala Theatre, watching the performance with HRH Princess Louise from the Royal Box.

After Wakefield's retirement to Hove, Fogerty regularly visited him and his family after her teaching sessions at Roedean. Wakefield's son, the playwright Gilbert Wakefield, described their relationship as that of a teacher and his favourite pupil and recalled his father forever teasing Fogerty about: '...all those eccentricities about which other people smiled affectionately behind her back. My father did it to her face...and Elsie obviously adored it! ...No longer was she the great 'Miss Fogerty', or even the beloved, but respected, Elsie, but (and I haven't a doubt of this) a young girl being playfully and affectionately teased by the man for whom throughout her life she had felt something very like adoration: the young Sydenham clergyman who had never – in her eyes, anyway – grown any older.'

Fogerty's dear friend, Muriel (Bousfield) Wigglesworth, wrote in a personal memoir that when Wakefield died, Fogerty 'quite went to pieces'. In the spring of 1933, Lillah McCarthy and her husband, Sir Frederick Keeble, came to Fogerty's emotional rescue with an invitation for yet another Greek cruise, but upon their return, Fogerty went back to her punishing schedule, never showing or sharing her private and overwhelming grief with those around her.

VERA SARGENT

Vera Sargent – 'Sarge' to colleagues and friends – was born on 29 May 1908 in Sittingbourne, Kent. At 20, she moved to London for a secretarial course, and upon completion was hired by Central to assist Jane Gavin and Hazel Thompson, and to be private secretary to Elsie Fogerty. Sarge's earliest assignment was to assist Fogerty in the organisation of the 1929 Summer School. Enormously able, within four years Sarge was listed as Summer School Registrar. She became Central Registrar and Company Secretary in 1938, and for the next 30 years was responsible for all financial aspects of the School, the arrangement of all timetables, and any and all administration concerning students' lives. Sarge organised Central's evacuation to Exeter in 1939, its return to the Albert Hall in 1942, and its 1957 move from the Albert Hall to the Embassy Theatre. She retired in 1968, and she and Gwynneth Thurburn moved to a small cottage in Surrey.

• • •

In 1934, at a time when very few decorations were given to anyone in the theatre, Elsie Fogerty was awarded the Commander of the British Empire (CBE) in the Birthday Honours. Ostensibly in recognition of her many contributions to the theatre and teaching, the award also surely honoured Fogerty's many other achievements: speech clinics, the Oxford Recitations, the Central Summer School, International Speech Conferences, her work towards forming the British Drama League, her tireless work both towards a Diploma in Dramatic Art and towards the formation of a National Theatre. Fogerty's CBE was the first time that Speech had received recognition at such a public and formal level, and on the night of her investiture, the Pivot Club gave a reception for over 300 guests to celebrate and honour her achievements. Although the country was still in a financial depression, the Albert Hall caterers donated champagne; invitations were printed free of charge by a Mr Milner, whose printing works were located in the outer walls of the Albert Hall; and flowers from guests' gardens adorned the Crush Room.

•   •   •

At the time of her investiture, Fogerty was 69 years old, yet she was still showing a willingness to embrace the most modern of ideas. Jacques Copeau's nephew, Michel Saint-Denis, had presented a ground-breaking London production of Obey's *Noah* with his famous Companie Quinze, and he was now being urged to stay in England to start his own school of acting. Fogerty began talks with him to see if an interchange of classes between their two institutions could be arranged – to provide Central 'with a more direct approach to the theatre'. In 1935, the *Viva Voce* reported a Central visit by the celebrated French producer, and at the Summer School in Malvern, Saint-Denis gave a lecture on his Companie Quinze, which the *Viva Voce* reported was delivered in English 'with little arabesques and flourishes of French'. Nothing formal came of these initial meetings, but Saint-Denis would have a profound impact on Central thirty years later, when the teachers and students from both his pre-war London Studio and his post-war Old Vic School directly influenced Central actor training.

When talks with Saint-Denis foundered, Fogerty instead arranged a joint three-year training in acting and the 'arts of the theatre' with the Old Vic Theatre, on the understanding that, upon completion of the course, selected students would be invited to join the Old Vic Company. The Old Vic had apprenticed young actors since the 1920s, but their training had mostly consisted of playing walk-ons or small parts. Esme Church had taken over direction of their training school in the early 1930s, and had begun to offer a wider and more rigorous training. The collaboration with Central would serve both institutions, but world events dictated that this first Central/Old Vic collaboration would be short-lived.

•   •   •

In 1935, as well as involving itself in negotiations with Saint-Denis and setting up the new joint course with the Old Vic, Central also became involved in an historic theatrical event. The poet T S Eliot's first project for the theatre, *The Rock*, was a pageant play performed at the Sadler's Wells Theatre for the London Forty-five Churches fund. E Martin Browne agreed to direct, and he enlisted Fogerty to provide and train the mixed chorus. Fogerty was quick to see the advantages of drawing the chorus from Central's own students: 'The one impossible thing with a chorus is to take a group of people who have had no common technical training together, who are strangers to each other and are unused to an accepted type of movement with speech, and hope to make of them a united

ISHBEL MACGLASHAN FOX (1910–81)

Ishbel MacGlashan Fox was on the Stage Course from 1929–31. After ten years as an actress, she joined Central as Wardrobe Mistress while the School was still at the Albert Hall.

      ❝ My first encounter with the remarkable lady [Fogerty] took place in what was known as the Lower Crush Room at the Albert Hall – one of those curiously shaped, concave-walled rooms which lay round the building outside the dark passages which circumnavigated the auditorium of the Hall itself, and in several of which at that time the school had its home. Saturday morning recitation classes were held there – the victim of the moment required to stand on a small rostrum at the end of the room, with the rest of the class ranged down both sides along the wall or under the enormous windows, freezing in winter, scorching in summer, and the lady herself behind a small table at the other end.

I recited my prepared piece, and there was dead silence for a moment. 'Why have you come here?' she asked brusquely. Speechless and appalled, I had no idea. 'Come down here,' she said, and I tottered down to stand before the table. 'You have come to learn all we have to teach you, and that is a great deal. INSIST that we teach you.' I couldn't have insisted on the simplest arrangement of any kind, and watched enthralled her pencil making violent marks all over my neatly copied out poem, culminating incredibly in the enormous VG, to which we were all to aspire. I was, of course, totally devoted to her from that moment on, although our relationship with her was one fraught with panic. We walked in awe.

Miss F's lectures on Dramatic History took place in the little theatre, also that strange curved shape, and these ranged over a variety of subjects which would perhaps not assist us in our examination, but were of immense fascination, including I seem to remember on one occasion, French cooking. She directed a play a term herself, which seemed to include almost all the school, men being played by girls in default of enough students of the requisite sex. We were delighted to slap on crepe hair beards in the tiny dressing rooms beneath the stage, which shared the mezzanine with the cloakrooms and the canteen...

We took Mime and Greek dancing (in little grey tunics) with Miss Breukleman, who always wore a long black dress and an elegant hat, and who was rumoured to have been taught the minuet at the last French Court. She carried a long, rolled umbrella, which she used for demonstration purposes on any too prominent behinds, and the classes culminated in a court curtsy: left toe four inches behind right heel – 'Bend your necks to your sovereign, girls'; which some of the class were of course actually to do, wearing the three little white feathers in their hair.

And then there were the productions of the Greek plays – Gilbert Murray's translations of course, 'And forth lo, the women go – the crown of war and the crown of woe – To bear the children, (pause, pause, pause) of-the-foe, And weep, weep for Ilyon.' Rigorously conducted by the lady, we would weep for a breath in the wrong place, as well as for the sad about-to-be-enslaved ladies, and woe for the false stress and over-emphatic emphasis.

On one occasion, we were performing a play at a rather celebrated girls' finishing school at Richmond (in the open air), and some inaudibility was complained about. Miss F appeared and lined us up as far away from her as possible. 'Have you filled in a form?' she required us to whisper, then louder and louder 'Roll it across the lawn to me! She demanded. 'Have you filled in a fooooooorm?' We rolled. No more problems, I think it was mesmerism...   [*continued...*

> I find it is so often said that people of dominant personality, who manage to bully, coerce and persuade others into a course of action that will achieve their own ends, have a 'method'. I am sure this is not true. The inspiration of the moment is what counts and each situation is judged and coped with on its own merits and within its own context. As far as I was concerned, E F was totally unpredictable.
>
> I learned from her never to be satisfied with the job in hand and that there is always 'a little more to give'. She had a horror of anything smug, and when you thought you were doing something rather well, you would receive a very sharp reminder that in her opinion the situation was quite the reverse. Although she could indeed be devastatingly cruel and we dreaded her disapproval, it was of the moment and immediately forgotten. ...I think that we carry a mark of integrity and open-ended interest through our lives which she helped us achieve. 〞

whole. Among the many great services of the Ginner-Mawer School was their capacity for giving just this background to students' work. There is no shadow of drill in the teaching; where unison action exists, it comes from a marked united impulse on the part of the whole group, and it will be harmonious – yet they remain individuals, not acting under a uniform command. And we started with the advantage of having just such a homogenous group.' [Fogerty, *Fogie*]

Marion Cole says in *Fogie* that Gwynneth Thurburn was made responsible for 'maintaining' the choruses for *The Rock*, but Thurburn remembered her involvement as more than merely maintenance, and her private papers include 'Some Recollections of T S Eliot', written in 1966 for E Martin Browne: 'We rehearsed the choruses in isolation, with you coming to many of the rehearsals and keeping them in line with your production. I had to filch time from my own classes in order to do the groundwork in between. Eliot often came too, seemingly enjoying himself, but shy and difficult to draw out if one wanted to know anything... I can remember, soon after I met Eliot, making some fatuous remark about his impressions of his first excursion into the theatre, and I well remember his reply, which was to the effect that he had not the same responsibility to himself of writing poetry – if it turned out poetry that was very good, but it didn't have to be. This made a profound impression on me at the time.'

The Rock was a dazzling success, but it paved the way for an even more important collaboration – Eliot's new play about Thomas à Becket, *Murder in the Cathedral*. Also directed by Browne, it was to open on Trinity Sunday and perform during Canterbury Festival Week. Again Browne came to Central for his Chorus, but this new work presented new challenges, as Fogerty recalled: 'The great popularity of Eliot's choric work was the way individual threads of character ran through the whole of the chorus... The problem was to find the exact number of speakers needed for each phrase in the chorus, and very soon we realised that we were doing not strictly choral work – but orchestral work; each speaker had to be like an instrument, in harmony with the other voices during the ensemble passages, but repeating a recurring phrase in an individual tone – just as a flute or horn would do in an orchestra…' [*Fogie*] Thurburn added: 'To keep it exact in repetition would have needed a conductor. I think, too, that today we understand better what use [Eliot] made of punctuation, or absence of it. Then, I had great difficulty in making the students appreciate that this mattered at all and that absence of punctuation was, in fact, a signal, so that the use of a comma or a full-stop had real significance. (On one occasion he came up to me during rehearsal and murmured very confidentially, "That should be a colon, not a semi-colon." I think this was the only spontaneous remark he made in rehearsals.)' ['Some Recollections of T S Eliot']

The original Chorus for *Murder in the Cathedral* was made up entirely of female students from the Teacher Course, and one of these, Peggy Innes, wrote: 'We arrived at Canterbury on the morning of the dress-rehearsal, and tried the effect of the choruses in the Chapter House, where the play was to be performed. At first, nothing was audible, all the sound penetrating up into the high roof and producing volumes of inarticulate noise. However, in an hour or two we became accustomed to the acoustics of the place, and before long we did not have to consciously think of audibility. In the evening, at the dress-rehearsal, the play was played straight through for the first time. It says a great deal for our producer, Martin Browne, and for the actors, professional and amateur, that the parts of the play fell into place

E RUDDICK STAGE MID-'30S

" So far as the speaking of English verse was concerned, Saturday was the Day of Judgment. I remember a long narrow room. At one end of the room there was a figure, somewhat larger than life, and floating about ground level, rather like the mediaeval painters' vision of God. It was Miss Elsie Fogerty. Facing her, at the opposite end of the room, and a long way off, was a dais. The floorboards were stained black. The neophytes sat round the walls of the room on gilded chairs, waiting their turn to step onto the dais and recite their poems. According to their merit, some would be awarded crowns of gold, and would float, in glory, back to their places. Others would find themselves in Purgatory with the hope of ultimate elevation, and some would be cast into the bottomless pit.

There were some passages from poems that Miss Fogerty loved so much that she couldn't resist speaking them herself. For instance, I don't remember anyone ever managing to 'get through' Hilaire Belloc's *Tarantella* without interruption. On the lines 'Hip, Hop, Hap,' Miss Fogerty would be on her feet, 'with the clap of the hand,' with 'the twirl and the swirl of a girl gone dancing,' she would be 'backing and advancing,' and 'Snapping of the clapper to the spin; out and in.'

You would think that the spectacle of the elderly lady, with her underslip showing, and her uncertainly pinned-up hair, performing these gyrations would be highly comical. But that was not so at all. It was magical! Everyone was caught up in the excitement and rhythm of it all. Except perhaps the poor girl on the dais, who stood with a fixed smile on her face, feeling disconsolate and isolated, hoping that she would at least be allowed to say the last verse of the poem which she had studied conscientiously for a whole week. **"**

and fitted like a jigsaw puzzle, even at the first consecutive rehearsal. In fact, so well was everything visualised and planned beforehand that very little had to be changed. The Cathedral Players – an amateur organisation, who devote as much time to drama as the average professional – the professional actors, and the chorus, representing the student element, worked together with complete understanding.' [*Viva Voce*]

Gwynneth Thurburn remembered things a little differently: 'The first performance in the Chapter House at Canterbury was something of a nightmare for me. In the first place the acoustics made unison speaking well nigh impossible, and in the second place we had hardly met the rest of the company and had not rehearsed long enough with them to know the continuity. On the first night I sat behind one of the screens and gave the leader her cues by tapping on it.' ['Some Recollections of T S Eliot']

In *Murder in the Cathedral*, a chorus of cleaners and scrubbers of Canterbury comment on the action of the play with text that swings from great poetry to modern prose and includes a 'Gloria' spoken by the chorus against a 'Te Deum' sung by the choir. In this first production, Robert Speaight played Becket, and Browne not only directed but also appeared as the last Tempter. The set consisted of a platform, screens painted to look like the Chapter House walls, and a hand-held cloth to represent the Altar. Played without an interval, the two acts were divided by the reading of the sermon preached by Becket four days before his martyrdom.

After its success in Canterbury, *Murder in the Cathedral* moved first to the Mercury Theatre in Notting Hill and later to the Fortune Theatre in the West End. A longer run necessitated a change of cast, so that the teacher-students could finish their Diploma work, and two eight-member choruses were cast from stage students and recent graduates. Each Chorus member could play any of the eight parts, and over the course of the three-year run, the Chorus repeatedly changed as students graduated or found other employment. Responsibility for the training and rehearsing of the Chorus and its duplicate was handed over to Thurburn. An estimate in the *Viva Voce* claimed that, including graduates who played small parts or understudied, over 42 Central students had at one point been in the cast before the show finally closed with a visit to America in early 1938.

• • •

That the teacher-students would also be professionally engaged as actors was typical of Central. Fogerty believed that all aspects of speech training were complementary, and the three strands of her Central training had from the earliest days of the School been interwoven. Teachers became actors, and actors became teachers. However, teachers also became speech therapists, and it was now becoming apparent to everyone but Fogerty that, if Central were to keep up with an ever-expanding field, changes would have to be made to the 'remedial speech' syllabus. Until 1936, teacher-students interested in Speech Therapy had specialised only in an extra third year of the Diploma course, which gave them teaching practice and qualified them for teaching but that also provided courses in Anatomy, Psychology, Phonetics, Voice and practical work in hospital clinics. In recognition of the quality of Central's course provision, the University of London had always endorsed this third year Central Diploma with the words 'Remedial Speech Training' without any further examination.

In 1934, a Committee of Medical Officers and a number of therapists working in London hospitals had approached the University of London to institute a separate Diploma in Speech Therapy. This request was refused, but the writing was on the wall. If a separate, specialised Diploma in Speech Therapy were to be offered elsewhere, Central would have trouble enrolling students interested in this emerging field. Central would have to choose between leading and following. Leading meant creating a separate and dedicated course in remedial speech. This fell to Joan van Thal (Teacher '22).

Joan van Thal had trained under Fogerty at Central, was her Assistant Director at the St Thomas's Hospital Clinic, taught remedial speech at Central, and was herself a therapist of international standing: 'It was only natural that in the early days the training for Speech Therapy was a matter of inspired improvisation: but [Fogerty's] many other preoccupations led to the improvisations becoming crystallised… It was not that she failed to appreciate that reforms were needed, but a certain ambivalence that made her waver between delegating power to others and continuing to try to carry an overwhelming burden of responsibility herself. It transpired that it was not that she disapproved of proposed reforms so much as that she could not face the work involved in introducing them herself.' [Fogie]

In the end, Fogerty yielded to pressure from her colleagues. In 1936, Central began to offer a one-year Speech Therapy Course, which was open to students who had either completed two years of Central Diploma work, or could prove equivalent knowledge from practical work in the field. The next year, students' clinical work was extended to patients at St George's Hospital. Central was beginning to lay the groundwork for an entirely separate Speech Therapy Department.

• • •

In 1936, friends, ex-students and colleagues commissioned R G Eves to paint Elsie Fogerty's portrait, which was hung in the Royal Academy Exhibition. A party was held in the Upper Crush room at the Albert Hall for its formal presentation to the School, and Peggy Ashcroft, Ruby Ginner, Irene Mawer, Geoffrey Whitworth, Walter Ripman, many 'Old Hallites', and Pivots past and present stood near the veiled painting for poet Laurence Binyon's speech:

> …A generation has grown up in our time to which the telephone and the wireless have
> already ceased to be a wonder. They are taken for granted. But still less do we pause to
> wonder at the primary marvel of speech: at words

Sweet articulate words
Sweetly divided apart

which in the living voice can take on such intimate and such infinite modulations, and which in the nature of speech can become so sensitively alive that they communicate all the subtleties of thought and feelings, from mind to mind and from heart to heart, invisibly, but with perfect exactitude. Speech surely is man's greatest achievement. And as it is something universal, which concerns us as a necessity from birth to death, I think nothing in education is more fundamental...

Binyon concluded by saying that Fogerty's portrait would 'keep an eye of authority and affection on generations of students still to come and remind them of a great teacher and a great woman', and he unveiled the painting. The next *Viva Voce* reported that everyone agreed it was 'a most striking resemblance'.

• • •

Fogerty was now in her seventies, and her health was failing. She had gradually given up her teaching at the many private girls' schools in and around London, but she now gave up the last of these, Roedean. Mab Gulick, educated at Roedean and then at Central during World War One, had gradually taken over the main body of Fogerty's teaching there, and Fogerty's visits had become mostly private tutorials. Gulick wrote in the Elsie Fogerty Memorial *Viva Voce* 1945:

She came to Roedean School as a visiting member of the Staff in 1907, and I was one of the half dozen girls to take 'extra elocution' with her – that was all the speech work there was to 'take' in those far-off days. Within a few terms Miss Fogerty had instituted her system of grading, and speech training was part of the school curriculum. The grading took place once a year, and Miss Fogerty herself heard every girl in the School read a passage of prose and a short poem. From that test girls were classified in three grades.

The 'A' girls were those who showed promise and ability in the subject as an art, and they were persuaded to learn privately or in small groups; the 'Bs' were moderately good and represented the bulk of the School – they needed no further speech work unless they asked for it; the 'Cs' were below standard in reading or in speech, and a period a week was devoted to their speech training.

By this time the School Authorities had fully realized the value of this work, and a period a week was given to the three younger forms.

When Miss Fogerty retired from the Staff in 1938 [sic], the speech work of the School had become of a traditionally high standard, and more than ninety girls were taking verse and drama as an extra subject, while a small proportion only needed to take the 'C' classes.

NATIONAL THEATRE

Foremost among Elsie Fogerty's many projects was lobbying for the formation of a National Theatre. A National Theatre committee had purchased a site behind the British Museum for this purpose as early as 1913, but with the outbreak of World War One all plans were halted. The site was leased to the YMCA to be used for the entertainment of the troops, and in 1922 it was sold to the Rockefeller Trust. In 1929, the foundation stone of the Memorial Theatre at Stratford-upon-Avon was laid, and the 'Shakespeare Memorial National Theatre Committee' drew up a proposal which would be presented to the Prime Minister by Central's future President, Lord Lytton. Even by 1937, little had been accomplished, and there was growing dissent about what should be done with the money already raised. In February 1937, Fogerty wrote to the Editor of *The Times*:

> Is it too much to ask those generous friends who are proposing to erect a mock-Tudor playhouse of the type which Shakespeare despised, and an unneeded library in a quarter of London unsuited to theatrical enterprise, to reconsider their decision and give us instead the help so desperately needed elsewhere?
>
> The needs of a summer festival theatre are amply and appropriately served at Stratford. Every year will see the growth of a better tradition there, and the atmosphere of a festival playhouse is already well established.
>
> The Old Vic is gallantly playing the part of a theatre with 'guest' stars, and even that, with a tradition of service and enthusiasm which can never be duplicated, finds it impossible, on the wrong side of the river, to subsist on Shakespeare alone. No great company of first-rate players can possibly be formed or maintained on the work of one dramatist, or even on archaistic principles of any kind. France proved that.
>
> The maintenance of a theatre permanently giving great plays, with great acting, first–class production, employing the greatest living artists and dramatists, and constantly enlarging its repertoire, is not a commercial proposition in any country in the world to-day. I believe that in 10 years the conditions necessary for such a theatre will have actually ceased to exist in England as they ceased in 1649.
>
> Only a national theatre can establish and secure them…
>
> [However] The Bankside scheme will be the death-blow to any realization of a national theatre in England till it is too late to gather together the elements necessary for its initiation.

Fogerty was certainly mistaken on a number of points, but Geoffrey Whitworth, who so appreciated Fogerty's help in the formation of the British Drama League, had this to say of her valuable contribution: '…She was to become my colleague on the Appeal Committee of the National Theatre, and it was she who brought to the notice of my wife the imminent auction of the site in Cromwell Gardens which was subsequently acquired by the National Theatre Committee. Although this site was finally exchanged for a larger one belonging to the London County Council on the South Bank of the river, the purchase of the Cromwell Garden site was of primary significance in that, at a time when there was grave danger of our capital being dissipated on other enterprises, it thenceforth became safely locked up in a piece of landed property beyond the clutch of envious marauders.' [*Fogie*]

The Cromwell Gardens site was purchased in 1937, and the exchange for the South Bank site occurred in 1942. The National Theatre Bill was passed in Parliament in 1949 empowering the government to give up to £1 million, and the foundation stone for the National Theatre was laid in 1951 during the Festival of Britain. The National Theatre's first Director was appointed in 1962 – Fogerty's favourite student, Laurence Olivier.

After her first serious illness in 1937, Fogerty suggested that the Governors appoint Gwynneth Thurburn as Vice Principal, and Thurburn took over many administrative responsibilities. However, Fogerty was by no means retired. She still taught classes at Central, but with no outside teaching and fewer administrative duties, she used any free time to complete her most respected publication, *Rhythm* (1937).

In this book, Fogerty defines rhythm as equal to Time, Force and Space: 'When these three elements are synchronized with perfect success, the result is rhythmical, the time period being isochronous, the force continuous, and the spatial adjustment regular throughout.' Rhythmic action is the only action that can be habitual; and – bringing it back to the voice – only with practice, by creating a habit, can one gain the capacity to breathe without effort. Fogerty describes the perfect upright stance, and matching the modern concept of 'the inner game', points out that the harder we try to do something, the less success we can expect. When *Rhythm* came out in 1937, Thurburn reviewed it for the *Viva Voce*:

> The work is, I venture to think, a contribution to knowledge and philosophy. ...Her vision has apprehended Rhythm as the principle which welds all created things into a single entity...
>
> In the Introduction we are given a clearer understanding of the words so often used in connection with Rhythm; repetition, periodicity, recurrence, pattern, and their relationship to the whole. She demonstrates in the works of nature and of man the blending of the three factors Time, Force and Space into a unity which is often felt, though seldom understood...
>
> Perhaps the most arresting idea lies in the establishment of the contrast between movement in a closed circle and movement in a spiral. 'Rhythm in a fixed and determined circle of unvarying action is not capable of vital or aesthetic development. Not only the rhythm of machinery, but all repetitive human movements carried out solely under pressure of economic necessity are of this order. To escape from the closed circle of repetition into the open spiral of creation man must, at some point in his performance, obey an impulse from within himself. No human being, of his own free will, will go on indefinitely repeating an action which has attained automatic perfection. Rhythmic action is effortless in itself, but it always stimulates to further effort. Its maintenance calls out a desire for some progressive increase in difficulty of performance – a delight in creative activity.'

Thurburn later wrote: 'I remember at the time of its publication an eminent psychologist who had been closely associated with the work of the School, remarking to me that *Rhythm* was about ten years before its time and that many of her conclusions could not then be appreciated. It is interesting now to note that there appears to be an increasing tendency on the part of biologists and physiologists to talk about 'pattern', and rhythm is held to be of much greater importance in co-ordinated movement than formerly.' ['The Elsie Fogerty I Knew']

• • •

The number of students in the last pre-war session at Central, 1938–9, was 156, and the total fee income for the School was £6,895 19s 6d. Central Registrar, Jane Gavin, was busy with administrative duties: booking tutors, collecting fees, allocating rooms and creating timetables for Central courses and extension lectures, as well as organising the Summer School. A petite university graduate from Scotland, Gavin had been hired in 1924 as Company Secretary to assist Registrar Hazel Thompson in reorganising Central for incorporation. Enormously able, she had put the books in order, allowing Thompson more time to work with students on productions and in the classroom, and she officially took over as Registrar in 1937. After a 1938 summer holiday with her close friend, Gwynneth Thurburn, Gavin was diagnosed with a terminal illness. Vera Sargent – Sarge – had assisted Fogerty, then Thompson and finally Gavin. She took over the positions of both Central Registrar and Company Secretary in the autumn of 1938.

• • •

ADDITIONAL CENTRAL FACTS

1930
- Elsie Fogerty's pay rises to £300 per year.
- 96 full-time students each pay £16 16s 0d per term.

1931
- Central offers single, part-time courses in Recitation, Mime, Voice-Training, Public Speaking and Cure of Speech Defects.
- The Government's Teachers Registration Council accepts the Central Teacher Course.

1933
- Elsie Fogerty's pay rises to £375 per year.

1936
- HRH the Princess Marina, Duchess of Kent, becomes Royal Patron of Central
- September: Gwynneth Thurburn broadcasts programme of Elizabethan songs and sonnets for the BBC.
- November: Broadcast of *Hippolytus* arranged by Gwynneth Thurburn and directed by Elsie Fogerty.

1937
- April: Broadcast of *Trojan Women* choric parts by ten Teacher and Stage 'A' (third-year) students, directed by Gwynneth Thurburn.
- June: Two broadcasts of choric speaking by students.

1938
- Central purchases its first microphone and recording apparatus. (This was sold upon evacuation to Exeter and replaced after the war.)

1939
- June: Thurburn broadcasts two programmes of selections of Shelley, with E Martin Browne.

6
1938–1942

LATE IN 1938, the Albert Hall gave notice to Central that, should war be declared, rooms would not be available. Elsie Fogerty was convinced that war was imminent. She cancelled the 1939 Summer School and immediately began to look for alternative premises.

Considering her long-term relationship with the Shakespeare Memorial Theatre, it was inevitable that Fogerty would explore the possibility of accommodation in Stratford-upon-Avon. When it became clear that the area could support too few students to be a feasible option for evacuation, she consulted the External Registrar of London University about other possible locations. The most promising suggestion was the University College of the South-West (now Exeter University), and Fogerty went to meet with the Principal of the College, Dr John Murray. In June 1939, parents of existing students were polled about a possible evacuation, and when fifty students instantly agreed to a move, Central began to organise classrooms, offices, a library and student lodgings in Exeter. In July, Fogerty's portrait, a piano and essential records were sent by train, and when war was declared in September 1939, Central was already safely in residence at University College of the South-West. Twenty-three new students enrolled for the 1939 autumn term, and when they graduated three years later, their Central memories would be only of the campus in Exeter.

Resident staff and 73 students were housed in either Hope or Lopes Halls, with academic classes held at Lopes. Movement and rehearsal classes were held in the Washington Singer Building (now Laboratories), and productions and presentations were given there on a small stage at one end of the auditorium. Eighteen months later, Central headquarters moved to the vacant men's residence, Reed Hall. This beautiful building, with its sloping grounds and stone steps would provide an idyllic setting for outdoor productions.

Resident staff took over all teaching and administrative duties. Fogerty taught verse speaking and theatre history, and continued her Monday Lectures on Theory. Vice Principal Gwynneth Thurburn taught voice and verse speaking, as well as taking over wardrobe responsibilities. Ruby Ginner and Irene Mawer had recently evacuated with their own students to a holiday home in Boscastle, Cornwall, and they occasionally came to teach movement to Central students. Vera Sargent handled administrative and organisational duties. Hazel Thompson had been a mainstay of the Central staff for over twenty years. In 1940, Fogerty urged the Governors to appoint her Director of Dramatics for as long as the School remained in Exeter, and in the spring of 1941, Thompson finally accepted the official title that formally recognised the work she had done for so many years. Nancy Brown taught

1939	Royal Opera House becomes a dance hall for the duration of the war
1940	Battle of Britain and the Blitz. Within two weeks of the first bombing, all West End theatres close
1941	Old Vic Theatre bombed
1942	ENSA applies for military deferment for actors

phonetics and provided general supervision and emotional support for first-year students – who called her 'Nanny B'. For these full-time duties, each of the resident staff received £330 per year, and in recognition of her achievement in organising the evacuation, Vera Sargent's salary was increased from £300 to £330 to remain in line with her colleagues. At a meeting in December 1939, Fogerty urged the Governors to make a gift of £10 to each of these women, as a token of appreciation for their hard work in so efficiently moving the School to Exeter.

Courses and activities at Central continued much as they had before the war. Thurburn organised practice teaching for the teacher-students in a wide variety of schools. Fogerty and the School Medical Authority arranged remedial speech clinics in Exeter, and in March 1940, a well-attended 'Remedial Conference' was held at Hoddesden. In spring 1940, the Royal Free Hospital was also evacuated to Exeter, and so Dr Lilian Dickson was able to continue her Anatomy lectures for the teacher-students. Ex-student Janet (Lewis) Philip (Teacher '34), lived in Exeter, and was hired to take rehearsal classes and direct student productions, and by the end of the year, Dr Joyce Partridge, Dorothy Allen and a Miss Radcliffe had also joined the staff. Visiting teachers, outside examiners and adjudicators visited on a regular basis, and actors on tour in the area often gave guest lectures. Christine (Hayes) Caldwell (Teacher '40) joined the staff immediately after her graduation, and she recalls a production touring at the Theatre Royal, Exeter, from the New Theatre, London: 'At one point, there was a touring production of The Cherry Orchard, with Nicolas Hannen, Athene Seyler, and some of the most distinguished actors of their day. Athene Seyler – there was no better actress on the stage, very plain but "serviceable", as she described herself, and she'd got the gift – she and Nicolas Hannen gave us a week's course on The Cherry Orchard. It was wonderful. Lillah McCarthy lived down in Fowey, Cornwall, so Fogerty drew her up to do some work with us, too.'

Enrolment was less than half that of 1938–9. The only man in training – Yorkshireman Arthur Sanderson (Sandy) – completed his training in August 1940 and then joined the British Army (returning after the war to live in Exeter). His piece for the Viva Voce, 'A Lone Male in a Women's Hall', gives a picture of that first year of evacuation:

...Here I am at the end of the Autumn Term, 1939, having lived through nine weeks of the aforesaid miracle. Thus being the very 'odd man out', I can view the school activities impartially.

The students of the University of the South-West received us in October with open arms, particularly the males, and many envious glances were cast in my direction by these gentlemen. However, the risk of jealous attacks soon ceased, when they had ample opportunities of fraternising at 'bops', debates, concerts, inter-hall luncheons, etc., with our students. Some of the fellows have proved a great help by taking various parts in plays, but whether it is art for art's sake, I do not know.

As two-thirds of the girls have seen me for a year or more, I am taken for granted and can come and go in peace. Only when I have the intrepidity to attend Mime classes do I create a stir, because to see a man playing an evacuee mother with three children, a nurse-maid in Hyde Park, a lady in sables shop-gazing in Bond Street, must be to say the least, diverting.

The School has made its presence felt in Exeter, and already much excellent work has been accomplished. Miss Fogerty was quickly instrumental in starting some valuable clinical work. She, as well as the students, have given a number of recitals to blind evacuees. Most of the 'A' Teacher students are doing good work in practice schools. Upward of five hundred soldiers enjoyed an excellent show by the students on November 29th, which they said was one of the best they had had in Barracks.

The actual work this term has been more intense than in peace-time, and the girls have all shown great enthusiasm – in fact, they are keen enough to do land-work and study horticulture in their spare time...

The red soil of Devon is becoming more and more fertile due to the sterling effects of the Central School Land Army. Thus, in these unsettled times, the school is pulling its weight splendidly, and even though certain females bullied me into writing these few lines, I really do feel a privilege to be...A Lone Male.

Christine Caldwell elaborated on this land work: 'When we arrived as evacuee students at the University College, there were already a lot of students there, and they were very nervous of us. They called us 'The Glamour Girls'... Well, we wanted to give our thanks to the University College of the South-West, as it was at that time, for taking us in. John Caldwell, eventually my husband, was Professor of Botany and was running the university grounds. He was determined to make the University College self-sufficient in food – to show that the country could, in fact, feed itself – and all the grounds were used for food production. We turned ourselves into a little team and helped.' The Glamour Girls potted, raked, weeded, sowed, dug, picked, pruned, cleared and, of course, spread manure, as well as taking their normal classes.

When Caldwell started her training at the Hall in 1938, there had been sixty students in her class: 'When I finished, there were very few students who got their Diplomas, only four of us, maybe six, but just a handful. People were so distracted and so much was happening. I finished my third year of training, and for two years I was on the staff – teaching any subject that was needed… I mostly taught the first-year people, so I did voice, phonetics, movement, drama and producing.'

• • •

When war was declared in September 1939, Prime Minister Chamberlain announced the closure of all theatres and cinemas, and although the decree had only lasted a week, restrictions remained on how late theatres could stay open. By the next year, few London theatres were capable of remaining in business as many had either been destroyed or badly damaged in the Blitz. Tours, however, continued, and in spring 1940, a deferment list of several leading actors was drawn up (although many enlisted, preferring instead to fight). During the first years of the war, some tour managers required that their civilian actors at the end of a run spend an obligatory period with the Entertainments National Service Association (ENSA). The Minister of Labour, Ernest Bevin, finally recognised the importance of theatre and entertainment in maintaining morale, and when Lord Lytton took over the Entertainments National Service Committee in 1942, it became a requirement for all actors to give six weeks a year to ENSA or some similar organisation. Everyone was expected to contribute to the war effort, in whatever capacity. Central was no different.

The Central School had never needed the admonishment or even the encouragement to 'contribute'. Although Central was busy with classes, teaching practice and clinics, throughout the war it continued to provide a full calendar of performances, entertainments and distractions for those who needed cheering up. On 29 November 1939, the 'A' (third-year) students presented their first troop concert in the barracks gymnasium, for an audience of 650 soldiers and children. The show consisted of sketches, songs, poems and dances by 'Les Girls', the Lone Male, and two male volunteers from the college. Before Christmas that year, the School gave three performances of *Hundred Years Old* by the Brothers Quintero at the Theatre Royal. The Pivots produced a revue in February of 1940, raising £14 to provide funds for the their annual autumn Slum Party – this year given for children of the south west.

The first Exeter school year ended in June 1940 with a 'Gaudy Day', which replaced the usual Public Matinee for graduating students. The day's activities started with a Governors' meeting and the Annual General Meeting, and finished with a presentation of plays by the 'A' students on the little stage in the Washington Singer Building. Lillah McCarthy and Caryl Jenner (Stage '34, nee Pamela Ripman, daughter of phonetics teacher, Walter Ripman) judged and awarded the medals. At the end of June 1940, an exam was held for the Pivot Scholarship, and the winner, Margaret (Margot) Braund, would graduate from the Teacher Course in 1943. She became a beloved long-time staff member, and would be the key architect of Central's one-year Postgraduate Voice Course.

In 1940–1, the number of students fell to 65, but all of them must have been very busy all of the time. Joan van Thal came from London to join the resident staff, and she helped open a number of new speech clinics in the area for her teacher and remedial speech students. The Pivot Club was active, that autumn giving shows at the Orthopaedic Hospital, the local Mental Institution and the Exeter Prison. Hazel Thompson directed a troop show, *Everyman*, in December 1940, which was attended by Queen Mary, and the next year, directed *The Distaff Side* by John van Druten at the Theatre Royal, Exeter – in aid of the Royal National Lifeboat Institution. Central students or old Pivots took most of the parts, and the Exeter Dramatic Club and the University College provided actors for the men's parts.

In 1942, Thompson and Thurburn led two companies of 'A' Teacher and the 'A' Stage students that presented shows in Exeter at the Higher and Topsham Barracks and at Mardon Hall, as well as in Lyme Regis, Chagford, Aldershot, Crediton and the Marine camp at Exton. Together the companies gave an original revue, *How's About It*, at Washington Singer, to raise money for the Pivot Scholarship fund (£11). *Reed Pipes* was presented two weeks later, also in aid of the Scholarship fund (raising £9).

In spite of these contributions, Central students often wondered if what they were doing was enough. Fogerty captured their dilemma in a 1942 *Viva Voce*: 'A year ago, Pivots in training at the Central School were getting worried. Did our work justify the peaceful life we were leading? Were we lucky ones shirking the responsibilities of an active war service? It was a difficult problem and many of us carried on only with a very uneasy conscience, half envying the older Pivots who had finished their training and were free to serve as they wished, and half feeling thankful that we could still carry on with our chosen work. Now things are different – our choice has been made for us and we can continue our training with an easier mind. The Government decided that students were more valuable in their capacity as trained citizens who could undertake essential jobs, than they would be in positions that could be filled equally well by others. This has decided the fate of Universities and Training Colleges all over the country, and we hope that Pivots in war jobs will be glad that we can carry on the Pivots trades and traditions which you have temporarily sacrificed.'

• • •

By leaving London before the Blitz, Central had hoped to escape the harsher realities of the war. No one had really expected Exeter to be bombed, but as Christine Caldwell recalls, the city was to suffer German retaliation for the Allies' bombing of Dresden: 'It [Dresden] was a beautiful old port city – so Hitler said, "I will take five jewels in the crown of the King, and I will destroy them." Exeter, Norwich, Canterbury, York and Bath. They were called the Baedeker Raids – Baedeker in those days being the name of a famous guidebook. The centre of Exeter was wiped out. By chance, the Central School was up on the hill outside, and they watched Exeter burn. At that, the School thought, "We might as well be bombed in London as in Exeter." '

The heaviest bombing in London had taken place from September 1940 to May 1941, and in spring 1942, London was quiet. The parents of the students were again polled, and all were in favour of a return to London. Hostels were inspected, and it seemed certain that accommodation for students could be found. The new manager of the Hall offered to make a temporary donation to the School of £200 per year, in addition to the old donation of £100, which reduced the annual rent to £450. The government urged people not to return to London, but the Central School moved back to the Royal Albert Hall in July 1942.

• • •

ADDITIONAL CENTRAL FACTS

1941   • Embassy Theatre bombed

7

1942–1945

ELSIE FOGERTY BELIEVED that each person must recognise the unique contributions he or she can make and co-operate with others to achieve them. She was committed to improving the world she lived in, and she had spent her life encouraging her students and colleagues to use their talents to do the same. However, although she may have in the past inspired generations of students to act, to teach and to heal, she was now less able to connect with her young students. Growing frail in mind as well as body, she found it difficult to dress herself and to fix her hair, so became almost comically untidy. Even before the evacuation to Exeter, at a Pivot Scholarship Recital in London observers had noticed the shake of Fogerty's hand, her memory difficulties and her confusion. By the time Central had moved to Exeter, Fogerty's lectures, disjointed even in her prime, began to resemble the ramblings of an old lady. Nevertheless, whenever the Governors sent someone to audit her classes, she would call forth her previous genius and again confound them with her brilliance.

Fogerty was still the titular head of the School, but Vice Principal Gwynneth Thurburn made more and more of the decisions. Friction grew; rapport weakened; tensions within the School intensified. Whether it was Fogerty's decision alone or whether others pushed her into it, in 1942 Elsie Fogerty retired as Principal at the age of 76. Those alive to remember don't wish to speak candidly of that time, but in *Fogie* Marion Cole intimates that the retirement may not have been altogether voluntary. 'The truth was blown on the wind with the bomb-dust of Exeter. Priorities were distorted by the stress of war; hearts were torn every day; things changed.' [*Fogie*]

Fogerty had wanted to see Central safely back to London and resign her position at the end of the 1942 autumn term, but the Governors felt the new academic year should begin with a new Principal in place. There is no indication of rancour in any of the minutes of Governors' meetings at this time. At one such meeting Fogerty formally suggested Gwynneth Thurburn as her successor. When Central moved back to the Albert Hall, Elsie Fogerty was no longer Principal of the institution she had founded 36 years before.

On 30 November 1942, many of Fogerty's friends, former colleagues and students presented a Jubilee Benefit Matinee at the New Theatre, London, to honour her life, accomplishments and over a half century of teaching. Ex-student Olga Katzin, the *New Statesman* satirical poet known as 'Sagittarius', wrote the Prologue, and Clifford Turner spoke Laurence Binyon's poem, 'To Elsie Fogerty', as an epilogue. Some of the biggest names in theatre contributed to the show: Edith Evans, John Gielgud, Peggy Ashcroft, Sybil Thorndike, John Laurie, Nicolas Hannen, Jack Hulbert and Laurence Olivier. There were others less famous who took part, but even in the middle of the war this was unquestionably a celebrity celebration. Friends presented Fogerty with a fur coat, the Governors gave her a watch, and she received £538 profit from the Benefit. The Governors named her birthday, 16 December, as Founder's Day.

ELSIE FOGERTY ONCE SAID...

" A girl over 5' 7" has little chance in the dramatic world. **"**

" Many Americans speak beautiful English, better than most of our own triflers with their mother tongue. Our 'refaned' English accent is now worse than the 'Oh yeah' of the films. **"**

" There is nothing in the construction of a woman's voice that makes it unsuitable for broadcasting. The reason women do not come up to the standard of the BBC mike voice is because the BBC do not take the time to tune their mechanical devices to bring out the individual qualities of a woman's voice. **"**

While in Exeter, Fogerty had kept her South Kensington flat, and she now moved back there to write her memoirs. Sadly, most of this work has been lost. Fogerty's friend Muriel (Bousfield) Wigglesworth managed to save copies of the first two chapters, but the memoirs in their entirety have disappeared. A few fragments are quoted in *Fogie*, but most of these reminiscences come from Fogerty's earlier articles written for the *Viva Voce*.

There were rumours that even in her retirement Fogerty remained a constant unwelcome presence at the Albert Hall, but there is no evidence of this. She attended the Inaugural Meeting in the autumn of 1942 to welcome her successor, and she was invited to meetings and events organised by the Pivot Club; but her regular teaching days were over, and the School was firmly under the guidance of its new Principal. Fogerty certainly wrote letters with suggestions and advice, but this was understandable. She had written letters every day of her professional life – to *The Times*, to her colleagues, to her ex-students and to her friends. Nevertheless, no matter how little she was around, it was perhaps too much for those who believed she shouldn't be there at all. Central was changing, and Fogerty belonged to another era.

Fogerty continued teaching to supplement her pension – holding classes at the British Drama League and at Toynbee Hall in the East End, and giving private lessons in her small flat. In 1943, she worked on speeches for a film of Shaw's *Caesar and Cleopatra*, later writing to a friend that she was in discussion with someone, somewhere, about the foundation of a school for film acting. Nothing further was ever said of this venture.

1942	The German SS kill over 50,000 people in the Warsaw Ghetto Sir William Beveridge proposes a post-war social security
1943	Mussolini is deposed and Italy signs military armistice Part-time war work becomes compulsory for women 18 to 45
1944	Troops land in Normandy on 6 June, known as D-Day Olivier's film of *Henry V* opens Conference of Repertory Theatres (CORT) founded
1945	War ends, and Allies carve up post-war Europe at Yalta Britain turns on the lights after 2000 nights of blackout and dim-out Hiroshima and Nagasaki destroyed by first atomic bombs Beatrix Lehmann becomes Equity's first female President

In 1944, the Germans once again began bombing London, this time with the V-1 flying bombs, known also as Buzz bombs or Doodlebugs. In August, Fogerty's flat and most of her possessions were destroyed, and she moved into a small residential hotel, The Cromwell, on Cromwell Place, SW7. As the bombing continued, she spent every night, and most days, in a nearby shelter – clutching her memoirs. When her health declined further and an operation became necessary, she insisted that the only doctor she would trust to perform it was Dr Gerald Alderson, husband of her first godchild, Marguerite Pasteur. She was moved to Leamington Spa, and on 4 July 1945 – a few months shy of her 80th birthday – Elsie Fogerty died of cancer. She was cremated in Birmingham, and her ashes were placed near her mother and father at a crematorium in Woking. A Memorial Service was held for her at St Stephen's Church, Gloucester Road, London.

Elsie Fogerty had known, among others, Eleanora Duse, Sarah Bernhardt, the Terrys, Henry Irving, Herbert Beerbohm Tree, Marie Tempest, Yvonne Arnaud and Lillah McCarthy. She had worked with some of the most well-known and respected actors and directors of the first half of the 20th century and been involved with some the most innovative movements in theatre of her time. She had worked most of her life towards establishing a National Theatre, had fought for academic recognition of speech and drama, and was a pioneer in both speech therapy and voice- and drama-teacher training. She was a world-renowned expert on voice and speech training. As her legacy, she left not only the Central School of Speech-Training and Dramatic Art, but also the students she taught and the training they would pass on to others.

When Fogerty died, the Pivot Club elected Principal Gwynneth Thurburn as its new President. In October 1945, Thurburn suggested to the 70 Pivots who attended the Annual General Meeting that the Club's functions had over the years gone through 'certain modifications'. She pointed out that it was no longer necessary to give numerous entertainments, and that the Club's 'outstanding usefulness lay in maintaining interest and sympathy between past and present students and staff of the Central School'. Fogerty's directions to her earliest Pivots to 'have some definite object to work for', and to 'form a fund to give training to those who had talent but no means to develop it' were now forgotten.

Whether because its original 'pivot' was gone, because their prime directive was no longer in force, or more likely, just because the world was different after the war, by 1949 the Pivot Club no longer existed. In the summer of 1947, the *Viva Voce* reported only six members at its most recent meeting, and there seemed little interest in continuing the Club. At the next sparsely attended meeting in spring 1948, the main aims of the Club were officially altered. The Scholarship was listed as an objective, but instead of Fogerty, the Central School itself became the Club's 'pivot', and the Club's purpose became to provide a link between the School's past and present students, even if that meant reorganising or renaming the Club. An extract from a May 1914 *Viva Voce* is reprinted in the final issue of the *Viva Voce*, Easter 1948: 'The strength that is given by such bodies as the Club is a very difficult thing to measure; it often seems to the individual students rather a superfluous act to join such things, and we sometimes hear, "I cannot see the good of my belonging; I cannot see what I get out of being a member." Those who started the Club knew what has proved to be the case in our experience. It is those who do most for the Club who in the long run get the most from it, not only in actual material help, but in that feeling of corporate action, of comradeship and solidarity which is one of the greatest sources of human strength. The force of such institutions is cumulative; if they survive the first reaction which follows on the enthusiasm of their

'TO ELSIE FOGERTY'
BY LAURENCE BINYON

True ease of speaking comes from Art, not Chance;
Love moods need music, Wit asks Elegance.
To every Passion they attune their Speech
Who had a Fogerty that art to teach.
When she resolved, her earliest Laurels won,
To carry Diction into Kensington
(Which Borough had not previously heard
True Intonation of the Spoken Word)
She banished Elocution once for all
From the chaste Threshold of the Albert Hall.
From Earth's four corners, students filled the School,
From Rio they arrived, and Istanbul;
Full many a Miss with faulty Diction went,
None ever left with an Impediment.
And from the Bar, the Rostrum and the Stage,
There Leading Lights have long made Pilgrimage.
Poets may murder their own lines and claim
They lisped in numbers, for the Numbers came;
It's otherwise with actors in a Play,
If they should lisp, then Numbers stay away.
But Voices Elsie Fogerty has passed,
Fill any Theatre, however vast,
In love-scenes, mob-scenes or Soliloquies –
Speak Verse or Prose, or anything you please.
Such various craft in Acting must combine
That Stars, though born, must still learn to shine!
Bright Constellations of the Thespian Heavens,
A Thorndike, and an Ashcroft, and an Evans,
The London's Ear enchant in every Part,
Owe something to this Mistress of their Art,
While some of the Applause belongs to Her
When babbling Gossips cry, 'Olivier!',
And in a one-time Pupil she delights
When Audiences rise on Gielgud Nights!
Today they come, a famous company,
All these and more, to grace her Jubilee;
Upon this stage they pay her Homage due,
Her they acclaim, and so good Friends, do you!

founders, they begin to form a body of tradition and of history which in a few years is a driving force for all concerned.'

A new student publication, *Prompt*, replaced the *Viva Voce*. Its first issue in February 1949 gives notice of application by the 'Central student organisation' to the National Union of Students. *Prompt* lasted a couple of years, and was replaced by another student publication, *Encore*, and that in turn was replaced by *Q*. Over the years, other student magazines would be published for brief periods, but none has rivalled the 42 years of the Pivot Club *Viva Voce*.

• • •

When Central returned to the Albert Hall in the summer of 1942, the School classrooms and the West Porch theatre had been shut for three years. There was debris from collateral bomb damage, and the windows were boarded up and blacked out. If the autumn term were to begin on time and with a minimum amount of chaos, rooms had to be cleaned, cleared, mended and decorated. The old Manager of the Albert Hall, Mr Askew, had retired, but the new Manager, C S Taylor, became a staunch supporter of the School.

Besides the physical organisation, Central also underwent an internal reorganisation. The only staff members in place were Hazel Thompson, Joan van Thal, Gwynneth Thurburn and Vera Sargent. After tensions between Thurburn and Nancy Brown in Exeter, Brown had taken a position at RADA, as she 'would not be in agreement with the future policy of the School'. Thurburn not only had to interview and audition students for the autumn term, she had to find new tutors to teach them. By hiring two previous students, Joyce Wellburn and Audrey Bullard, and with Hazel Thompson remaining Director of Dramatics, Thurburn was able to build upon and consolidate the training, all the while retaining continuity.

Like Fogerty, Thurburn had a work ethic and dedication to service, and as Fogerty had done, Thurburn would put her stamp on the School she ran for the next 25 years. She was quoted in the Programme for her own Memorial Service in October 1993: 'If I were asked to sum up what I believe in as few words as possible, I would say, "Work as hard as you can at anything that can be worked at. Think and feel all you can. Imagine that you are the vehicle of somebody else's creation." '

• • •

Gwynneth Thurburn was born on 17 July 1899 in the outskirts of Buenos Aires, the daughter of banker Robert Augustus Thurburn and his wife, Bertha Loveday. Thurburn said of her childhood in an interview for *Woman and Home* magazine in 1959: 'As a child I always wanted to go on the stage, but it was as a dancer that I saw myself holding audiences spellbound… Anything to do with dancing attracted me enormously, and the best memory of my childhood was travelling in the same ship as Nijinsky and the Russian

'SPEECH IN THE THEATRE' BY ELSIE FOGERTY

Reprinted from the *Theatre Arts Monthly* in the October 1931 *Viva Voce*.

It will be found that in the subsequent history of the theatre there is a natural swing of the pendulum from realism to conventionality. The naturalists of one generation being the pedantic formalists of the next.

There are natural reasons for this, apart from the changing taste of successive generations. The human voice is at its best between 25 and 40. Utterance is composed of audible movements, and delicate movements grow more clumsy and rigid after maturity. The constant habit of using selected diction, in parts which tend more and more to reflect the player's known individuality and achievement, leads to the development of a fixed quality of tone and cadence. At its best this may be very beautiful, and the player who maintains such a standard throughout a long career is held up as a model to youth and is followed by a host of imitators, but often this very beauty may take on the effect of a mask. It may express the art of a player, not the real range of personality or of character required. This is the tragedian's essential danger: Mounet-Sully, Sara Bernhardt, Duse and Forbes Robertson all in their turn succumbed to it. 'Tragedy is essentially a drowning and a breaking of the dykes that divide man from man. It is on these dykes that Comedy keeps house.' (from Yeats' Introduction to *Plays for an Irish Theatre*.) Here we get the opposite difficulty. In the case of a young actor full of talent whose only voice training has been derived from the comments of various producers and critics on his rendering of individual parts, there is a tendency to make every part a 'character' part. He feels that the voice must be changed with every part, like costume and gesture. Every act soon demands a deliberate variation in the whole character of speech. Usually he mimics some individual in every impersonation. He has no real voice or speech of his own, and takes no pains to improve his whole diction in a broad way on sound principles. Such a performer is an impersonator or mimic rather than an actor; his various deliveries are like gramophone records slipped into his throat and mechanically recording superficial impressions. Usually he believes himself born to great tragedy in the same way, and his one ambition is to play Hamlet. Comedy of Humours, and in a lesser degree Comedy of Manners, foster such forms of speech. The voice deteriorates quickly under such treatment.

If the risk of the character actor is that he disintegrates and diminishes his personality, the risk of the straight actor is that he always plays himself. We meet the young player who has been praised for having a 'beautiful voice' – sometimes the jig of rhythm badly directed has led to a monstrous artificiality. This speech is not unlike a dancer's acting. One vocal pose succeeds another, each plastically beautiful; we are distracted from the significance of the performance by admiration for its graceful facility. If the brilliantly gifted young player is a disciple of stylism, such a one falls into the habit of using speech as if it were a toy to play tricks with. Striving after a difficult effect, a fortunate little trick seems to accomplish just what is required. It registers itself as a very present help in time of trouble and recurs at first sparingly, then more often in all such emergencies, and people begin to 'love the funny way she talks'.

Modern science has come to understand that the voice needs as careful training for speech as for song if it is to endure physically, let alone if it is to please. Once its central quality is established strain need not be feared, but such training will be useless if fashion exalts errors of production under the impression that they are treasures of 'personality'. The true stage voice is a voice physiologically faultless, in which breathing, note, vowel resonance and articulatory movement are [continued...

physically balanced. Hoarseness is a disease, not a charm! Nasality a vulgarism, not a brilliant touch of individual genius; muffled articulation suggests the need for a visit to the dentist, or the advisability of serving out ear trumpets to the audience with the ices, not an ingenious simplicity on the actor's part.

It must be frankly admitted that the voice trainers have themselves to blame in a very large degree: they have taught on no clearer principle than imitation, and they have nearly always been ignorant of one side of their subject, either of the scientific, the aesthetic or the dramatic necessities of speech. Speech in the theatre is one of the four aesthetic uses of utterance; of these the greatest is song, the next, lyric verse speaking, the next drama, and the next ordered oratory. The singer has sole authority on the question of vocal tone; the lyric poet alone understands the perfect meaning of rhythmic emphasis, the speech which can stress without shouting, hurry without cluttering and keep a tune without losing character; to the drama belongs the whole field of characterization and of the shift and play of action in speech; the orator disdains all arts but that of logical significance.

If we are to have a perfect training for the stage our players must 'make' their voices first by acquiring the principles of their art, not with reference to their own profession only, but as they underlie every one of these great means of expression. The finest speakers on the stage have generally had a singer's training. Technique must be sound enough to become completely unconscious and inevitably resourceful – a matter of at least three years' training before freedom can be achieved. Copy no one; preserve unbroken the line between thought and tone; work till breath, note and articulation balance as perfectly as the limbs, body and head of a dancer; cultivate no defects for the sake of so called 'character'; it is not necessary to grow a hump to play Richard III or suffer from senile dementia to portray the witches in Macbeth.

The principles are very simple – poised and accurate action in a few tiny movements – but the application is never ending. Skill must pass beyond all conscious knowledge of self-congratulatory enjoyment into inevitable sureness. So the work must be begun young. Fiddling criticism of the 'accent' must give way to automatic purity in general vocal resonance.

High voices are not better or worse than low ones; Edinburgh does not speak better or worse than London; Whitechapel does not possess a 'charming dialect', only a confined tendency to adenoids and a woeful lack of pocket-handkerchiefs.

Strong nerves, perfect physical co-ordination, intelligence and self-control lie behind all perfect speech, and where such speech is at the service of genius – how rare a combination! – we have the greatest of all human joys in the theatre. The conditions of acting are so unnatural that they demand relentless training. The result of such training should be perfect naturalness of effect. Perhaps acting is in reality at its best in youth. A self-denying ordinance like that which ruled the Russian Ballet might benefit the speech of the theatre. Years of adequate training, a brief period of splendour and – compulsory retirement at 29 – with a state pension. In the meantime, we might experiment with a National Theatre.

Ballet. We were living in the Argentine at the time and on this occasion we were on our way from Rio to Buenos Aires… I met most of the Ballet Company, though I never met Nijinsky who was extremely aloof and kept very much to himself. But I used to get up early in the morning to watch him practising alone on the deck. I can see him to this day, repeating the same thing over and over again as though he could never be satisfied with it.'

Thurburn might have had a young girl's dream to be a dancer, but a fall through bad flooring in a dance class left one ankle weakened, and she would always walk with a slight limp. More noticeable to her students was her staring and cloudy right eye, which had been blinded when she rolled onto a knife as a baby. Generations of students were never clear if she was looking at them or the person next to them (a handy attribute for any teacher). Only the most candid of photos would ever capture her right eye. All official photos were taken in profile.

As a girl, Thurburn was sent to England to be educated at Birklands in St Albans. After graduation, she completed a two-year secretarial course, and started training on the Stage Course at Central in 1919 at age 20. She soon found her true vocation lay in teaching, and easily switched courses to focus on teaching and remedial speech work. Shortly after her graduation from Central in 1922, she was hired to assist Dr Aikin with his voice classes, and she took over from him when he retired in 1928, becoming head of all voice work at Central in 1935 and Vice Principal in 1937. All through these years, she had only ever been employed part-time at Central, so she had had to find other ways to supplement her income. Always a gifted seamstress and embroiderer, from 1925 to 1935 she owned and ran a private theatrical costume hire business, Thyrtis, that provided reasonably accurate period costumes in children's sizes for dramatic work in schools or clubs.

The 1930s were productive years for Thurburn. From 1930 to 1939 she lectured at Board of Education courses for teachers, taught privately, and did occasional broadcasting work with Central students. She was responsible for training and maintaining the choruses for Eliot's The Rock in 1934, and Murder in the Cathedral from 1935 to 1938, and she published her first book, Voice and Speech, in 1939. New Speech would be published in 1949.

When she became Principal in 1942, Thurburn was already recognised as a leader in the field of speech and voice, and over the next 25 years her reputation continued to grow. She was asked to attend or read papers at conferences organised by the Ministry of Education, the Institute of Education, the Society for Education in Art, the Women's Employment Federation, the London Association of Teachers of English, the Incorporated Association of the Teachers of Speech and Drama, Birmingham and Midlands Federation of University Women, and the Standing Conference of Drama Associations. She was on the Council of the British Drama League (later the British Theatre Association) and was made an Honorary Life Member of that organisation. She was made an Honorary Fellow of the College of Speech Therapists, and an Honorary Member of the Guild of Drama Adjudicators. She served on a number of Committees, including: the Diploma in Dramatic Art of London University; the Institute of Education; the Society for Theatre Research and William Poel Centenary; and the Youth of the British Theatre Centre. Thurburn conducted courses for Speech teachers in Cape Town and Johannesburg in 1955, and in

1955 and 1956 worked with the Stratford Shakespeare Festival in Ontario, Canada, on the problem of the adaptation of Canadian speech for Shakespearean performances.

In her later years, Thurburn could seem forbidding, but friends appreciated her quick humour and her lively curiosity about those around her. Known to her friends as 'Thurb' or 'Thurbie', she often jokingly referred to herself as the 'Fundamental Principal'. Like Fogerty, she worked privately with those at the very top of their professions, whether they were actors or just active in public life. In the early 1950s, photographer Cecil Beaton went to her for private lessons to help with an impending speaking tour, describing her in his book, *It Gives Me Great Pleasure*:

> Miss Gwynneth Thurburn appeared unglamorous. She looked somewhat like a gaunt schoolmistress, with her sallow complexion, grey, short-cropped hair, and thrush-like eyes. She wore a cretonne dress. One large, formless and bony hand was garnished with a man's leather wristwatch. There was absolutely nothing theatrical about her.
>
> …As the days passed, I came to appreciate more and more the innate dignity that Miss Thurburn possessed. And how could I have judged her as looking like a schoolmistress? I remember that, one day when she had occasion to pronounce the name 'Dior', she conjured up such richness, such a luxury and opulence of sound, as no mere lady of fashion could ever have done.
>
> I learned, too, that Miss Thurburn had a sparkling sense of humour. …But what always impressed me most was her mackintosh quality of being impermeable to distracting moods. She was always alert; nothing could interfere with the task at hand. …Her powers of concentration were endless. If she sat on the window seat, laid her face in her hand and said, 'I'm putting myself in a state of complete receptivity,' I believed her. Her listening powers were so highly developed that it seemed she had some extra sense with which she judged the vast area of reading lines, of giving colour and music to the voice.

By 1942, Central was recognized as a leading institution for actor training, and the respect earned by Thurburn in the fields of speech therapy, speech and voice training for teachers helped maintain a high profile for the School. In August 1943, Thurburn was asked to give a paper on the 'Physiological Basis of Voice Training' to the Conference of the Association of Speech Therapists, and she emphasized that for basic training speech therapists should first use preliminary relaxation exercises for the whole body, to allow for correct posture, and then proceed to developmental exercises for capacity and control of respiratory, vocal and articulatory functions. She suggested appropriate ear training with a rhythmic basis – such as verse and prose – to stimulate the imagination and extend vocal range and expressiveness. This would encourage phrasing that is not based on breath groups, pauses, and a greater and lesser force of speech, but instead established as a focused means to convey thought.

In 1943, in her capacity as an educator, Thurburn wrote a 'Summary of Speech' to address the Government White Paper on 'Educational Reconstruction', and the Norwood Committee's Report on Curriculum and Examinations in Secondary Schools. She made clear that speech training had been sidelined and isolated in secondary schools as a 'frill' subject, only taken by children whose parents could afford it. Quoting the White Paper's essential requirement for 'training in clarity of expression and in the understanding of the written and spoken word', she forcefully insisted:

> Power of expression in speech is acquired, it is no mere technical accomplishment but the ability to communicate lucidly and audibly with clear intention and adequate vocabulary…
>
> The Norwood Report makes very clear the necessity for greater attention to the English language on the part of all teachers. There is great insistence on training in speaking, but the inference to be drawn is that all teachers should be able to do it. Since most teachers are insufficiently equipped vocally to meet the exigencies of their profession it is not likely that they will be able to set and maintain a high standard of performance in speaking. Nor are they qualified to deal with the delicate mechanism of children's voices.
>
> The needs of the children are briefly:
>
> a, The development of good speech habits for everyday life by means of organs which function harmoniously;
>
> b, The ability to communicate with ease and spontaneity, either in the form of simple communications (taking and delivering messages, giving simple explanations), or to use the extended vocabulary of formal speaking such as is required in making speeches, reading aloud, verse-speaking and acting.
>
> Speaking poetry and acting plays should be a part of literary study but, before either of these is possible, preliminary training is required in posture and control of movement and speech. The transfer from the language used by the child in his everyday life to the language of authors should be gradual, in order that full enjoyment may be experienced instead of the meaningless gabble and awkward meaningless gestures which so often pass for acting to-day.
>
> …The teacher must have control over his own voice and be able to demonstrate good speech with ease. He must arrest and hold attention by his manner of speaking in order to give his class full benefit of his matter. The specialist will care for the voice of the child and help him to use it in such a way that he is not aware that his voice is being cared for.
>
> …Training in breathing and of the vocal apparatus is not something to be given only to specialists but is no more than the vocal counterpart of physical training for the body and therefore the right of every individual.

George Hall, Director of the Central Stage Course from 1964 to 1987, said of this remarkable woman: 'Thurbie wanted the world to speak. She thought people were impoverished if they didn't have richness of vocabulary and freedom of voice.'

• • •

Thurburn's first year as Principal began with the 1942–3 Inaugural Meeting presided over by Lord Lytton. L A G Strong gave the Lecture and one of the Governors, Mrs Laura Henderson, presented the School with a pastel portrait of Ellen Terry. Central's General Regulations and Rules for students were presented to the students as follows:

1. No outside classes without permission of the Principal.

2. No professional engagement without permission of the Principal.

3. No absence from classes without leave from the Registrar.

4. All fees to be paid in advance of term and 'notice of withdrawal in writing 14 days before the last day of the current term' or ensuing fees will be charged.

Central had been in profit during its years in Exeter but, because of the higher rental expenses and an increased staff, the School ran at a heavy deficit its first year back in London. Always generous with her time and money, Joan van Thal relinquished part of her salary, so that additional lectures could be provided for her remedial speech students. There is little additional information on 1942–3, and there is no record of courses offered, but the prospectus for the next year, 1943–4, can perhaps give an indication of life at Central after it returned from Exeter.

Many of the courses remained the same as they had been under Fogerty. Lord Lytton remained President of the Governing Council, and John Gielgud was Vice President, as he had been since 1933. Council members included: Lewis Casson, Phyllis Foot, Mabel Gulick, F Mauris Pasteur, Geoffrey Whitworth, Aileen (Wyse) Dance, Lillah McCarthy, Muriel (Bousfield) Wigglesworth and staff representatives, Hazel Thompson and Joan van Thal. Now that Central was back in London, enrolment again began to grow. There were 68 first-year Stage students alone in 1943–4.

Fees for all three courses remained £16 16s 0d per term throughout the war years, with an entrance fee of £1 1s 0d. Three terms ran for 11 weeks – from the first week in October, from the third week of January and from the end of April. Still separate from the fees, an annual library subscription was £1 1s 0d. The School provided costumes for shows, but the student was expected to provide their dancing/mime costumes, textbooks and plays. The Registrar provided a list of hostels for accommodation, but students were responsible for finding their own housing.

Hazel Thompson remained the Director of Dramatics for all courses and oversaw the Stage Course, which students could attend for one, two and now three years. Stage students took courses in Acting and Rehearsal; Production and Stage Management; Theatre Craft and History of Costume; Greek Dancing; Mime; Diction; Voice Production; French – with a special study of selected plays; and Lectures on Drama History and Literature. Performances were given several times a year, with external examiners grading the students at these in-house performances, and a student would be awarded either a 1st or 2nd Class Dramatic Certificate upon completion of their training. A final public West End matinée performance was re-instituted – for agents and potential employers, as well as friends and family.

Thurburn oversaw the three-year course for Teachers of Speech Training and Dramatic Art, which included classes in Theory and Practice of Speech Training; Elementary Anatomy and Physiology as applied to Movement, Voice and Speech; Elementary Psychology as applied to Movement, Voice and Speech; Phonetics; History of Drama; History of Theatrical Art; Poetics; French, with a special study of selected plays; Verse Speaking, Acting and Rehearsal classes; Greek Dancing; and Mime. No full-course teacher-student was obliged to enter for the University Diploma, but if he or she wanted to, it had to be done by the end of the second year of training. In the optional third year, there was teaching practice and remedial work undertaken at Clinics, both under supervision. Graduates were eligible to join the Incorporated Association of Teachers of Speech and Drama (IATSD), and if students successfully sat examinations and gained their University of London Diploma in Dramatic Art, they were also eligible to apply for admission to the Royal Society of Teachers after 'one year of satisfactory experience in teaching'.

From 1937, qualified teachers who wanted to teach drama, to become county drama advisors or organisers, to lecture in training colleges, or to work freelance doing speech training and drama, could attend a one-year course to acquire the University of London Certificate of Proficiency in Diction and Drama (CDD), which replaced the old CDA. This CDD also gave eligibility for membership in the Incorporated Association of Teachers of Speech and Drama (IATSD).

Joan van Thal oversaw the remedial speech training, which offered a Certificate of Proficiency in Speech Therapy as a specialised third year – either after completion of two years of teacher training or as a two-year course for anyone over 21 who had professional experience or training. The Course included Speech Therapy and Clinical Observation and Practice, and required courses included Biology, Anatomy, Physiology, Neurology, Neuropathology, Psychology, Theory and Practice of Voice Training, Phonetics, Rhythmic Movement, Theory and Practice of Therapeutic Relaxation. There were lectures and demonstrations in Orthodontics; Plastic Surgery; Diseases of Ear, Nose and Throat; Oral Surgery; and Paediatrics. If a student completed this course after the initial two years of teacher training, they were also eligible for a Teacher's Diploma.

There were only three scholarships available to Central students. The £50 bursary was for men only (though not during the war years). The Kendall Scholarship was awarded either to a Stage or a Teacher Course student every three years for three years, and the Pivot Scholarship was awarded to a teacher-student for a specified time.

There were also a number of prizes and medals for students in training. A Gold Medal was awarded to a second- and a third-year Stage student with the best results throughout the year. The Sylvia Strutt Memorial Prize – a complete edition of Shakespeare – was awarded to a Teaching Diploma student for verse-speaking and literary appreciation. The Clifford Bax Cup was given to a third-year student for the best performance in the Diction Examination. The Dawson Milward Cup was presented for the best performance in a short modern scene by a first-year Stage student; and the Ben Greet Cup went to a first-year teacher-student for the best performance in a short Shakespeare scene. Thurburn awarded a 'Cup for Beautiful Speech'; and a prize of £3 was given for the year's best work in Stage Management. The Jane Gavin Memorial Prize of £5 was endowed by the Pivot Club and given to a female student in her second year who 'has proved her worth to the School'.

• • •

Stage students could expect to walk-on in professional plays at outside theatres throughout their final year, and Thurburn and Central were always looking for new performance opportunities. At a Governors' meeting in 1943, Lord Lytton suggested reinstituting collaboration with the Old Vic Theatre, to relieve them of the necessity of running their own training school and to give Central students the opportunity to gain more practical experience. A brief alliance had been attempted before the war, but again a course was offered for the 1944–5 academic year, which was billed as 'The Old Vic Course at The Central School of Speech Training and Dramatic Art'. Two new staff members – John Burrell and John Sullivan – were hired to help with the additional Old Vic students, and classes were offered in Voice, Diction, Literature, History of Drama, Costume and Theatrical Art, Musical Appreciation, Movement, Stage Management, Improvisation and Elements of Acting, Make-up, Stage Lighting, Rehearsal Classes and Performance. It was much the same training as that offered to Central students, the fees were the same, and as at Central, Old Vic students had to qualify at each successive stage of the three-year course to remain. At the end of the final year, a few students were invited to become student-members of an Old Vic Company – either in London, Bristol or on tour. Students with a technical aptitude would be helped to make 'contacts' within the business, and students who held the necessary educational qualifications could enter for the London University Diploma if they so wished. The course remained connected to Central until 1946, when the Old Vic again started its own school, this time under Michel Saint-Denis, but students continuing from the old joint course were allowed to complete their training at Central. Thurburn again had to look for opportunities for professional experience for her actors. Brief collaborations with Anthony Hawtrey at the Embassy Theatre and, in 1948–9, with the People's Palace were discontinued within a few months.

• • •

Britain had been at war for five years when Thurburn described the activities of the Central School in December 1944:

> This year has been one of the most disturbed in the history of the School, from the point of view of external interference, but neither the High Explosives of the spring nor the Flying Bombs of the summer seriously interfered with the work. In point of fact, progress has been made in several directions… The number of students has greatly increased, so that the Hall, instead of seeming spacious, now feels tight at the seams.
>
> We were heartened by the visits of two distinguished actresses, Dame Sybil Thorndike and Mme Francoise Rosay at a time when the outlook was cold and bleak. Mme Rosay came just after the windows had gone and her inspiring lecture gave us all a sense of renewed hope. When Dame Sybil gave her enthralling recital we were temporarily evacuated to the Imperial Institute, and again we felt that there are more permanent things than bricks and mortar.
>
> We are very grateful to the University of London and to the British Drama League for so kindly lending us rooms during our short evacuation from the Albert Hall…
>
> For the past 18 months co-operation between the West End Hospital Speech Therapy Training School and the Central School Speech Therapy Department has been closely maintained. Lectures on ancillary subjects such as Orthodontics and Laryngology are shared by both groups, and an exchange is effected in certain basic subjects, such as Neurology and Voice Training. The first joint examination was held this year.
>
> We welcome the establishment of the College of Speech Therapists and extend our good wishes to its members in the very valuable work they are doing. [*Viva Voce*]

Just as the formation of the College of Speech Therapists in 1945 was momentous for the profession, the most significant event for remedial speech teachers at Central was the official formation of the Speech Therapy Department. Unofficially in existence since Central's return from Exeter in 1942, it now completely separated itself from the Teacher Course. Joan van Thal was appointed its first Director.

• • •

ADDITIONAL CENTRAL FACTS

1944   • Flying Bombs blow out windows and damage the Albert Hall. The School briefly evacuates to Imperial and Toynbee Halls.

1944–5 • Special classes are held for members of the Old Vic Company, and for 'ratings' and WRNS of the Royal Canadian Army appearing in *Meet the Navy*.

8

1945–1954

JOAN VAN THAL (Teacher '22) was born in Rotterdam on 9 June 1900. Poor eyesight had made her desired career in medicine impracticable, but van Thal's interest in medicine and her great talent for languages (she spoke seven fluently) found their perfect 'pivot' in Elsie Fogerty. In 1919, van Thal became a student at Central. After her graduation in 1922, she went into private practice in remedial speech, and began her clinical work at the Royal Dental Hospital. In 1924, she was made Assistant Director at the St Thomas's Clinic under Fogerty, became Director after Fogerty's death in 1945 and remained in that position until 1951. Joan van Thal was awarded an MBE in 1950.

Van Thal had long been aware of the international work being done in remedial and therapeutic speech, and her understanding of continental methods and investigations was unique in Great Britain. In 1930, she was the only British delegate to attend the prestigious Fourth Congress of the International Association of Logopedics and Phoniatrics in Prague, and in 1937 she officially became the representative for Great Britain. This International Association had been founded by Dr Emil Froeshels for research into defects of speech and voice, and had grown out of a meeting of 65 international representatives in Vienna in 1924. Van Thal would later become its Vice President, its General Secretary, and finally its President, the first woman and the first non-medical member to hold that office.

Van Thal recognised the need for formal professional organisations. She had been a member of the ATST since her graduation from Central, but when in 1934 the ATST became the Incorporated Association of Teachers of Speech and Drama (IATSD), it was clear the needs of the teachers of speech and drama and the requirements of those working in remedial and therapeutic speech had grown in very different directions. Van Thal was instrumental in forming a subgroup of speech therapists within the new IATSD – the Remedial Speech Section – which would a year later break away to become a totally separate organisation: the Association of Speech Therapists (AST). In 1934, a separate, more medically orientated remedial speech organisation, the British Society of Speech Therapists (BSST), had also been created. Van Thal immediately saw the need for these two groups to join forces, but any plans she might then have had to accomplish this unification were interrupted by the war. In 1940, she joined the Central School in Exeter.

CONGRESS OF INTERNATIONAL ASSOCIATION
OF LOGOPEDICS AND PHONIATRICS

Joan van Thal reported to the *Viva Voce* that at the 1930 Fourth Congress of the International Association of Logopedics and Phoniatrics 40 papers were submitted on a wide variety of topics. They included: tuition of deaf-mutes, 'rhotacism' (defective 'R'), intelligence and other testing for speech defective children, acoustics and experimental phonetics, the inter-relation of infectious disease and defects of speech, word deafness, and the teaching of singing. There was also a 'lantern slide' of palatograms showing correct articulation of a number of lingua-palatals, and van Thal reports on the use of film and X-rays as a useful and 'innovative' adjunct to the lectures. The Congress convened biennially, and van Thal wrote of the next, which took place in Vienna:

...I cannot in the space of an article give a full report of the proceedings, but am only able to mention the more important points of some of the papers, so that I must be satisfied with mentioning that Prof Potzl gave an interesting account of Aphasia in individuals who speak several languages, that Prof Marburger gave us the benefit of his recent research on cerebral pathology, and Dr Feuchtwanger did us a great service in bringing with him a gramophone record of a case of Amusia (loss of musical ability)...

The shorter papers of the afternoon session dealt with stammering. M Meresz wished to attribute this disorder of speech exclusively to a mother complex. His point of view did not meet with much favour. [*Viva Voce*]

The Sixth Congress in Budapest in 1934 was devoted to stammering, and Elsie Fogerty was invited to give a paper on the 'harmony between the aesthetic and physiological standard of speech'. She no doubt met with a more favourable response than M Meresz.

When Central returned to London in 1942, van Thal took her first steps towards creating a single professional body of Speech Therapists. Until this time, members of both the AST and the BSST could become qualified to practise as speech therapists only when they had successfully completed their own organisation's examination requirements. For the 1942-3 academic year, van Thal set up interim joint courses for both the AST and the BSST with the West End Hospital for Nervous Diseases, and for the first time the two separate groups recognised a single organisation as examiners for their prospective members. The 'new Qualifying Body', mentioned in a Medical Press Circular as the 'College of Speech Therapists', first provided Joint Diploma exams in August of 1943.

This successful cooperative alliance led to the official merger of the AST and the BSST in 1945, when Joan van Thal and seven other Central graduates helped make up the 18 Founder Fellows of the College of Speech Therapists (now the Royal College of Speech and Language Therapists).

Meanwhile, van Thal was also ensuring Central's place in this emerging profession. While in Exeter, she had laid the groundwork for a separate Speech Therapy Department and begun to formulate the first specialist training course. Central's first Speech Therapy

1945	World War Two ends
1946	Standard repertory contract agreed by Equity
	The wartime organisation, The Council for the Encouragement of Music and the Arts (CEMA), officially becomes the Arts Council of Great Britain on 9 August
	Wartime rationing reimposed
	Bristol Old Vic and London Young Vic founded
1947	February sees non-stop blizzards and fuel shortages
	First University Drama Department created at Bristol University
	First Edinburgh Festival
	Marshall Plan instituted
1948	Mahatma Ghandi assassinated
	Twelve-year-old Lester Piggott is youngest jockey to win race
1949	Bill passed to create National Parks
	World's first jet airliner makes maiden flight
1950	Frank Sinatra sells out London Palladium
	George Bernard Shaw dies
1951	Spies Burgess and MacLean disappear
	Festival of Britain
1952	Death of George VI
	The Great Smog
1953	Ascension of Elizabeth II to the throne
	Theatre Workshop at Stratford East begins
	Conquest of Everest
1954	First BBC TV Equity contract agreed
	Food rationing ends
	IBM announces development of 'electronic brain' calculator for office use
	Under Milk Wood first performed on BBC Radio

students started this new course in 1945; they would graduate in 1947. They no longer sat for their University Diploma with the teacher-students, who had specialised in remedial speech only in their third year of study. They now trained separately and were examined solely by the College of Speech Therapists. Their 'degree' was a Licentiate, and they could be given permission to practise only through this new licensing body.

During the department's developmental years, van Thal gradually led the Speech Therapy Course away from its traditional base in speech training and dramatic art. Van Thal had always had a keen interest in drama and was very active in dramatic societies, but she recognised that her students were becoming overburdened with the more specialised academic and clinical requirements and could no longer spare the time for drama courses in their syllabus. Therefore, after 1947, Theatrical Art and Dramatic History lectures became optional subjects, and students were encouraged to spend more time on Social Sciences. Nevertheless, they could not help but be influenced by being part of a small, arts-based institution at the Royal Albert Hall, and for years a focus on normal voice and speech remained in the curriculum.

There are no personal reminiscences from Speech Therapy students from this exact period, but even though their course was evolving and changing each year, the experience could not have been too different from that remembered a decade later by Cynthia (Harries) Young (Speech Therapy '55).

I found myself being ushered into a darkened room... A shaft of sunlight filtered through partially drawn curtains on to a diminutive figure wearing thick pebble glasses and seated behind an enormous desk. (It was the)...brilliant Therapist and Linguist, with a passion for exotic hats from Paris, our much loved head of department, Joan van Thal.

The Speech Therapy Department was always small in comparison to the rest of Central, but what fun and how much we achieved. In the first year all students were integrated for certain classes such as Voice with Gwynneth Thurburn; of all the Therapy Schools in London (and there were four at that time) we had the best foundation in normal voice and speech, something now sadly lacking in modern Speech Therapy training.

Central School was vibrant. It was not unusual to find ex-students who were on the brink of glittering careers, such as Claire Bloom and Virginia McKenna, popping in, or to find Hermione Gingold holding court in the student canteen, having come in to see Stephen Joseph, who was on the staff. Every term the key question was who had been back in the holidays to receive voice coaching from Gwynneth: 'Oh! My dear, haven't you heard? It was Larry!!'

With so much to distract us it is amazing that we managed to fit in formal lectures, sometimes combined with the students from the West End Hospital for Nervous Diseases, or anatomy demonstrations at Gray's Inn Road, as well as our practical work in Hospitals and Clinics...'

Van Thal's vision in creating the Speech Therapy Department at Central was certainly to leave its mark on the profession. When she retired as Director of the Department in 1960, Principals of three of the seven other training schools for speech therapy in the United Kingdom were her former students.

● ● ●

Joint courses with other institutions – such as those for Speech Therapists at the West End Hospital for Nervous Diseases – provided some financial relief for Central's post-war economic distress, but the only way seriously to address this ongoing problem was for the School to enrol more students. A partial solution came from an unexpected source.

In the spring of 1945, the American Army Education Division approached Thurburn to request a Summer Refresher Course for American service men and women with previous experience or training in theatre, and so in 1945, and again in 1946, summer courses were given to personnel of the American Army. Rooms at the Hall had to be paid for whether it was term time or not, and giving courses during term breaks was a useful sideline, if in this case a not particularly lucrative one. In November, Lord Lytton had to write to the American Ambassador concerning non-payment of the sum of £802. This must finally have been paid, as 20 American GIs were selected to attend Central full-time for the 1945 autumn term.

Brian Tipping Codd started the Stage Course in October 1945, and remembers his student years with affection:

...Although the war was coming to an end there were only half a dozen men in my year. However, what was interesting was that there were several American GIs who had taken advantage of a scheme which allowed them to opt for an educational course in the country they found themselves on demobilisation. Much to the delight of many of the girl students they opted for the Central...

Aged 16, together with Claire Bloom who also started that term, at that time we were the youngest students ever to be accepted. In the second term we appeared together in *The School for Scandal* as Sir Peter and Lady Teazle... Claire took her studies extremely seriously and even at that early age showed signs of the qualities that would turn her into an outstanding actress. She was well chaperoned by her mother, who delivered and picked her up from the school every day.

Probably because of the war, lessons started at 8:30 am and finished in the early afternoon. At first, being so young, I found the course very daunting and for the first few months I was literally speechless with nerves when asked to read aloud.

I started a diary in '46 and some of the entries make bizarre reading but help to identify members of the teaching staff. Tuesday: Hensie Raeburn – Strangling. Miss Raeburn was a rather flamboyant actress who taught other stagecrafts as well as strangling! Thursday: Miss Richmond – Laughing. I was rather taken with Miss Richmond as she'd been a member of Sir Frank Benson's Company, a well-known Actor Manager from an earlier era. Miss Sadler and Miss Wellburn took Diction and we spent many hours practising with a bone peg clenched between our teeth.

We were extremely busy as students. As well as attending classes and rehearsing for end of term productions, we stage-managed for productions given by other years. I have a note that a performance of *The Beaux Stratagem* I worked on was attended by Dame Sybil, who took a great interest in the school. Performances were given on the tiny stage of a theatre in the Albert Hall rooms, which only had less than half a dozen rows of seats in its auditorium...

After VE Day there was a feeling of optimism throughout the country, and this was reflected in the life of the school. I remember it as a very happy time. Things could only get better, and we looked forward to working in our chosen profession. Food was still rationed, and we usually ate lunch at Slaters in Kensington High Street. Slaters was one of a chain of restaurants, rather like Lyons Corner Houses but not as expensive. There was an elderly Irish waitress who either had a grudge against the management or a soft spot as far as students were concerned. Whatever we ordered, she only charged us for the cheapest dish on the menu; needless to say, she did very well for tips. Occasionally, we went further afield, and I have a note of lunch at The Six Bells in Chelsea, which cost four shillings and seven pence (including coffee). There was a great perk in being in the Albert Hall – in between lessons one could watch the orchestras rehearse. I have a diary entry to 20 February '46: 'Watched John Barberolli and The BBC Concert Orchestra rehearsing Verdi's *Requiem* and listened to it on the wireless later that evening.'

CRYSTAL PALACE,

GRAND SUMMER DINING ROOM, NEAR LOW LEVEL STATION.

Miss ELSIE FOGERTY'S

Dramatic Recital, (Fogel)

ASSISTED BY PUPILS OF

Mr. E. THEODORE GILMER,

TUESDAY, SEPTEMBER 27th, 1898,

8.15 o'clock.

Enderby, Sydenham, S.E.

TOP LEFT: Portrait of Elsie Fogerty painted by R G Eves for the Royal Academy Exhibition and presented to the Central School in 1936. TOP RIGHT: Elsie Fogerty as Estrild in Swinburne's *Locrine*, directed by William Poel (1899). BOTTOM: Elsie Fogerty's first Dramatic Recital given in the Grand Summer Dining Room of the Crystal Palace. Theodore Gilmer later taught dance at Central in the Albert Hall.

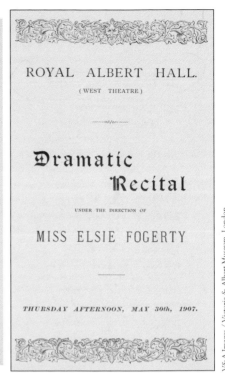

ROYAL ALBERT HALL.

(WEST THEATRE)

𝕯ramatic
𝕽ecital

UNDER THE DIRECTION OF

MISS ELSIE FOGERTY

THURSDAY AFTERNOON, MAY 30th, 1907.

TOP LEFT: Fogerty as a young woman. TOP RIGHT: Dramatic Recital in the West Theatre of the Albert Hall (1907).
BOTTOM LEFT: Actor John Laurie, Central 1919–20, who taught at Central and was for many years a Central Governor (1930).
BOTTOM RIGHT: *Mystery (Miracle) of the Rose* by Elsie Fogerty, presented on the steps of St Paul's Church, Covent Garden.
The cast included Lewis Casson as Prologue, James Dale as the King and Iris Baker as Lady Laura. Mary Casson was the
young child; and Central students (including Gwynneth Thurburn) appeared as the crowd (1919).

CENTRAL SCHOOL OF SPEECH TRAINING AND DRAMATIC ART.

TIME TABLE, SPRING TERM, 1921

MONDAY.	TUESDAY.	WEDNESDAY.	THURSDAY.	FRIDAY.	SATURDAY.
10-0.—Clinic.	10-15.—Classical Dancing. 2nd year. Miss Ginner.	10-30.—Physical Training. 2nd year. Miss Harvey.	10-30.—Voice Training. 2nd year. Dr. Aikin.	9-45.—Phonetics. 2nd year. Mr. Ripman.	10-0.—Recitation. B. and C. Miss Fogerty.
10-30.—Voice Training. V.B. Dr. Aikin.	10-30.—Voice Training. V.A. Dr. Aikin.	10-30.—Voice Training. V.B. Dr. Aikin.	10-30.—Dancing. 1st year. Miss Ethel Radmar.	10 15.—Voice Training. V.B. Dr. Aikin.	10-0.—Rehearsal. A. *Mr. Herbert Marshall.
	10-30.—Recitation. V.B. Miss Fogerty.	11-30.—Voice Training. Dr. Aikin.	11-30.—Voice Training. V.A. Dr. Aikin.	11-30.—Phonetics. 1st year. Mr. Ripman.	
	11-45.—Classical Dancing. 1st year. Miss Tucker.	11-45.—Physical Training. 1st year. Miss Harvey.	11-30.—Recitation. A. Miss Fogerty.	11-30.—Fencing. 2nd year. A. and B. M. Tassart.	
12-0.—Theory Lecture. All Students. Miss Fogerty.	11-45.—Voice Training. 2nd year. Dr. Aiken.				12-0.—Recitation. U.E.L. Miss Fogerty.
2-0.—Recitation. A. Miss Fogerty.	2-0.—Recitation. C. Miss Fogerty.	2-0.—Crafts. 1st year. Mr. Norris.	2-0.—Recitation B. Miss Fogerty.		
2-30.—Rehearsal. B. and C. Mr. Herbert Marshall.	2-30.—Rehearsal. A. Mr. Athole Stewart.	3-0.—Crafts. 2nd year. Mr. Norris.	2-0.—Fencing. C. M. Tassart.	2 30.—Crafts. All Students. Mr. Norris.	
			2-30.—Clinic. A.		
	4-0.—Rehearsal. B. and C. Miss Fogerty.		4-30.—Rehearsal. A. and B. Miss Fogerty.		
5-0.—Mime. A. Miss Irene Mawer.		5-30.—Anatomy. A. 2nd year. Dr. Hogarth.	5-0.—Ear Training. C. Miss K. Salmon.	5-30.—Voice Training. U.E.L. Miss Dexter.	
			5-30.—Voice Training. U.E.L. Miss Dexter.		

CENTRAL SCHOOL OF
SPEECH TRAINING
AND DRAMATIC ART
ROYAL ALBERT HALL

DRAMATIC CERTIFICATE

This is to Certify that

Laurence Olivier

Student of the

Central School of Speech Training & Dramatic Art

has satisfied the Examiners and has been awarded a
Certificate of

THE First CLASS with a Star

Examiners   Margaret Halstan

Assessor   Edith Craig.

Date July 23/25   Principal   Elsie Fogerty

TOP: Spring Timetable 1921. BOTTOM: Sir Laurence Olivier's Central Certificate,
complete with misspelling of his name (1925).

TOP LEFT: Hazel Thompson, 'The Bournemouth Graphic' (1904).
TOP RIGHT: Lee Matthews, a supporter of the School from its inception, was also one of Central's earliest Governors.
BOTTOM LEFT: Elsie Fogerty (second from right, middle row) and some of her students, at the wedding of Muriel Bousfield Wigglesworth (1922). BOTTOM RIGHT: Peggy Ashcroft, from a 1930 Central Programme.

TOP LEFT: George Bernard Shaw and Elsie Fogerty on the lawn at the Malvern Festival (1930s).
TOP RIGHT: Gwynneth Thurburn and Elspeth March at the Malvern Festival (1930s).
BOTTOM: 1936 Summer School Programme and Receipt for 1936 Summer School.

TOP: First production of T S Eliot's *Murder in the Cathedral* in Canterbury (1935).
BOTTOM: The last Public Matinée at the Arts Theatre before the School's evacuation to Exeter (1939).

TOP: Reed Hall, Exeter University (*courtesy of Exeter University*). BOTTOM: Central's 'Land Army Girls' (left to right: K Macrae, J Ewart, Christine Hayes (Caldwell), D Bissell, M Cockle, M Alston, A Peacock).

REED HALL 1940-41

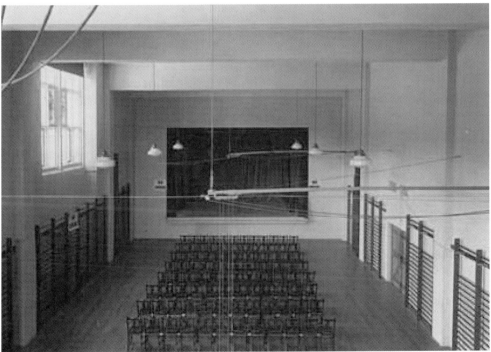

OPPOSITE TOP: Greek dance class, Exeter. MIDDLE: Les Girls and Lone Male in 'Wa-di-da-di-do' (left to right: M Cockle, D Bissell, M Houghton, R Christie, J Pritchard, J Evans, S Eliot, M Alston, J Harris, R Trump, M Vanderburgh, J Ewart, A Peacock, M Hunter, R Spenser, Sandy Sanderson (lone male) and M Mannion. Missing: C Read and C Hayes). BOTTOM: Central School at Reed Hall, 1940–1. The photo also includes evacuated female medical students from the Royal Free Hospital (starting sixth from left to right in second row: Christine Hayes (staff), Vera Sargent (staff), Nancy Brown (staff), E Fisher (warden), Elsie Fogerty (Principal), Gwynneth Thurburn (Vice-Principal), H Spalding and A Gurney-Dixon (medical representative).
THIS PAGE TOP: Exterior of Lopes Hall (courtesy of Exeter University).
BOTTOM: The little stage in Washington Singer Building (courtesy of Exeter University).

ELSIE FOGERTY JUBILEE

GALA MATINÉE
MONDAY, NOV. 30th
AT 2.15 P.M.

At THE NEW THEATRE
St. Martin's Lane, W.C.2
(by kind permission of Messrs. Howard Wyndham and Bronson Albery)

THE PROGRAMME WILL INCLUDE
An Informal reading of Poetry
By PEGGY ASHCROFT, DOROTHY BLACK, EDITH EVANS,
JOHN GIELGUD, JOHN LAURIE, LAURENCE OLIVIER,
SYBIL THORNDIKE, ROBERT SPEAIGHT,
J. CLIFFORD TURNER

A "Rag"
By STUDENTS OF THE CENTRAL SCHOOL OF SPEECH TRAINING
AND DRAMATIC ART

Scene from "Twelfth Night"
With PEGGY ASHCROFT and NICHOLAS HANNEN

Scene from "Way of the World"
With EDITH EVANS and JOHN GIELGUD

The following have also consented to appear:—
ROSALYN BOULTER, HENRY GASS, O. B. CLARENCE,
MABEL CONSTANDUROS, THEA HOLME, HENRY OSCAR,
ANN TODD

Presentation to MISS FOGERTY on the stage

Tickets may be obtained from:—
The Earl of Lytton, 3 Ladbroke Road, W.11. Tel. Park 7233 & 5700
Keith Prowse Offices. New Theatre on day of performance only

PRICES—Boxes £10 10s., £8 8s., £6 6s., £3 10s. Stalls £1 1s., 12/6, 7/6, 5/-.
Dress Circle 12/6, 8/6, Upper Circle 6/-, 4/-, 3/-. Gallery 2/-.

Elsie Fogerty Jubilee Matinée
Chairman of the Matinée Committee, The Rt. Hon. The Earl of Lytton, K.G.
Monday, Nov. 30th, 1942, at 2.15 p.m.

Programme

1 PROLOGUE by Sagittarius
Spoken by DOROTHY BLACK

2 POETRY READING
PEGGY ASHCROFT
EDITH EVANS
JOHN GIELGUD
JOHN LAURIE
LAWRENCE OLIVIER
HENRY OSCAR
ROBERT SPEAIGHT
SYBIL THORNDIKE

INTERVAL OF TEN MINUTES

3 STUDENTS' RAG
STUDENTS of the Central School of Speech Training
and Dramatic Art
Written and produced by DIANA MORGAN

4 MABEL CONSTANDUROS

5 "TWELFTH NIGHT," Act II, Scene 4
Viola ... ... PEGGY ASHCROFT
Orsino ... ... NICHOLAS HANNEN
Feste ... ... FREDERICK RANALOW
Curio ... ... ANTHONY BAZELL
Produced by John Gielgud
Setting of Song by Dolmetch

6 "THE WAY OF THE WORLD"
Millamant ... ... EDITH EVANS
Mirabell ... ... JOHN GIELGUD
Mrs. Fainall ... ... THEA HOLME

7 "HAMLET," Act I, Scene 3—In Modern Dress
Polonius ... ... O. B. CLARENCE
Laertes ... ... HUGH BURDEN
Ophelia ... ... MARGUERITE VAN DER BURGH
Members of the Household
Produced by Nicholas Hannen

8 JACK HULBERT

PRESENTATION TO MISS ELSIE FOGERTY, C.B.E., ON THE STAGE
Ode by LAURENCE BINYON   Spoken by CLIFFORD TURNER

TOP LEFT: Elsie Fogerty Gala Matinée, November 1942
TOP RIGHT: Gala Matinée Programme
BOTTOM: Gwynneth Thurburn

TOP: Vera Sargent and Gwynneth Thurburn in the audience of the Central Theatre in the Albert Hall (front row).
BOTTOM: Central displayed graphic designs of course work and costumes in its booth at the British Drama League's week-long Theatre Exhibition in Birmingham (May–June 1949).

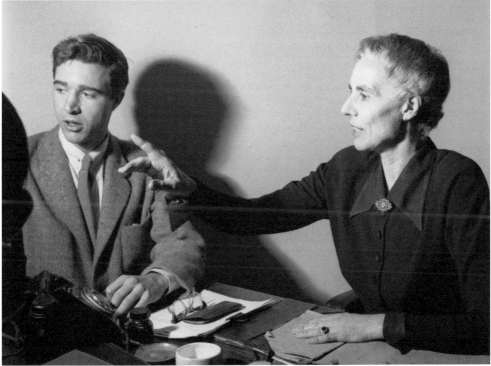

OPPOSITE TOP: Second-year students doing verse choral speaking. BOTTOM: Michael Danvers-Walker and Heather Sears, second-year students. THIS PAGE TOP: Margaret Edgecome teaching movement to first-year students Neil Curnow and Anne Barker. BOTTOM: Timothy Findley and Gwynneth Thurburn.
FOLLOWING PAGE TOP LEFT: James Valentine, Pamela Strong, Carmen Veliz, Benedikt Arnason, Valerie Dunlop and Don Brown in the Common Room of the Central School at the Albert Hall. TOP RIGHT: Mary Peach, Brian Smith and Anne Barker. BOTTOM: John Flexman and Wanda Ventham prepare the Central Theatre for a production by 'A' students.
All photographs on these three pages copyright © Desmond O'Neill, 1954.

TOP: New John Davis Wing (1961). BOTTOM: Actors in John Davis Wing using bone props (back row, left to right: Hugh Rose, Peter Nordeen, Caroline Monkhouse, Fiona Walker, Keith Darby, Noelle Finch, Caroline John, Douglas Ditta, Barry Justice; front row, left to right: Valerie Cutts, Rosemary Nicholls, Peter (Bette) Bourne).

TOP: Granada Library, John Davis Wing (1961). Staff member at desk; student at desk is Anna Sweeney. The couple at the back with a book is Julie Christie and Timothy Carlton.
BOTTOM: John Davis Wing, Pilgrim Trust Reading Room (front centre: Kate Lansbury).

'52'

52 Hyde Park Gate was described in the July 1947 issue of the *Viva Voce* by an anonymous student:

66 Apart from the obvious advantages of our new annex, there are many minor ones involved; including the provision of another excuse for unpunctuality, 'Oh, I thought Voice was down at 52 so I had to come all the way back to the Hall again!' Incidentally, the distance between Hyde Park Gate and the Albert Hall is conveniently elastic – it can be traversed in a matter of seconds, or stretched to occupy any time up to ten minutes, according to requirements.

When we first used 52, one of its greatest assets was that it enabled us at last to see daylight; we looked through glass doors and windows out onto Kensington gardens in the front and our own private garden at the back (filled though it was with air-raid shelters, the subsequent removal of which has lost us half the garden wall as well). Now that the windows have been replaced in the Hall however, we take this luxury for granted, but we have not forgotten the winter pleasure of coming from the draughty Hall to have a Phonetics class round a cheerful coal fire in 4/52. It is also a great help when practising relaxation on the floor of Room 1, to gaze up at a cloud-decked ceiling – a thoughtful relic left to us by our predecessors.

It is doubtful whether the Victorian family who once lived in the house would entirely approve of the changes they would find today. Would they recognize the 'Spanish lounge', bereft of all its stuffed birds and antimacassars and left instead with some wooden chairs, a piano, a blackboard and some cigarette ends lying on the bare floor, and on the wall, instead of the daughter's sampler, a cryptic motto – 'No Smoking'? Mama would doubtless be very shocked to see the 'best bedroom' used as a Common Room, filled with groups of men and women, sitting on the floor, the table, the window sill – and the chairs. She would be gravely mystified to see them gesticulating and muttering in corners, or gazing at their tongues in little mirrors. Upstairs in the 'cook's bedroom' how would she greet dear Billy Bones (Magog to some generations) as he leers from behind the blackboard or affectionately rests his footless fibula on the lecturer's chair? The horrified matron would retreat, with as much speed as her crinoline allowed, down the stairs towards the kitchen. Here, however, she might become involved in that midday phenomenon – the canteen queue.

There are two ways of coping with this obstacle: one is to take the line of least resistance and give oneself up to the purely social aspect of queuing, taking care not to become too involved in theatre discussion to forget whether one is 'meat or sweet'. If, however, the aim is purely gastronomic the second method is sometimes used – called queue-barging. But this is considered to be a very drastic and unpopular action, unless it is performed by a member of staff when it is, of course, quite another matter.

Alas, I fear the transformation scene would probably prove too much for our predecessors! On the other hand, it provides us with much for which to be thankful; the extra rooms, which can be used for other purposes than those indicated on the timetable – Pivot dinners, dancing and social evenings – the library, which is not used as a classroom as well but is run with professional efficiency by Miss Ross, whose work there is greatly appreciated. And above all, we are thankful for Mrs Gibson and her helpers, who work under frustrating conditions in the canteen and are yet able to provide Christmas dinners and seasonal feasts all year round.

The final word about 52 must inevitably concern the Corporal, who embodies all the cheerfulness and friendly atmosphere we find there. Yes, we have plenty to crow about, all you Pivots who spent your student life wandering in the blacked-out mazes of the Albert Hall. And do we crow? No of course not, we grumble as much as you did. **99**

I think the emphasis at the time was on the teaching of Speech Therapists (which was probably quite right). Gwynneth Thurburn came over as very much an academic, and one of our set books was her book *Voice and Speech*, dedicated to Elsie Fogerty. I may have been wrong but I always thought of Elsie Fogerty as more a woman of the theatre, perhaps it was because she was famous for coaching Laurence Olivier. There is a story, perhaps apocryphal, of her falling down the main staircase of the Albert Hall. As people rushed to help this elderly lady, she picked herself up, brushed herself down and said, 'One must always remember to relax.'

Within a short time after the war, Central enrolment had reached nearly 200. A victim of its own success, the School now desperately needed more classrooms, extra office space, a room for its library and more student facilities. Central took a seven-year lease (at £750 per year, exclusive of rates) on 52 Hyde Park Gate, which students soon referred to simply as '52'.

Joan van Thal had her office at 52, as did the Principal. Cecil Beaton remembered the room vividly: 'Miss Thurburn's quarters were on the first floor, up a circular staircase. The building itself had once, doubtless, been intended for domestic purposes, probably as the home of some ordinary middle-class Victorian family. It was a remnant of days when people lived spaciously. The paint was shabby now, and students ran up and down the bare treads of the stairs. I entered a room as sparsely furnished as the office of a mother superior. There was an Adam stucco decoration of medallions around the ceiling, and walls painted the colour of Devonshire cream. There was a photograph of Mrs Kendal (wearing an hour-glass ball gown of black velvet and jet) as she appeared in *A Scrap of Paper*; and some certificate of merit on the wall, signed by Christopher Fry and other notables of today's theatre.' [*It Gives Me Great Pleasure*]

As welcome as the space was at 52, it was not enough. The Manager, C S Taylor, allowed Central to also lease additional space at the Hall. Vera Sargent moved her office into a stabilised lift shaft to the right of the West stairs, and small Stage and Teaching offices were created above part of the theatre and the general office. It may always have been broke, but the Central School was a bustling success.

• • •

In 1946, Thurburn stated the aim of the Stage Course at Central as '...an education for the theatre in which every student may develop as an individual member of society in addition to learning the elements of his craft'. 'Learning the elements of his craft' would now set drama schools apart from their emerging competition – university drama departments.

University drama departments had long been in existence in the United States: Harvard's Drama Department was formed in 1912, and Yale's in 1925. When Thomas Taig opened the Drama Department at Bristol University in 1947 – with university personnel teaching academic courses and the staff of the Bristol Old Vic Theatre Company and School giving practical classes – it was the first of its kind in Britain. In 1950, Taig spoke of the beginnings of this Department at a meeting for the IATSD: 'The students would, of course, do practical work in speech; but it must be remembered that the course would not, by intention, produce speakers or actors. A university student was first a scholar, and was more concerned with exploring and pioneering than in becoming an executant.' When asked what was the use of the course at Bristol, he replied: 'For educating the students. Education produces integrated people. The study of art, of any art, does this. Art is the outward embodiment of imagination. An arts degree is not ever a qualification for a job. They will earn their living in engineering, in business, some in teaching, some one or two in films or the BBC; but if the educational value of drama comes from the expression of imagination, then the specialist is not the only person who should do it.'

From 1923, a University of London Diploma had given an indication of professional status for teachers and for the few actors who also sat the exams. Now, if drama schools were to continue successfully to attract students, they would have to focus on the practical training they offered and accept that those more interested in a degree would be lost to the emerging drama departments. At a spring 1947 Central Academic Board meeting, Eileen Thorndike proposed that emphasis be laid on practical rather than theoretical work for Stage students, and from October that year there were no more written exams during the third year. However, practical tests were still held in Acting, Diction, Mime and Movement during the second year, and admission to the third year still depended on the aggregate marks obtained.

Two years later, Thurburn and the Principal of RADA, Kenneth Barnes, were responsible for the first major changes to the University of London Diploma syllabus since 1923. French, Music and Physics were dropped, Poetics became optional, and a class in Shakespeare was added. Significantly, the London University Diploma was dropped as an option for Stage students, and for the next 45 years, the lines became more and more clearly drawn between a university degree in drama, and practical actor training for the professional theatre.

• • •

Another change immediately after the war greatly affected an entire generation of Central teacher-students. In 1946, the Central Teacher Course was the first of its kind to receive recognition from the Ministry of Education. This was more than a pat on the back. Students accepted onto this course now became eligible for the new Local Education Authority grants that had been instituted by the 1944 Education (Butler) Act. However, not only would the teacher-students receive financial assistance to train, when they graduated with their three-year Diploma, they were also automatically given Qualified Teacher Status. This mark of excellence translated into the higher rate of pay laid down by the new Burnham Scale. Students could only gain Qualified Teacher Status from two other places besides Central: the Royal Academy of Music and the Guildhall. There was, however, a down side to this new pay scale.

The Burnham Scale (and the Pelham Scale for Training Colleges) also brought up the unwelcome question of adequate rates of pay for Central staff, whose pay was well below the outlined scales. From 1946 onwards, the Governors continually tried (and usually failed) to keep up with these new suggested rates, with student fees having to be raised accordingly to cover the increases.

Staff salaries had always been meagre, and in the spring of 1948, the Board of Governors finally raised them to:

Lecturers: £1 1s 0d per hour
Part-time staff, practical classes: first hour, £1 1s 0d then £0 15s 6d per hour
Play reading classes remained: £1 11s 6d for 2 hours
Producers pay remained: £2 2s 0d first two classes per week, then £1 11s 6d per class
Special lecturers: approximately £2 2s 0d per lecture.

At a Board meeting in November 1952, a Governor pointed out that the School was being subsidised by the staff, whose salaries were greatly below the Pelham Scale for Training Colleges, and he moved that this situation should (again) be remedied. At a 1957 Board meeting, the inadequacy of staff salaries was again discussed and an increase of 25% for staff members was agreed, with visiting lecturers to receive £1 7s 6d per lecture – a hardly princely 6s 6d rise in pay from a decade before. Yet the appalling remuneration somehow didn't seem to matter, and Central's reputation continued to attract quality tutors and lecturers. In 1947, L A G Strong, John Burrell, Athene Seyler, Alec Guinness and James Forsythe gave special lectures, and Helen Best, Muriel Judd, Mrs P Smith, Mrs Worth and Marjorie Frances joined the staff.

As new tutors arrived, old tutors left. Hazel Thompson had been the Director of Dramatics since 1941, and when she resigned from that position in 1947, Hal Burton was appointed to replace her at a salary of £500 per year. William Devlin took over a year later, with Assistant Director, Mary Crossley, filling the position during Devlin's many absences. In 1950, Walter Hudd became Director, with Devlin agreeing to deputise for him as their professional engagements might dictate. Thompson retired from the remainder of her teaching duties in 1949, and connections to the past dwindled – even the Albert Hall Commissionaire, Captain Hook, isn't mentioned after 1950. Nevertheless, incoming classes of students had always created their 'own' Central, and post-war students were no different.

A new Student Association took the place of the now defunct Pivot Club, and out of this organisation grew a student performance group. Mask and Dagger was created to contribute money to a fund for a new Central theatre (they made £100 the first year) and the group's inaugural production in autumn 1949 was Marlowe's *Dr Faustus*, with a

WILF TAYLOR POST-WAR TEACHER COURSE

Wilf Taylor wrote in 2005:

    ❝ Claire Bloom, who stayed only one year as she did not like the ladies who ran the place, says in her autobiography, 'The Registrar had the ominous name of Sargent.' All of us chaps on the Teacher Course starting in 1946 had just come out of the Armed Forces and Vera treated us with a good deal of deference. Perhaps she realised that we had had enough of sergeants, however they spelled their names.

    Two of us even persuaded her to let us have some money to buy tubular steel and cartridge paper to build sets for our Diploma Plays. The theory was that if the set were attractive enough, the adjudicators' attention would be diverted from the acting!

    We had to perform in five different plays, including a modern one. Personally I was very lucky with this one, which was Harley Granville-Barker's translation of a Spanish play. Lucky, too, with the producer, that splendid Hazel Thompson. She, in fact, had been a protégée of Harley Granville-Barker. The set, which I designed, was of a Spanish patio, with Moorish arches, etc. Johnny Sanders and I set about building this with the steel and cartridge paper, which we had bought.

    The only time we could have for erecting it was the night before the performance. We worked away until I said, 'They must be thinking of closing up. We had better get going.' 'What do you mean, Wilf?' said John, looking at his watch. 'It's half past eleven.'

    I remember we managed to get released by attracting the attention of a passing policeman who, somehow, got us out. The reward came when the curtain went up on *The Kingdom of God* the following morning and a gasp went up from the audience. Nothing like it had been seen on that stage before.

    Thurb was a splendid speaker of verse, but rarely gave us a treat by speaking any. I recall that one day she spoke Browning's 'A Toccata of Galuppi's' superbly, then followed it with a ballad she had found somewhere – but refused to tell us where – called 'The Ballad of the Bleeding Nun'. Each verse ended with the line 'Twas the Bleeding Nun'. We were rolling in the aisles long before she had finished.

    There was a 'red letter' day when Christopher Fry turned up with just one act of a play he had written and asked a producer called Stuart Latham to read it and tell him if it was any good. Stuart went into raptures about it and got the 'A' Stage people to act it. Ann Jellicoe in the female lead and John Van Eyssen (a South African) in the male lead made a splendid job of it. Then it was a part of the programme of the annual matinee for the 'A' Stage group at the Globe Theatre. John Gielgud was there to observe the talent and was so taken with this one act that he asked Fry to finish it as soon as possible because he wanted it for the West End. Fry did. But because he had to do it in a hurry, I fancy he did not have time to work out a good title, so gave it what I consider to be the worst of all his titles, *The Lady's Not for Burning*. I have no hesitation in saying, however, that Ann and John out-acted Gielgud and Pamela Brown by a distance...

    There are so many memories of Central and Albert Hall that linger in the mind. Another, when one of my colleagues, Peter Hills, said he had found out there was a bar in the basement. So that's where the orchestra disappeared to during intervals in rehearsals! Whenever we had time – and sufficient pennies – we went down for at G & T.

    One final memory – the voice of Clifford Turner still rings in my ears as he encouraged us 'chaps' to utter one or other of his mantras. His favourite, 'He jests at scars that never felt a wound'. We could never emulate him. ❞

cast that included Richard Pasco and Virginia McKenna. Five more productions followed that term. One of these, *The Provok'd Wife*, opened the National Union of Students' Arts Festival in Birmingham during the Christmas holidays, and received a glowing review from the *Manchester Guardian*: 'It was the dramatic comet, to which the rest cannot hope to be more than a rather precarious tail.' Stephen Joseph was the director.

Stephen Joseph was born in 1921 and trained on the Central Stage Course from 1937 to 1939. After service in World War Two (he was awarded a Distinguished Service Cross for action in the Mediterranean) and demobilisation, he read English at Cambridge, and in 1949 Thurburn invited him to become a member of the Central staff – along with Heather Black, Hazel Potts and Carol Sairfield. As well as undertaking directing and teaching duties on all courses, Joseph also became the first leader of the new Stage Management Course.

Stage management skills had always been taught to the teachers at Central, with courses in costume and prop construction, and 'Physics, as applied to Stage Lighting'. Stage and teacher-students were expected to participate as stage managers as part of their training. While teacher-students continued to receive minimal instruction in these subjects from Caryl Jenner (Stage '34), specialisation in the technical branches began in earnest in 1947 when Central accepted two Stage Management students. (One left after only one term.) Two more students were accepted in 1948. (Only one remained for the whole year.) Stephen Joseph initiated a full Stage Management Course in 1949, and although the small Central Theatre over the West Porch offered limited technical facilities and elementary lighting opportunities, by 1953 there were ten Stage Management students learning stage lighting, scenic design, prop-making and wardrobe management.

Students respected and liked the young director, and one, Shirley Cooklin (Stage '52) recalls: 'I was a pupil (and admirer of) the late, great Stephen Joseph. I complained bitterly to him when I was cast as "the little page" in *The Merry Wives*. I think I had one line. He told me that his mother, Hermione Gingold, had made her name in the part and produced me outrageously as a scene-stealer – a performance for which I was highly praised.'

However, not all of Joseph's student productions were as well received as Mask and Dagger's *The Provok'd Wife* and *The Merry Wives of Windsor*. Bridget (Evans) Davies, Caroline (Parkin) Cornish, John Clotworthy and Patty (Haworth) Miller (Teachers '53) remember a catastrophic production of Purcell's *King Arthur*, with a stellar cast that included Wendy Craig, Jeremy Brett and Harry Landis (now President of Equity). Paul Scofield was in the audience for the presentation, to see a student who was serving as his dresser in the West End. A proud Hermione Gingold was there to see her son's highly praised directorial work.

Whether he was attempting to expand upon the limited technical horizons of the little Central Theatre or just trying to give his actors more light, Joseph had lowered an extra lighting bar on Stage Left. When the curtain went up, a procession of proud actors marched onstage wielding banners, which immediately tangled on the low-hanging lights. The banners caught fire, the line ploughed forward, and actor tumbled over actor into a smouldering pile. Things went from bad to worse, but even as Antonia Grimaldi, as Britannia, visibly bobbed and crawled behind the cutout waves to make her upstage appearance, the audience maintained its decorum. Torn newspaper 'snow' drifted from above, with an entire sports or financial section occasionally thudding to the stage. Still, the teacher-students in the audience maintained respect for their fellow professionals. Everyone still agrees that Jeremy Brett's performance as an Iceberg was memorable, but when Wendy Craig appeared in baggy tights to announce, 'I've left all right behind!' the entire audience – including Gwynneth Thurburn and Vera Sargent – could no longer stifle their guffaws. Choking with laughter, Scofield later admitted: 'That has to be one of the most enjoyable afternoons I have ever spent in the theatre!'

Stephen Joseph remained at Central only part-time after this memorable production, and Helen Dorward (Stage '55) claims he always held *King Arthur* attributable for his demotion. It didn't do much to slow his career, though, and in 1955 in Scarborough, he opened the first professional Theatre-in-the-Round in Britain, leading to the formation of Studio Theatre, Ltd., and after his early death, the Stephen Joseph Theatre. When he passed away in 1967, he left over 1000 of his theatre books to the Central library.

Through the years, the Mask and Dagger Society continued to contribute to the fund for a new Central Theatre. In 1955, its President, Ian Hendry, added to the constitution an additional purpose for the society, and students were given the opportunity to produce and act in shows of their own choice. Once these shows were approved by the Society, £5 was awarded for production costs. Cynthia (Harries) Young (Speech Therapy '55) recalls: 'Second-year students of all disciplines assisted with front of house duties when the third-year drama students were performing in the little theatre. The coffee making facilities were formidable, however, and Jeremy Brett and I just about mastered them by the interval! In addition, there were performances by Mask and Dagger to raise funds for a new Central School Theatre. We were asked to give generously to the silver collection at the end of a performance.'

Mask and Dagger was sponsored by the Student Association, which in 1949 also put out a student publication, *Prompt*. In the second issue, Helen Best contributed an article, 'How to Do It' – specifically for the few students on the new Stage Management Course. There was a report of an inter-School event: the Old Vic Theatre School versus Central School Fencing Match (Central won by four hits), stating, 'Mr John Blatchley and Mr Glen Byam Shaw were very enthusiastic about the idea of more association between the two schools.' The same issue had another, equally prophetic article, proposing that British Equity 'should consider giving students from Theatre Training Schools the opportunity of becoming members of Equity on terminating their studies.' This suggestion would take over thirty years to accomplish, and only after even more restrictive entry rules came and went.

• • •

Central's teacher training provision had been the first to receive Ministry of Education recognition in 1946, but in spite of the School having remained in the forefront of drama teacher training, in 1949 the Teacher Course was only given temporary recognition by the Ministry. Immediately Gwynneth Thurburn and Vera Sargent met with Mr Fleming of the Ministry, who explained that all specialist teacher-training was now under review, and when new governing regulations were put in place in 1951, the School would again need to be inspected. The Ministry was moving towards sponsoring more youth clubs and drama work and would need teachers for them, and he encouraged Central to further develop their drama training in the syllabus. Both Fogerty and Thurburn had run the Teacher Course as part of their duties at Principal, but in response to possible future requirements from the Ministry and the resultant administrative duties, in the spring of 1949 Central officially formed a separate Teacher Training Department. In 1950, ex-student Marjorie (Siratsky) Frances (Teacher '33) took over as the first part-time Director, and began to organise the course structure to suit the Ministry's demands. By 1952, the Central three-year Diploma course included:

1ST YEAR: Voice; and three of following: Poetry, Dramatic History, Theatrical Representation, Anatomy. Students also had to achieve a satisfactory standard in Diction and Dramatic Tests.

2ND YEAR: Voice Training; and two of following: Poetry, Dramatic History (two papers), Theatrical Representation (two papers). Students had to achieve a good standard in Diction and Dramatic Tests.

3RD YEAR: Practice Teaching; Elementary Theory of Education; Voice training; Phonetics. Students also had to achieve a satisfactory standard in practical Diction and Drama.

The Teacher Course remained in flux for the next several years, buffeted by changes both internally and externally. A 'Plays in the Parks' scheme was developed to address the Ministry of Education's suggestion to develop the drama provision within the course, but by the time Marjorie Frances left Central in 1952 to take up a full-time lectureship at Goldsmiths' College, it was becoming clear that that may not be the best strategy. In her last meeting with the Academic Board, she suggested that, in order adequately to address the external changes in the world of teacher training, the department would in the future need the services of someone experienced in the educational world – someone who had contact with Training Colleges and the latest ideas and methods of teaching, rather than someone who was simply a specialist in Speech and Drama. Central set about finding such a person. Vera Fraser replaced Frances in 1952, and a year later, Dr C J Phillips replaced Fraser.

At an interview in 2005, John Clotworthy, Patty Miller, Bridget Davies and Caroline Cornish (Teachers '53) were critical of the Teacher Course, remembering it merely as a watered-down version of the Stage curriculum. They spoke with admiration of their phonetics teachers, Heather Black and the young Cicely (Cis) Berry. Both women had trained at Central. Black had been on the staff since 1949, and Berry since 1948. Berry would remain at Central for over twenty years, leaving only to become the resident voice specialist for the Royal Shakespeare Company. The RSC was the first UK company to have a full-time Voice Department, and Berry became their Head of Voice in 1970. Arguably the most famous voice teacher in the world, Berry is the respected author of a number of seminal books on voice, and is without a doubt one of Central's most esteemed alumni. It is no wonder this group of teachers remembers her with affection and respect.

Teachers '53 also remembered another Central voice 'star', Clifford Turner, who taught voice in the room behind the Albert Hall organ that, when played, used to vibrate so loudly you 'couldn't hear your own voice'.

WALTER HUDD

Walter Hudd, Central's Director of Dramatics from 1950 to 1960, first appeared on stage in 1919 as Monty Missit in *The Manxman* at the Theatre Royal, Aldershot. He toured internationally with Fred Terry's Company, and in 1925 opened at the Kingsway Theatre in London as Guildenstern in *Hamlet* – one of the first modern dress productions of Shakespeare. An array of parts followed in a number of plays, both on tour and in London. In 1939, he played in *Julius Caesar* at the Embassy Theatre, and from 1942 to 1945 toured his own company for the war effort, again appearing at the Embassy Theatre, this time in *Little Eyolf*. After the war, Hudd was associated with the Shakespeare Memorial Theatre in Stratford-upon-Avon and the Old Vic, both as an actor and as a director, on tour and in London. He directed a number of commercial productions in the West End (including *Turn Two Pages* at the Embassy Theatre in 1950), and worked on film, radio and later television in a range of supporting roles. As well as writing several one-act plays, his full-length play, *Snow in December*, was presented at the Whitehall Theatre (now Trafalgar Studios) in 1935.

Turner was stern, serious and sometimes insulting, particularly to the girls – 'You've been here two years, and you still have linen draper's vowels!' Margaret Rubell taught movement and dance (the girls had to wear green tunics) and, to her students, seemed ancient – 'Even though she was in her 50s, she knew everyone's name!' Muriel Judd, known irreverently as 'Pixie', taught sight-reading, but it seems she had little control over her students and is remembered mostly for stroking her top lip, yawning and falling asleep while she herself was talking. Betty Shaw rattled off her lectures on Costumes (Theatrical Representation) from a book: 'If you dropped your pencil, you missed a hundred years.'

The terrifying, yet highly respected, Gwynneth Thurburn taught diction and verse speaking – 'She *was* verse-speaking' – which was held for two hours each Friday. As had Fogerty, Thurburn required her students to learn a poem every week, culminating in the end of term Diction Test given on the Central Theatre stage. Like generations before, students left the audience for the dressing rooms beneath the stage and, one by one, were called up the staircase and through the trapdoor on the stage to perform, standing in front of Elsie Fogerty's carved wooden chair.

By the end of the second year of training, these Teacher '53 students felt they had been 'knocked down', and there was only one teacher who took the time to build them back up – L A G Strong. Strong was extremely popular with Central students for his entire tenure at the Hall. A teacher before his success as a novelist and poet, Strong came to the Hall first as a part-time lecturer and then, in the early 1950s, as a part-time instructor in drama and voice. He remained at Central until his death in 1958.

The students of '53 also had distinct memories of Queen Alexandra's House, home to a number of Central's female students over the years. A wide, sweeping staircase led to the living quarters, which in the 1950s consisted of either single bedrooms or two single bedrooms with a shared sitting room. There was a hall for occasional dances, and piano practice rooms at the top of the building. Residents were given breakfast, lunch, afternoon tea, supper and a room for £52 per term. (Central's fees were £25 per term.) The administrator for the House at that time was Charis Frye. From a naval family, she was known as 'The Admiral', and she ran Alexandra House with military precision – even to the extent that she insisted one of the girls 'pipe' her into the dining room. There was a male porter, but boys were not allowed upstairs into the rooms, nor even permitted to place a foot on the steps. As a consolation, rooms 5 and 5A were referred to as the 'Boy Boxes', and girls could book them for visitors – for a whole half-hour at a time.

A number of memorable events marked the lives of these young students. HRH Princess Marina, the Duchess of Kent, paid an informal visit in November 1951, and the Manager of the Hall, C S Taylor, promised the Governors he would have the Goods Lift furbished and manned for the event. In December 1952, the Great Smog of London was particularly unforgettable: over 4000 people died in four days from the combination of low pressure, fog and smoke – smog so thick that at a production of *The Lady's Not for Burning* it was impossible to see the Central Theatre stage from the auditorium. The Underground was closed, and Bridget Davies tells of her blind friend, Hal, who was riding a bus in London. The driver stopped, unable to go further in the thick fog. Familiar with the route, Hal got out and led the bus the rest of the way, tapping in front with his white cane.

Delena Kidd (Stage '55) wrote of those years:

It's been fifty years since I left the Hall with two jobs – a TV and six-month contract at Ipswich Rep as the juvenile lead – without even an interview. How much easier it was for us in those days! I think we all had a theatre job to go to. It was a wonderful time, and it was always exciting to go to work at the Albert Hall and stand at the back watching concert rehearsals.

ALEXANDER TECHNIQUE

In 1952, Thurburn and the Central Staff began to make investigations into F Mathias Alexander's method of posture and breathing as applied to voice training. In 1956, Thurburn requested funding from the Board of Governors to undertake serious research on the Alexander Technique, projecting it would take four or five years to produce findings. However, more pressing financial needs meant the research was never undertaken. The following is from a History of Central, compiled by Thurburn and Sargent in 1967:

> With the agreement of the Governors a pilot investigation was undertaken by Dr Barlow with Gwynneth Thurburn, some members of staff and students as guinea pigs. The immediate findings were not unpromising and it was agreed that more work was desirable. Unfortunately funds did not permit further investigation. Gwynneth Thurburn and some of the voice staff and students felt that they had personally derived great benefit from the experience and, though it was not possible directly to incorporate the principle into training, there was no doubt that their thinking on questions of voice and movement had been enlarged. It is to be deplored that through lack of means a promising venture had to be discontinued, especially as other specialist training schools were later able to pursue the value of the Alexander Principle, largely as the result of Gwynneth Thurburn's initiative, to their great satisfaction and benefit.
>
> One interesting fact emerges. In 1910 Elsie Fogerty had met and learned from Sir Charles Sherrington. In 1946 Sir Charles Sherrington commended the work of Matthias Alexander.

We had a remarkable staff then: Cis (Berry), Clifford Turner, Stephen Joseph, Thurb herself and Ollie Reynolds; but the whole tone was set for us by Dickie (Walter) Hudd who was Head of Drama. He was as meticulous a teacher and critic of our work as he was an actor, with tremendous attention to detail. He really wanted us to understand the importance of discipline in the theatre – we must never walk between the director and stage and we must stand in the director's place whilst he was demonstrating for us in a scene – and he was fierce about punctuality. Once, when I was late on a Monday morning, having been to Stratford to see some plays, he said, 'Now, Delena, do you want to be an actress or a weekender?' He was a well-known, working member of the profession, as were Guy Verney, Harry Latham, Joan White and Michael Langham, and they all directed us in term plays.

On the social side, lots of us shared flats around Kensington and Knightsbridge; the Serpentine was near for swimming in the hot weather; and we drank inordinate amounts of Merrydown cider in the Scarsdale. I think we made a lot of spaghetti at parties, and at one of these a young soldier, Julian Bream, played the guitar. I remember a big group of us slept out all night in the Mall to watch the Coronation. Looking back it was such a post-war period, but we certainly didn't feel part of a 'lost decade', as the BBC is now describing it. There was plenty of everything.

Sadly so many of my group died young, and I think the only ones still acting are Helen Dorward, Philip Bond and myself. We were a very happy but disparate group, with students from South Africa, Canada, New Zealand and the US, lots of boys released from National Service on grants, and quite a few middle class girls who paid.

• • •

In the early 1950s, the Central School consisted of Stage, Stage Management, Speech Therapy, and Teacher students – from both the three-year and the one-year courses.

Graduation from the one-year Teacher Course provided a Certificate of Diction and Drama to qualified teachers who wished to specialise in speech and drama, and was taken either after two years of teacher training college or as a separate year's specialisation after at least three years' teaching. Alan Lyne was one of 14 students on this course in 1950–1. He wrote in 2004:

> An interesting, and surely unique, outcome of our CDD year was the declared desire to maintain a group connection as we prepared to go our separate ways at the end. We decided to present a play in London in the forthcoming Christmas season 1951, and this we did. Cutting a long story short, we followed up with a three-night tour the following year, and this became the precursor to the formation of a drama company – we invited talented friends to join us – which, in 2001, celebrated 50 years of taking important dramatic works to various venues. And it still goes on, though far more proficiently than in our early days.
>
> Although I am not now a member, I am kept in touch with their activities and, as the Company's first 'Director', to give a grand name to the mundane task of keeping everyone involved and making on-the-spot decisions, I was invited to the 50th anniversary dinner. An interesting sidelight is that the company is called The Riverside Players, simply because another CDD student and myself, sharing the organisational role back in 1952, both lived in that part of London, which in those days had a telephone number with the prefix RIV which stood for Riverside.

The Central School Diploma (CSD) replaced the CDD in 1954, and this new CSD qualification could be obtained by satisfying examiners in either: Voice (written and practical) and Oral Phonetics: or Acting, Production, Stage Management and Dramatic History. The Voice Paper was taken at the end of the spring term and a Viva in the summer term. Any teacher who obtained this new CSD was also immediately eligible to join the IATSD, as were the graduates from the three-year course.

After the war, Central's enrolment had increased steadily, and by 1954, there were 233 students – a 33 percent increase from pre-war enrolment. 52 Hyde Park Gate, the Church Hall of St Stephen's Church, and a building behind Harrods were able to handle some of the overflow from the Hall, but Central desperately needed additional premises. There were insufficient funds to purchase a suitable space, but the Governors recognised that

SHIRLEY (JACOBS) JAFFE STAGE '54

❝ I was a Central School Stage Course student 1951–4. This was the era of Stephen Joseph, although during our first year, all we had was older students saying, 'Of course, you haven't had Stephen Jo, he's on sabbatical in the States'. During our second year I was amazed he cast me in a play we took to the first Student Festival, which was opening the Student Theatre at Leeds University. We did an obscure Restoration comedy, *The Careless Husband* in which I was the wronged wife, married to Harry Landis. Working with Stephen was a step to growing up on my part – I learnt enormously about all sorts of things from *Guys and Dolls* being the best ever musical, to putting wine in packet chicken noodle soup, with bits of literature, architecture and theatre history thrown in. Our one night stand at Leeds was very successful, in spite of the new lighting box catching fire while we were on stage, and Paul Massie, my current love-of-my-life (not that he knew that), manfully beating out the flames while we continued playing – and I led students and cast in a conga round the streets of Leeds as the 1953 New Year came in.

That summer (1953), Harry and Stephen organised a tour to a Festival of Peace and Friendship in Bucharest, behind the then solid iron curtain, and to an NUS conference in Warsaw. We were all in a film, *One Great Vision*, about the Festival, made by Antony Simmons and Walter Lassally (Oscar winner for *Zorba* some years on). We flew to Prague where God, from our Mystery Play about Noah's Ark, was whisked away from us into a sort of Limbo, because his name (Clive) was written as Olive on his visa, so making him female! We were all mightily concerned about arriving behind the iron curtain and losing God, but he was restored to us on the train to Bucharest next night. He did miss one performance through illness (or possibly hangover) and we must have seemed very advanced in that night's show, having a young woman stage manager playing God. The other play we performed was Stephen Joseph's *The Key*, a strange comedy set in modern, Victorian and Elizabethan times that must have been even more incomprehensible to our international audiences. We played in West End type theatres, and once we did The Flood as part of an international performance in an open-air stadium seating about 3000 people and the President of Romania, sharing a dressing room with wonderful Chinese jugglers. In Warsaw, we were taken on tours of the still bomb-damaged city, to the ghetto, and out into the forest to Chopin's house, where one of their best pianists played for us, and to a student hotel in the woods where Polish students performed for us and vice versa. We were made very aware of our lack of party pieces for such an occasion. There was no song or performance dance taught at Central – and I distinctly remember someone being told, 'If you want to do singing, you should go to Webber Douglas', in a most derogatory tone!

Again I gained enormously from this experience – playing on huge stages, coping with all sorts of regulations, and being ready to perform at short notice. We became politically aware – in Romania, putting the Western case, but when we returned, the Eastern one against so much prejudice from people who only had the papers' words for everything. Harry spoke some Yiddish, which gave access to some uncensored opinions of the regime there, and we found out the locals had gone short of food for months to store up for the delegates of the Festival. We had been warned if we wanted to work in the States, currently in the thralls of McCarthyism, not to have our passports stamped – but though visas were pinned inside, I was often stopped when going abroad subsequently, and questioned. (They obviously didn't think I represented much danger, though, because they didn't transfer any to-me visible mark to my married passport.) Stephen made me props mistress for the tour, saying I needed to have responsibility – even though I knew I had a singularly inefficient memory for knowing where things were. I managed alright, but on the morning following a fire on the train on the way back from Warsaw, as we crossed the East German border, I saw something that looked surprisingly like our costume skip on a distant platform. Of course, when we got to Ostend it had been, indeed, the skip with all our costumes and props inside. It took about three months to get them restored to Central, and prevented us doing our show the following term... ❞

an alternative to the Albert Hall must be found to accommodate the School's expansion. What seemed merely a good idea in 1954 would two years later become imperative.

• • •

ADDITIONAL CENTRAL FACTS

1945   • Clifford Turner resigns from British Council to rejoin the Central staff and teach at RADA.

1946   • February: The BBC broadcasts a programme of Choral Speaking, *A Time for Verse*, by the 'A' Teachers – arranged and directed by Thurburn and John Laurie.

         • The student Public Matinée is presented in July at the Globe (Gielgud) Theatre.

1947   • Laurence Olivier is elected to the Board of Governors.

         • The student Public Matinée is presented at the Phoenix Theatre.

         • July: The English Festival of Spoken Poetry is re-inaugurated after the war, with L A G Strong as Director. A Central student takes first place.

1948   • President of the School, Lord Lytton, dies, and Lord Esher is appointed to take his place.

         • June: The student Public Matinée is held at the Phoenix Theatre.

1949   • HRH Princess Marina, the Duchess of Kent attends the student Public Matinée at the Garrick Theatre.

1952   • With the popularity of television growing, at the urging of Laurence Olivier the Stage Course is extended to include lectures on Film and Microphone technique.

1954   • The student Public Matinée is held at the Scala Theatre.

9

1954–1957

AS EARLY AS 1934, Elsie Fogerty had recognised Central's premises were full to capacity and 'not one more student' could be taken. She approached the Governors to find a suitable site to build a theatre – one that could be licensed and let for outside performances, and that would provide at least seven large classrooms, dressing rooms, a canteen and proper office accommodation. The Governors began to search for vacant sites within a suitable radius of the Hall.

Premises were inspected at 4 Palace Gate, and rejected as too expensive. It was suggested that, should a National Theatre location be found, it might be possible for the School to acquire part of their site. Fogerty looked at 15 Kensington Gore, but the 1851 Commission was unwilling to sell individual freeholds. In 1936, a house in Queen's Gate seemed suitable. The London County Council indicated willingness to grant the necessary licence, but an estimated £50,000 was needed for the purchase and alteration. The School could not find the money. A building on Pelham Street was considered. In 1937, a corner house on Cromwell Road near the National Theatre purchase was inspected, but the lease was not available. Houses in Prince's Gate and Ennismore Gardens both proved too expensive. Then, when war broke out in 1939, all thoughts of a move were put aside.

When enrolment had increased after the war, the Governors again began to search for larger premises. In 1949–50, Central unsuccessfully pursued the Trustees of the Campden's Charities for both a long-term lease and permission to build a theatre in the adjoining garden of 52 Hyde Park Gate. Neither request was granted. Speden Tower in Hampstead was thought to be an ideal site, and Central applied for a £37,000 mortgage, but during negotiations the owner received a higher offer. Gwynneth Thurburn then found available premises in Highgate for £50,000, but when in November 1951 the Albert Hall Manager, C S Taylor, assured Central that their tenancy was in no danger, it was decided that no further search for premises would be made until sufficient funds were in hand.

A Building Fund Appeal Committee was formed, with Lady Balcon as Chairman and C S Taylor as Treasurer, and Central held a number of fund-raising events: a Square Dance, Christmas Fairs, Lucky Draws and Bazaars. In 1952, Bertha Hagart, ex-student Jill Balcon and her husband, Cecil Day-Lewis, gave a Recital of Poetry and Music. In 1953, there was a Coronation Seats Ballot, a Sunshine Competition for children to forecast the hours of sunshine in London on Coronation Day, and a Coronation River Party that cruised to the Port of London to see the illuminations and ships and returned for the firework display. In 1953 and 1954, students and friends of the School gave Verse Speaking recitals; and staff member Heather Black arranged Choral Speaking demonstrations in schools in various parts of the country. Mask and Dagger continued to contribute profits from their productions.

Then, in 1953, the management of the Albert Hall unexpectedly increased Central's rent from £450 to £1200 per year. Thurburn hurriedly inspected both Toynbee Hall in the East End (too small) and the vacant Old Vic School premises in Dulwich (too distant). Both the Teacher and Stage Courses needed to be in touch with the London theatre, and the Speech Therapy Department could not be too far from the hospitals and clinics so important to their students' training. An immediate move could not take place unless suitable premises were found, and the Albert Hall Corporation accepted Central's reduced offer of £800 per year from 1 April 1954.

For the next two years, means were sought to elevate Central's profile and to raise funds for alternative premises. When Sir Michael and Lady Balcon resigned from the Board, Governor Mrs Edward (Joan) Sutro (and subsequently Mrs Laura Jenkins) took over as Chairman of the Building Fund Appeal Committee. Dame Edith Evans was invited to join the Board. A Central Appeals Players' Club was formed in 1954 to give ten private performances on Sundays at a West End theatre. Emlyn Williams gave a Dylan Thomas Recital at the Wyndhams Theatre. A reception was held at the House of Lords. Joan Sutro gave a dance at her home in Oxted, and in 1955 she organised a Mask and Dagger Ball at the Mayfair Hotel, with Princess Alexandra in attendance. A preview of *Much Ado About Nothing* by the Stratford Memorial Theatre Company was held on 19 May at the Palace Theatre. In 1955, Audrey Russell broadcast a radio programme about Central in her *All in a Day's Work* series, which was re-broadcast on the Far Eastern Service.

• • •

Then, early in 1956, the Manager of the Royal Albert Hall notified the Principal that when Central's lease expired it would not be renewed. The year before, the Hall had hosted a trade fair and having found it a far more lucrative and far less troublesome use of their space than the housing of a training school, they now required Central's rooms to

JENNIE GOOSSENS STAGE '56

❝ I was just 17 when I entered Door 9 of the Albert Hall to start at Central.

C Stage was the lowest class and those in A Stage and in their final year were our gods! Jeremy Brett – too gorgeous to look at directly – Mary Ure, Wendy Craig, Heather Sears, Benny Arnesson... They were a world away from us chubby teenagers and I was terrified.

The teachers were even more alarming. Determined to break us of any preconceived ideas or fancies, they set about removing any vestiges of confidence that we might have had – and I had precious little to begin with! The only one who seemed human was our much-loved Cis Berry. She taught voice and poetry and gave me the greatest gift possible in a passionate love of verse and poets. She was doubly human in that we all knew the story of her romance and subsequent marriage to a former student [Harry Moore]. 'Shall I compare thee to a summer's day?' the story went.

Ollie Reynolds for Drama was my particular scourge. 'You're too bloody virginal,' he'd shout. Virginal? I scarcely knew what it meant! Gerda Rink for Movement found out that my mother had been a dancer. 'What WOULD Mummy say,' she'd moan, as I tried to master the tarantella. The girls bulged in their black tights and leotards and the boys, including one Peter, now Paul Bailey, just 'hung'. It was a nightmare that we tried desperately to view with some trace of humour.

As I lived in the country and we could not afford for me to live in London, this meant catching the 7:30 daily from Plumpton, squashed between the businessmen in their suits and bowler hats, wreathed in cigarette smoke. Then onto the 52 bus at Victoria – making sure that I had my packet of ten Olivier ciggies in my pocket for the day. I'd not thought of smoking until the first day of classes, when the tutor told us to break for a smoke – and I had to borrow one! But I soon caught on.

In my second year I shared a mews house with four others and life took on a rosier aspect, but at the end of the year came the assessments. Walter Hudd, pushing his glasses up the bridge of his nose with an elegantly curved finger, saw us one by one and told some – to their misery – that, in his opinion, we would not make it in the world of acting. I remained for a further term, but as I was what Gwynneth Thurburn called a 'long-term prospect', I decided to spare myself the humiliation of playing only maids in the Public Show and left early to allow myself to 'mature' and be paid for it in rep. I am happy to say I have never looked back! **❞**

provide hospitality and additional areas for similar future events. The race was on to find both alternative premises and the money to purchase them.

There were many events planned for Central's 50th Jubilee Birthday throughout 1956. They would now also be used to raise money for the Building Fund. In February, an hour-long BBC TV documentary on Speech, directed by ex-Director of Dramatics, Hal Burton, celebrated the three incorporated departments of the School. H M Tennant donated the £1200 proceeds from a preview of Noël Coward's *South Sea Bubble*, starring Vivien Leigh, on 24 April 1956 at the Lyric Theatre, Shaftesbury Avenue. Another Mask and Dagger Ball, with prizes, draws and tombolas, was held at Grosvenor House on 7 May 1956, and the event raised over £2000. The School held a Christmas Fair at 45 Park Lane on 21 November, which raised £1100.

The main theatrical celebration for the Central Jubilee was *Cavalcade of 1906* on 25 November at the Saville Theatre. The show was a tribute to Elsie Fogerty, Gwynneth Thurburn and the students and staff of the Central School's first fifty years. Tickets were available only through club membership of 5 guineas and 5 shillings, and the show raised £1600. In spite of the efforts to raise money, the Building Fund was still nowhere near sufficient to secure the School a new home.

• • •

Thurburn had replied to the Albert Hall Corporation in March 1956, 'We have one proposition before us and should this be found to be suitable the necessary alterations would probably take slightly more than 18 months, in which we might have to ask your Council to help us over the difficulty.' The Corporation responded that more than the necessary six-month notice had been given, and it was unlikely that any extension could be allowed. They would officially serve a six-month notice in March 1957.

This really should have been no surprise. The lease at the Albert Hall had been in question to a greater or lesser degree for over a quarter of a century. In 1925, the Hall had raised the rent by £100, and a clause was added to the lease that tenancy could be terminated by six months notice on either side. Unsuccessful efforts were made to get the clause altered. With a change of management in 1926, the rent was again raised – from £450 to £750 per year. Once more the Governors attempted to have the rent reduced and the six-month notice clause removed. However, although the Albert Hall Corporation was 'sympathetic to the idea of having the School on the premises', it was immovable on terms. The Governors accepted the rent rise and the clause, but agreed amongst themselves that they would search for more suitable premises. In 1929, the rent was reduced when the Corporation agreed to donate £50 per year to the School, in effect reducing the rent, and in 1930, they agreed to make a 'donation' of £100 per year to the School, which reduced the rent still further. When Central returned from Exeter in 1942, the Albert Hall Corporation increased the 'donation' to £300 for the duration of the war, and Central's tenancy had seemed secure. Nevertheless, though the termination clause seemed forgotten, it had remained in the lease.

The 'one proposition' referred to in Thurburn's reply to the Albert Hall in 1956 was the Q Theatre (since demolished) at Kew Bridge, Richmond-upon-Thames. The remaining lease on the theatre would cost £16,000, and another £40,000 was needed to build adjoining classrooms. The Governors considered this too expensive, and a sub-committee was formed to look for other premises. News of the Albert Hall notice was kept strictly confidential.

Sargent, Thurburn and Colonel Pasteur looked at Mount Clare, a large home in Roehampton (too inaccessible) and visited the Crown Commissioners in Regent's Park (too expensive). The School placed an unsuccessful advertisement in the Personal Column

EMBASSY THEATRE

The original Embassy Theatre was designed by Rowland Plumbe and built in 1888 as 'Eton Avenue Hall'. In 1889, it was developed to house the Hampstead Conservatoire of Music and School of Art, which had a Willis Grand Organ, a concert hall for performances and balls, lecture rooms, an Antique School and artists' studios. The lecture rooms and the concert hall were occasionally let – the most notable production, in 1900, being the newly-formed Purcell Operatic Society's production of *Dido and Aeneas*, which was designed and directed by one of Britain's and the world's greatest designers, Edward Gordon Craig. From 1907 until 1915, the Conservatoire shared the premises with the Hampstead branch of the London Academy of Music (later the London Academy of Music and Dramatic Art).

By the 1920s the Conservatoire had failed, and in 1927, architect Andrew Mather converted the building into a 700-seat theatre. It re-opened as the Embassy Theatre in September 1928, under the management of John Herbert Jay and Sybil Arundale – with a production of M E Hope's *Yellow Streak*. Jay managed the theatre for only six months, before he began to let it as a touring house. When A R Whatmore's Hull Repertory Theatre burned in 1930, the Company took over the Embassy, reformed itself as the Embassy Players and, backed by Alec Rea, successfully ran the theatre as a two-weekly rep. When the national depression set in, audiences dwindled, and Rea and Whatmore gave up their lease. There was talk of the theatre becoming a cinema, but Rea's business manager, Ronald Adam, stepped in and re-opened the theatre in 1932 with a new play, *Behind the Blinds*. It was only a moderate success, but Adam had been bitten by the experimental theatre bug. He produced *Miracle at Verdun* – with its 100 characters and 13 scenes, and the unlikely hit transferred to the Comedy Theatre in London's West End. This was the beginning of a string of successes and occasional flops. A good businessman, Adam started the Embassy Theatre Club, which offered discounts on tickets and provided a restaurant and bar for Club members. At a time when the Lord Chamberlain dictated what plays could be produced, making the theatre a Club allowed Adam to stage more ambitious projects. By 1933, there were 3000 subscribers, and he later reorganised the Club into the less-expensive Theatre Guild of London, which gave members concessions at any of the other theatres he ran in London.

In conjunction with Frank Rhoyde and Eileen Thorndike, Sybil's younger sister, Adam started the Embassy School of Acting in 1933. (Eileen Thorndike would later teach at Central, and one of her early Embassy students, William Devine, became one of Central's early Directors of Dramatics.) The Embassy School students served as walk-ons for the theatre's plays, and on Sundays presented their own productions.

In the 1930s, the Embassy, the Mercury Theatre (producing new verse plays by young poets) and the Lyric Hammersmith were London's most prestigious outer-London venues. Ronald Adam presented a production every two weeks: a mixture of politically radical plays and commercial successes – from Paul Robeson in Eugene O'Neil's *All God's Chillun* to Joan Hickson in the murder mystery, *Distinguished Gathering*. One of his more extraordinary productions was Shakespeare's *Cymbeline*, with the last act re-written by George Bernard Shaw.

Adam gave up his lease in 1938, after producing 110 plays, of which 28 were West End transfers. For the next three years, the Embassy came under the leadership of Jack and Beatrice Leon, who presented mostly light comedies, each running for only a week. The theatre was bombed in 1941, and its doors remained closed until the end of the war.   [*continued…*]

In 1945, Anthony Hawtrey, son of the actor Sir Charles Hawtrey, restored the Embassy and moved into the flat above the theatre offices. He re-opened the theatre with his production of J M Barrie's *Quality Street*, and continued to present a conventional programme of plays that were largely try-outs for the West End. The Embassy had no wings, no scene dock and a tiny stage, and Hawtrey once described it as a 'nursery theatre – a shop window where new actors, new actresses, new authors, and new ideas may be displayed for a limited amount of time'. Hawtrey lost money (by 1953, he was in debt by over £10,000) and in 1952 Embassy management was transferred to the Hampstead Theatre Ltd. This company limped along for two years, producing their own shows (their biggest hit was *The Boyfriend*) as well letting the theatre to others. In 1955, the Granada Theatre Group bought the lease, with plans to develop the Embassy into a television film theatre. Luckily, these plans were never realised, and Granada sold their lease to the Central School in 1956. Temporary partitions at the back of the Embassy Theatre stalls were made permanent when Central took up residency, leaving the Theatre with a seating capacity of nearly 400.

of *The Times*. Then in May 1956, Thurburn and Sargent found 218 Goldhawk Road, the most suitable and affordable space so far. With the purchase price and the additional expense of erecting a preliminary classroom building, the total came to approximately £74,000.

The Board quickly went ahead with negotiations. Then, in June, Central Governor Edward Symmons reported to the Board his conversation with Granada Theatres about the Embassy Theatre in Hampstead. Granada would accept £30,000 for purchase of the remaining 24-year lease, and they implied Eton College might be willing to sell the freehold. Building on the Embassy Theatre car park could provide classrooms, and the house next to the theatre car park on Adamson Road might also be for sale. The Embassy was thought to be an ideal location for the School and, as the total cost would be similar to Goldhawk Road, at around £75,000, negotiations on Goldhawk Road were allowed to 'rest'.

Central may have found an ideal location, but it would now have to find the money. The School's entire financial resources were about £13,000: the £7000 raised by the Building Appeal Committee, plus £6000 in the School's general reserves. Governors were urged to speak to anyone who would be willing to give or loan money to the School. Ever generous, Joan van Thal immediately offered to loan £3000, if sufficient money could not be raised elsewhere.

Due to failing health, in June 1956 Colonel Pasteur – long time supporter, Governor and Chairman of the Board since 1947 – submitted his resignation, and Mr Cyril Ross took over as Chairman. In July, on behalf of Central, Governor Edward Symmons offered Granada a £3000 down payment for the remainder of the lease on the Embassy. In September 1956, Central and Granada signed a contract, and £27,000 was due in January 1957.

At the same time, the Board approached the Eyre Estate with an offer for an additional triangular piece of land to the west (left) of the theatre. Development on this property could only go forward if the London County Council (LCC) granted planning permission. If the LCC turned down the application, the School would have to build additional classrooms on the car park to the east (right) of the theatre. However, this option had its drawbacks – the Embassy lease would become more expensive, and there were old covenants that restricted building on this land.

Central took out a bank loan to pay the balance owed Granada, but by January 1957, the LCC had still not given building permission for either the eastern or western site, and an urgent appeal was made to the Ministry of Town and Country Planning to secure building permission. Six months later, the School was notified that a decision on the western triangle would be reserved until plans were in place for future road planning, however the LCC removed the ban on the eastern car park. In fact, the delay hadn't really mattered. Central was in debt, and had no money to build anything anyway. The School needed a white knight.

Early in 1957, John Davis had expressed interest in the Central School, and at the March 1957 Annual General Meeting, he was appointed to the Board of Governors. At the time, he was assured that Board membership would mean no more than three or four meetings a year and certainly would not involve a great deal of work. It soon became clear that this was not really the case. Central was in financial difficulties, and Davis stepped into the ring. He was the perfect man for the fight.

• • •

Born in 1906, John Davis had become chief accountant to the Odeon cinema chain in 1938. When J Arthur Rank bought the company in 1942, Davis was made the joint managing director, and in 1948 he was promoted to managing director of the Rank Organisation. He soon had responsibility for over 500 cinemas in the UK and Commonwealth, wielding

DRAMATIC SCHOOLS JOINT APPEAL

In 1957, John Fernald (Principal at RADA), Michael MacOwen (Principal at LAMDA) and Gwynneth Thurburn organised a Dramatic Schools Joint Appeal scheme to raise funds from the entertainment industry. This money would not only support the day-to-day needs of their Schools but also provide bursaries for their students. Annual student performances were given at each of the Schools in turn, and the money received was split three ways: 37½ % RADA; 37½ % Central and 25% LAMDA. In 1960, the students gave a joint performance for the Queen Mother at RADA's Vanbrough Theatre, raising over £9500. Central used its percentage for scholarships, staff salaries and the addition of more public plays for their students. Eventually, RADA dropped out of the scheme. Television companies continued to donate money to Central and LAMDA until the fund was closed in 1970.

power over what films were made, where, and with whom. Within a short time, Davis had become one of the most influential figures in the British film industry. Then in the early 1950s, with the advent of television and the cessation of duty on American imports, Britain's film industry began to struggle against the competition from Hollywood, and the Rank Organisation went into a slump, ultimately going into debt by over £16 million. Never one to be beaten, Davis completely restructured the company, and during the next two decades of his control, he developed Rank into a massive and successful conglomerate. He became notorious as one of Britain's most ruthless and formidable businessmen, but he was almost as famous for his devotion and enthusiastic support of the arts.

When Davis joined the Board in the spring of 1957, Central urgently needed £19,000 for immediate building repairs so it could open for classes in September. Davis asked the builders if he might delay payment, and as head of Rank, generously offered proceeds from the September film premiere of *Campbell's Kingdom*, starring Dirk Bogarde. After raising £15,752 from programme advertising and £817 from ticket sales, he personally donated £5000 to the fund, and at the end of September, the builders were paid.

Davis also requested a financial survey of the School's resources, and when it was completed in August 1957, the gravity of the situation became starkly apparent. Approximately £50,000 had been estimated for the purchase and renovations of the Embassy, and only £22,000 had been raised. Any further delay in the move to the Embassy would incur additional expense, further damaging Central's already dismal financial position. The bank loan had to be cleared as soon as possible. When Chairman of the Board, Cyril Ross, became ill, Davis was immediately invited to become Acting Chairman. He seized the job with both hands and immediately requested a complete examination of the School's financial activities, so that the Governors might put a plan in place for future operations. The School had to become financially stable if it were to survive.

A Finance and General Purposes Committee was created to advise on administrative, financial and policy problems, and a small sub-committee was formed to deal with the day-to-day problems faced by the Principal and her associates. A House Committee was created to consider proposals, consult and advise the Academic Board, and to make recommendations to the Finance and General Purposes Committee. Davis had not sought the position of Chairman, but now that he held it, he would do what he did for Rank: restructure and develop. Without his business genius, Central might not have survived.

• • •

Meanwhile, even though the threat of closure hung over the Central School, student life continued much the same as it always had at the Albert Hall. There were rumours of closure, but when they began to impact on the students' lives and their training, Thurburn held a meeting to dispel the gossip and share her plans for the future.

Students from the 1957 Stage, Teacher, Speech Therapy, Stage Management, and CDD courses, were the last to graduate from the Central School of Speech Training and Dramatic Art at the Royal Albert Hall, and among them were two of Central's most famous graduates, Vanessa Redgrave and Judi Dench. Both would go on to illustrious careers in theatre, television and film, and both later became Central Governors. Judi Dench briefly served as President of the School. Both would send their daughters to train at the School (Natasha Richardson, Stage '83, and Finty Williams, Stage '94).

• • •

ADDITIONAL CENTRAL FACTS

1954   • There are thirty staff members for 230 students.

• In aid of the Building Fund, Mr and Mrs Edward Sutro hold an 'Invitation Subscription Dance' for 150 guests at their home in Oxted, Surrey. Guests include Googie Withers and Virginia McKenna, and a cabaret is presented by Nicholas Parsons.

1956   • A Golden Jubilee Charity Affair includes a sale of 'spare-time work' by famous people. Terence Rattigan buys a surrealist study of a nude woman by Marilyn Monroe Miller, for £40. (The picture of a young woman reaching for her toes was painted in Monroe's dressing room at Pinewood Studios.) Also sold are paintings by fifty famous people, including sketches of wrestlers by Peter Ustinov, 'Three Cats' by Gilbert Harding and a sketch of Diana Dors by Emlyn Williams.

• 2 February: Speech, a Limegrove Documentary with Edith Evans, celebrates the first fifty years of Central.

• 11 March: a party is given at 52 Hyde Park Gate to celebrate Gwynneth Thurburn's OBE. Guests include John Davis, Viscount Esher, John Gielgud, Margaret Rawlings, Mary Ure, Virginia McKenna, Robert Helpmann and Peter Brook.

• Michael Croft starts the National Youth Theatre. Supported by Gwynneth Thurburn, the Youth Theatre is given training by Central teachers.

• Aileen Wyse Dance resigns from the Board of Governors to make way for a Governor who can provide more practical help.

1957   • In October, Gwynneth Thurburn is a guest on the popular BBC Radio show, Woman's Hour.

10
1957–1963

THE CENTRAL SCHOOL of Speech-Training and Dramatic Art began classes at the Embassy Theatre in the autumn of 1957. Central's patron, HRH Princess Marina, the Duchess of Kent, officially opened the new premises on 28 May 1958.

For the next two and a half years, nearly 200 Teacher and Stage Course students crowded into the Embassy Theatre for classes and presentations. Two Church Halls were hired for rehearsals, with two more eventually added. Now that the School had its own theatre, Stage students could give a matinee and an evening performance of four plays per term, and the first Central student performances at the Embassy were in October 1957: *Music at Night* by J B Priestley and *Top of the Ladder* by Tyrone Guthrie. Invitations were still issued to agents and possible employers, but in the spring of 1958 seats for all performances were for the first time also made available to the general public.

The Speech Therapy Department, with its fifty students, remained based primarily at 52 Hyde Park Gate, as did half the library. The other half of the library moved to a small room off the Embassy foyer. Movement classes for speech therapy students, other than first-years, were given at the Embassy, but as the journey by bus between the two sites could take over an hour, timetables were drawn up so students and staff could spend at least a half-day in either location. More classroom and office space was desperately needed at the Embassy site if Central was to bring all three Departments together at the new premises, but more classrooms could not even be considered until Central found the funding to pay its existing debts. The move to the Embassy had not come cheaply, and Central began its residency at the Embassy owing over £30,000.

John Davis continued to find ways to support the School. He donated the new student brochure, and raised another £16,000 with a premiere of the Rank Organisation's *Robbery Under Arms*, starring Dirk Bogarde and David McCallum. Central Governors organised a West End preview of *My Fair Lady* that raised nearly £5000. By the summer of 1958, the School had reduced its debt to a little over £10,000. A year later, this debt had been totally cleared, and there was £14,000 in the Building Fund, but to help offset the annual running-cost deficit of over £3000, student fees were raised from £95 per annum in 1957 to £195 in 1958.

• • •

Undoubtedly the most important development in Central's first two years at the Embassy was the renegotiation of the lease agreement with Eton College. The Governors had originally hoped to purchase the Embassy freehold and build a £55,000 new connecting wing to house the Speech Therapy Department, but when in 1959 Eton College would only agree a lease extension of fifty years, the Board instead decided to erect a £20,000 steel, pre-fabricated, three-storey structure. The building had a projected life of fifty years, and came with strict instructions: 'No jumping or dancing permitted, because of the type of building.'

TAFFY

William Frederick Fisk (Taffy) was born in Swansea in 1901, and worked for twenty years at Garngoch No. 1 Colliery before leaving for London in 1935. He started at the Embassy as a stagehand in 1944, and within a year became resident stage manager, living in the little flat at the top of the theatre. Vera Sargent remembered, 'Taffy had a cat [Java], and he got it to come up on the first night we were having a student show. He came up into the house – to "see the house in", we said.' When Taffy passed away in 1961, Claire Fox (Stage Management '62), headed a Students' Association appeal fund to purchase a public bench for outside the Embassy.

Once the fifty-year lease with Eton College was signed, a new Building Appeal was launched, and all large endowments were allocated for specific purposes: the Granada Library, the Pilgrim Trust Reading Room, and the Columbia Pictures Workshop. Lord Rank donated several large sums of money, and John Davis organised yet another Charity Première in January 1961 – *The Singer Not the Song*, starring Dirk Bogarde and John Mills – which raised over £29,000. Foundations for the new building were laid in September 1960. The ground floor was set aside for stage management workshops, the second floor provided two large teaching rooms and two small offices, and the top floor offered a library and reading room as well as two small classrooms. All floors had large windows, and there was a covered walkway to link the new wing with existing buildings. A temporary workshop at the back of the theatre was demolished to create a new car park, and two trees were planted in front of the building named 'Thurbie' (left) and 'Sarge' (right).

• • •

The summer before the new building was completed, Joan van Thal retired as Director of the Speech Therapy Department, ending over forty years' association with the School. Van Thal was a leading figure in the world of speech therapy, and the Principal realised it was important to find a strong replacement. Betty Fitch (later Byers Brown) was appointed Department Director in the autumn of 1960. Fitch had graduated from Central in 1947, returned to serve on the staff in 1953, and in 1958, had become the first person to obtain the new qualification: Member of the College of Speech Therapists (MCST).

1958 *My Fair Lady* opens in the West End after two years on Broadway

1959 Buddy Holly dies in a plane crash

1960 Royal Shakespeare Company inaugurated, to be led by Peggy Ashcroft with Peter Hall as Director. Three-year contracts are instituted, and the company takes over the Aldwych Theatre as its London home

1961 Soviet Union puts first man in space
USA invades Cuba in Bay of Pigs fiasco
Stratford's Shakespeare Memorial Theatre becomes Royal Shakespeare Theatre

1962 National Theatre formed at the Old Vic under artistic director Laurence Olivier
Cuban missile crisis

1963 Profumo affair rocks British government
President John Kennedy assassinated in Dallas, Texas

Fitch would seamlessly bring the Speech Therapy Department to the Embassy site and its new building.

The gradual move began in the autumn of 1960 when the top floor of 52 Hyde Park Gate was sublet. What remained of Central's library was brought to the Embassy, and the small temporary library in the theatre foyer was altered to hold the additional books until the new building could be completed.

Named after Central's Chairman, the John Davis Wing was opened free of debt, and the first classes were held there in January 1961. For the official Opening on 24 May 1961, the Embassy Theatre was re-painted in white, blue and mushroom; and the School threw a party for students, staff and Royal patron, HRH Princess Marina, Duchess of Kent. Besides placing a gold key in the lock of the new 'J D' Wing and unveiling a plaque, there was another official Royal duty that evening that not only provides an interesting side-story to the grand event, but also ties the evening back to Central's earliest years.

When Elsie Fogerty directed her production of *Electra* in 1914, she had remarked that Aileen Wyse's performance as Electra was 'one of the finest ever given by a Central student'. Wyse had gone on to become a successful actress, working first with Sir Frank Benson's Shakespearean Touring Company, and later playing in the West End in, among others, *Tod the Tailor* at the Arts Theatre and *A Wise Child* at the Garrick. She married the (much older) well-known actor, Reginald Dance, and together they were chosen by Galsworthy to play the leads in his American tour of *The Skin Game*. In the 1920s, Reginald Dance became a part-time tutor and director at the Hall, and Aileen (Wyse) Dance re-entered Central, to retrain in Remedial Speech. After her husband died in 1934, Aileen Dance continued her remedial work in London County Council speech clinics. When war broke out, she took over the running of a feeding centre for the poor at St Martha's Kitchen in Paddington, but she always maintained a strong connection with Central, even serving as a Governor from 1940 to 1956. St Martha's Kitchen closed immediately after VE Day, and as Dance had been away from Remedial Speech work for six years, she permanently retired as a speech therapist and continued to work in catering. When Central moved to the Embassy, another ex-student, Phyllis Gow, had been brought in to run the student canteen. Gow left in 1960, and Central needed someone to take her place. The quiet, grey-haired ex-student, ex-actress, ex-speech therapist and ex-Governor stepped in.

In 1960, Dance had inherited a cottage in Wales from her aunt, and using the proceeds of its sale, she commissioned Patrick Phillips, the former head of the Byam Shaw School of Art, to paint a portrait of Gwynneth Thurburn. On the night of the gala opening of the JD Wing in 1961, Aileen Wyse Dance presented the portrait to Central, to be unveiled by HRH Princess Marina, the Duchess of Kent. This picture of Gwynneth Thurburn, wearing a gown and blue shawl and regally sitting in Elsie Fogerty's carved wooden chair, hung at the entrance to the Embassy Theatre for nearly 35 years. After a few years of relegation to a back stairway, it has been cleaned and restored, and it once again hangs in the foyer by the Embassy entrance.

A-R TV

In 1957, Associated-Rediffusion Television, an independent commercial company, not only donated a television for the student common room, but also offered a scholarship of £400 per year to two third-year Stage students. The only stipulation was that when these students graduated, they give A-R TV 'first-refusal' for their employment. A-R TV's Norman Marshall was appointed to act as Honorary Television Adviser to the School, and students in their final year received a one-week television course to compare and contrast acting for the theatre and for television. This consisted of lectures, talks, visits to studios and a dummy production.

• • •

In the early days at the Embassy Theatre, the Teacher Course had no performing space and was allowed only limited use of the Embassy stage. Out of necessity, they took their plays into parks, youth clubs, and schools. In addition to plays, in 1958–9 alone students visited 23 schools to give demonstrations on choral speaking, and in June 1959 staff and students gave demonstrations as part of the National Union of Teachers' Exhibition at Olympia. That same year, A F Alington, Staff Inspector of the Ministry of Education Department, took over from Dr C J Phillips as Director of the Teacher Department.

In 1959, a successful candidate for the 100 student-strong Teacher Course had to have the General Certificate of Education, with passes in five subjects, including an 'A' level pass in English. However, potential students were judged not only on their academic qualifications, but also on their 'suitability' to the profession. Applicants were auditioned through improvisation, were asked to read a poem and a passage of prose, and were then interviewed by two staff members and seen by half a dozen more. Central's emphasis on voice was evident and, by today's standards, archaic: 'They must have voices that are acceptable all over the country, so a regional voice may be a drawback.' [Thurburn, *Woman and House* magazine, 1959]

Once students were accepted on the three-year course, they could expect to study voice production, prose reading, verse speaking, phonetics, and the history of drama and theatrical design. They would take classes in movement, anatomy, theory of education and acting. They would learn how to stage a production in a variety of spaces, interpret text and direct actors. In their first year, students visited schools to watch drama teachers at work, in their second year they both observed and taught, and by their third year, they taught regularly two afternoons per week. Successful graduates still received the London University Diploma.

• • •

Thurburn outlined Stage Course auditions in a 1959 *Woman and House* article: '…We see sixty to a hundred drama candidates each year, of whom we accept thirty to forty in equal numbers of both sexes. There is a shortage of men, for we do not get as many promising young men applying as we do girls.' Candidates (who had to be under the age of 25) were given a short interview, and were asked to present two audition pieces, sight-read, and undergo an ear-test to evaluate voice modulation.

Once accepted, students spent the first two of the three years studying movement, acting and voice production: 'Control over the voice embraces pitch, tone, articulation, clarity of diction, phrasing, tempo and rhythm. …In my opinion all the initial stages of voice training should take place out of the theatre. The training should be on much the same lines as that of an instrumentalist. I prefer to balance a voice in miniature first, and then increase it in volume and scale afterwards.'

To encourage their power of concentration and communication, students spent the first and second term of the first year doing improvisation and mime. Members of the permanent staff rehearsed and directed scenes for first- and second-year students, and experienced professional theatre directors were brought in for their third year when, for the first time, students performed plays to the public.

• • •

The Central Stage Course had been under the Directorship of Walter 'Dickie' Hudd since 1950, and his resignation in the summer of 1960 not only shook up the training, but also triggered one of the most difficult periods in Central's history. Hudd was both a highly respected actor and a successful director. During his early association with Central at the Albert Hall, he had regularly directed student productions, but as professional engagements infringed on his time, he became more of an overseer. Nevertheless, he remained an important influence on the students' training. Bill Hobbs (Stage '59) recalls: 'Dickie Hudd was working in the West End, and used to come in to see our third-year productions. Afterwards, we'd sit in a circle and he'd give us our "crits" – and he would be spot on, very much to the point. The wonderful thing was, he didn't know us – it was a completely objective eye by someone we admired and respected. We revered him.'

In 1951, Hudd had brought in Oliver Reynolds to help reorganise the Central course. Reynolds had not only taught privately but had also worked with Michel Saint-Denis at his London Theatre Studio. Virginia Snyders (Staff 1956–68) remembered taking classes from Reynolds before she became a student at the Old Vic School: 'He was direct and honest about the process. He very rarely said, "Terrific." He tended to say, "What did you think of it?" And you'd start analysing what you'd done. Then he'd occasionally say, "Yes," and you'd feel wonderful. He would analyse the text completely, and be very thorough, and only then read it aloud. He expected you to take notes. Iris Warren did voice work; one afternoon a week Gerda Rink did movement with us. It was the most dense period of learning in my life.'

CLAIRE (BOUSFIELD) SIMPSON
SPEECH THERAPY '61

❝ One overriding memory concerns Phonetics lectures. Our tutor was endeavouring to introduce us to the Cardinal Vowels, devised by Daniel Jones, and she would play her prize possession, a '78 recording of him, pronouncing these vowels. At the same time we would look at photos of his mouth positions for the vowels in a textbook. A fellow student and I were convinced that our tutor was in love with Professor Jones. She would sit enraptured, as we listened to this well-worn record. We became hysterical about this weekly routine and would sit heads down, shoulders shaking from repressed giggles, terrified that she would notice.**❞**

As part of the reorganisation of the Central Course, Reynolds brought in Gerda Rink to teach movement and period dance. Rink's ballet background took the movement training away from the Greek dance taught for so long by Ruby Ginner, but even though her classes started with tough ballet barre exercises, they ultimately focused on relaxation and fitted comfortably in with the Central ethos.

When Hudd retired as Director of Drama in 1960, surprisingly Reynolds was not offered the position and, instead, both the Academic Board and Walter Hudd recommended John Blatchley to the Governors. Virginia Snyders had trained under Reynolds, taught with him, and admired him as one of the great drama teachers of her day, but even she had no qualms about recommending Blatchley as the more exciting choice to run the Stage Course.

• • •

John Blatchley was born in Melbourne, Australia in 1922. His parents were the variety artistes Jack and Ruby Wynne, and he, literally, grew up in the theatre. Blatchley won a scholarship to RADA, served in the RAF during World War Two, and worked briefly as an actor – playing small parts in the West End and spending a season at Stratford-upon-Avon – before joining the staff of the Old Vic School. When the Old Vic School closed, Blatchley became Director of Acting at Saint-Denis' school in Strasbourg, later returning to London to assist and co-direct with George Devine at the Royal Court Theatre. Blatchley was also on the staff at Sadler's Wells at the time of his appointment to Central, but according to Virginia Snyders, who had been taught by Blatchley at the Old Vic School and later worked for him as an actress in Canada, he was an inspiring and charismatic choice.

When Blatchley joined Central, Gwynneth Thurburn, Cicely Berry, Marjorie Phillips and Clifford Turner taught voice. Snyders remained on the acting staff, as did Berry's ex-student and American husband, the actor and director Harry Moore. William Harmer-Brown was fencing master, Teddie Gray continued to teach make-up, and Ishbel Fox ran the wardrobe department. Gerda Rink resigned, due to illness, and Oliver Reynolds retired a year after Blatchley's arrival, though whether this was his own decision or Blatchley's remains unclear.

Blatchley brought in his own team to add to Central's existing staff. These visiting directors included some of the best and the brightest talent in British Theatre: John Dexter, William Gaskill, Corin Redgrave, Christopher Burgess and Thea Musgrove. Blatchley himself taught acting and mask work; his wife, Catherine Clouzot, taught mime. Peter Streuli had been a director at the Shakespeare Memorial Theatre in Stratford-upon-Avon (1952–7) and an assistant director at the Old Vic. He would remain at Central until 1981, in 1963 becoming the Director of the Stage Management Course. Stanislavski disciple, actor Harold Lang, and his two colleagues, Greville Hallam and Nicholas Aymer, taught acting and improvisation – bringing The Method to Central students for the first time.

Blatchley's first year started well when John Schlesinger, then a director of the BBC television programme *Monitor*, filmed Harold Lang teaching an acting class to 'C' (first-year) Stage students. Shot in the 1960 winter break, 'The Class', took five days to complete. With no musical score, no commentary, and only two cameras focused mostly in the classroom, the show is described by William J Mann in his book, *Edge of Midnight: The Life of John Schlesinger*: 'It is a wonderfully quirky little film: not quite a documentary, for Lang and the students were re-enacting a class for John, stopping action when he called cut and positioning themselves for the best camera angles; but it is not a fiction film either, for these were the lessons Lang would have used anyway, and the students had no idea ahead of time what he was going to ask of them.'

The BBC gave a special showing for the students and celebrity guests on 6 April 1961 at the National Film Theatre, and transmitted the programme on 9 April. Robert Grange (Stage '63) recalls: 'John Schlesinger threw a private party for the students taking part. It was at his home... The guest of honour was Schlesinger's aunt, Dame Peggy Ashcroft, whose off-camera delivery of Portia's 'The quality of mercy' speech over the final captions was the climax of the programme. Incidentally, even then, the difference between the student speech patterns and Ashcroft's delivery was marked. A new post-war theatre was emerging and changing.'

Harold Lang was part of this post-war theatre, and the young theatre professionals emerging were causing a stir. Lang had known Gert Malmgren (known as Yat) since the beginning of the 1950s, and Lang's insistence on detail and specifics in an actor's work were a natural fit with Malmgren's theories not only on movement, but also on actor training. Blatchley included Malmgren (and later his assistant, Christopher Fettes) in his Central team. Over the next three years, Malmgren and Fettes taught physical re-education, improvisation on the elements of expression, building of character, characteristic rhythms and national dance, science of projection and the Laban-Lawrence theory of action. During this time, Malmgren developed and expanded upon the theories that he and Fettes later so successfully put in place at the London Drama Centre.

Yat Malmgren was an electrifying addition to Blatchley's team. Born in 1916 in Galve, Sweden, Malmgren first trained as an actor, but he gained renown primarily as a soloist dancer and choreographer. When he joined the Ballet Joos at Dartington Hall in Devon in 1940, he met Rudolph Laban, the German movement theorist who was also in residence – an encounter that would have a profound and lasting impact on Malmgren's thinking and future. After celebrated work with the International Ballet, Malmgren opened his own studio on West Street in London, and his reputation widened. In no time at all, his classes were filled with young stars and exciting new directors. In the 1950s, Malmgren worked with the English Stage Company at the Royal Court, assisted Brook and Gielgud on a production of *The Tempest*, spent a year on the staff of Laban's

PIERS YOUNG
STAGE MANAGEMENT '61

"I started on the Stage Management course in 1959, not long after the move from the Albert Hall – in fact some classes still took place there. At the time, the premises consisted of the old Embassy Theatre and a small new block next to it, which contained the centre of all SM activity: the workshop. This was presided over by Stan Parker, a Bristolian, a stage carpenter of the old school.

There were ten or twelve of us who joined that September. Our course head was the dreaded Tubby Hayes…and after Stan, we had the irrepressible Terry Chart as carpenter/resident stage manager. There was also Neville Brian, nominally Stage Director, a nice man who spent all his time being just that, and after him a chap called Sandy Black – very intense and something to do with the Ludlow Festival. Also, there was an unfortunate fellow called Lawrie Brooks who could not cope with us at all.

We as stage managers were also expected to do some voice and movement classes; for most of us, who had no intention of ever appearing on the stage with the curtain up, this was considered something of a joke; we used to entertain ourselves trying to work out which eye Miss Thurburn was using to look at us with that day!

In those days, we had three social centres: the Canteen, run by Judy; 'Gerry's', the Caff on the other side of Finchley Road; and, more occasionally, the public bar of the Swiss Cottage. Judy eventually gave up the canteen and Gerry took it over.**"**

Art of Movement Studio in Surrey, and taught at RADA. When he was invited to take responsibility for movement at Central in 1960, it presented an opportunity to further develop his ideas on actor training. In the autumn of 1960, first-year students at Central began Malmgren's first complete three years of actor training.

There are a number of opinions on what happened during this time. There are those who had great respect for Blatchley and Malmgren's teaching, and there are those who disagreed with their methods. John Jones (Stage '63, Staff 1966–88) recalls his student years:

> In many respects Central was an interesting place to be at that time, particularly with regard to the vocal, speech and text teaching, which was amazing, thanks to Gwynneth Thurburn, Marg Phillips and particularly Cis Berry. For me, it remains true that the real quality in the course lay in the vocal work. Some of us found much of the other stuff less helpful. We started to feel that there were other writers apart from Ionesco and Brecht. John Blatchley had some things of interest to say, but I was surprised to hear him say that we should not expect to work on Shaw, Restoration or 'straight-down-the-centre' repertoire. The course was strongly influenced both for good and bad by the work at the Royal Court. It was part of Blatchley's philosophy that when we left we should only work in communist-based theatre. We were mostly pretty left wing, but we were also aware that we had to go out and earn our living.
>
> Yat Malmgren arrived with a considerable reputation, but his training was found by many of us to increase our tensions – perhaps this was not so much the system as the personality of the teacher. A great deal of this training depended on the theories we were being taught. From early on in the course we spent Saturday mornings studying the theory, and in order to illustrate 'punching', 'dabbing', etc, we were presented with quotations from Shakespeare, which we had to read aloud without actually understanding what the text was saying. Less than helpful, I thought. There also seemed to be a suggestion that if you followed the theory a performance would be created. That is highly questionable, in my view.

Lionel (Hawes) Guyett (Stage '64) remembers:

> They basically said at the beginning, 'We think you have talent, but it is raw and what we will give you is that by the time you leave here, you will be able to act. But what we have to do first of all, you have to agree you cannot act. There has to come a point in your psychological make-up, where you can say: I cannot act. Then we can fill that void with our method, and if you accept our method at the end of it you will be able to act.'
>
> I think what they didn't explain to us, because we were their first group ever to complete their training, was that this training was there in case some or all of the rehearsal process didn't work. All actors are instinctive. You may change or swerve

from your first instinct, but when your instinct fails, that's where Yat's theories are useful. If you don't know how to do something, you go back to the theory. Does my character 'push'? Maybe he's 'that' and a bit of 'this' and a bit of 'that'. But what they said was, 'Follow this,' and because we were young, we thought, 'I must be able to do it because Yat and Christopher said this is the way it works. Maybe if I "dab" and I "flick", suddenly I'll be all right.' But it often didn't work.

He brought a student up in front – all the boys were dressed in leotards and tights and jock straps and little ballet shoes – and Yat said, 'Now you see, look at him…his pelvis hasn't yet freed itself, so I want one of you girls to take his virginity by the end of the term.' There were aspects, well… Yat and Christopher dominated us.

In no way will I ever denigrate what Blatchley, Yat and Christopher did, because if you look at the people who left to form the London Drama Centre – or on the other hand if you look at the people who decided to stay at Central – it's just that their training suited some people and it didn't suit others.

ALISON MILNE EDWARDS
TEACHER '51, STAFF 1954–66

❝ The staff were paid appallingly: I earned £365 per annum during my first few years, a desperate wage even in those days. Many classes at Swiss Cottage were held in various church halls of indescribable dirt and cold. I used to feel so sorry for the students who got filthy during class with nowhere to wash or have a coffee. But I loved it. Central students were endlessly interesting and though I obviously remember those Stage students who have become famous, like Judi Dench, Julie Christie and Jimmy Bolam, it is the teacher-students that I will always remember with greatest affection. We had two curiously different Heads of the Teacher Course during my time. Bobs Alington had a background of Eton and the Guards but had ended his career as the Senior HMI in the East End. He loved Central and the students made him laugh, which evaporated the disparity between them and him. He was succeeded by Clarissa Bell, also from the Inspectorate and utterly different from Bobs. She was totally faithful to the students and fought their corner at all times. Both had endless contacts in the education world and used them on Central's behalf at all times. ❞

There is no indication from existing records of Staff, Academic Board or Governors' meetings of friction within the Stage Department during this period, but it seems there were private doubts among some of the staff about what was happening with the actor training. The only recorded hint of things to come appears in minutes of Department meetings in November 1962 when a Stage student is sent to a laryngologist in the Speech Therapy Department. Two weeks later, the same student is sent to an osteopath. In May 1963, two students are sent to the laryngologist, both are diagnosed with inflammation of the vocal cords, and both are 'put on silence' for a week. That same week, another student is told to take care of his voice – 'no shouting, etc.' Virginia Snyders remembers ensuing events:

> Thurb began to get a bit panicked by this, and she talked to the Speech Therapy Department about it. They said there was an enormous amount of physical tension going on through the shoulders and the neck – because of certain exercises they were doing.
>
> So, Thurb got Yat in and said, 'I'm going to have to ask you to change some of these exercises, because at the moment they're damaging the voices.' …Yat said, 'I will not change anything.' At which point, Thurb said, 'Well, I'm sorry, but in that case I'm going to have to ask you to go. One thing I cannot allow is that we do anything that will damage their voices for life; that's the one thing about which this School feels very responsible.' So, Yat and his two assistants quit.
>
> At which point, John [Blatchley] said, 'If they go, I go.' Thurb said, 'I'm terribly sorry, but they will not change what they do, so I will have to accept your resignation.' He went, and Catty [John's wife] went. Lang and his people were working abroad, so they were not part of this. They had been brought in as outside teachers hired term-by-term, so they were never officially asked either to leave or to stay – they just weren't asked back…
>
> Yat used to exhaust the students; he worked them very, very hard. He did a lot of movement based on contractions, tense and release. Then, having left them choking with exhaustion, he'd lie them down on the floor and say, 'You'll never be an actor unless you follow this method.' They were so exhausted that they became convinced that their only hope of ever being an actor was to follow this particular system.
>
> Most of the staff didn't realise quite what had been going on until he left, and the students began to tell us. We had people screaming and crying all over the building. We had students who spat at Thurb in the foyer. …We had one girl who wasn't sure what she wanted to do, and such pressure was being put on her, we rang her parents to get them to take her home. Finally, we decided to disband the school before the end of term – there was only about a week to go, but we thought it might save her if we did. I know of three who left who all had breakdowns. It was an extraordinary time. I had a scene with one of them, who started yelling at me, screaming abuse. People were very strange over it.

Malmgren may have attracted criticism, but he also inspired fierce loyalty. When he and Blatchley 'left' Central, their admirers approached them with a proposition: if they could gather enough like-minded first- and second-year students who wanted to continue the training they had begun at Central, would Malmgren and Blatchley teach them? Guyett: 'Yat and Blatchley, to their credit, said, "We would be interested, but it must come from you."' Within days, Gordon Taylor, Carol Jenkins, Siobhan O'Casey and Amarylis Garnet had found nearly £6000 and had organised a lease on an old church in Prince of Wales

Road. Over the next few days, there were late-night meetings in student flats, and questionnaires were distributed. Answers would determine who wanted to be considered for Malmgren and Blatchley's new school – the London Drama Centre. Emotions ran high; loyalties and friendships were examined. Thurburn watched in desperation as student after student came to hand in their resignations. Some students wanted to follow Malmgren and Blatchley but were not invited; others wanted to go to the new school, but could not afford the fees. There were others who made the choice to stay at Central. Guyett recalls: 'I never went to any of the big meetings they had when they started the London Drama Centre, but we all remained friends. We all still lived around there;

THURBURN ON STANISLAVSKI

Gwynneth Thurburn once quoted Orson Welles on Stanislavski: 'The only thing wrong with The Method is the word "The".' This opinion suited Thurburn's egalitarian view of actor training: 'The Method, as we know it now, is only an extension of Stanislavski's principles which he formulated when he started his productions of Chekhov's plays at the beginning of the twentieth century. It was the time of reaction against anything rhetorical. If, as I believe, acting is a reflection of life, then its fashions must always be changing. We should probably be quite horrified by Mrs Siddons to-day, but she suited the life of her time. Therefore it seems possible that if Stanislavski were still alive he might modify his ideas to suit the needs of the theatre of our time. [Thurburn, 'My Life with Many Voices', *Woman and House*, 1959.]

we drank in the same pub. Everyone understood, and we just got on with it. There was no animosity. We went to each other's shows. I'm glad I was there at that time. It was historic. No drama school has ever imploded and then exploded before.'

The last few days of that 1963 summer term were indeed chaotic. The third-year students had left already, and some student first- and second-year showings had already taken place. Other showings had to be cancelled when too few students attended rehearsals, and Virginia Snyders called Litz Pisk and George Hall to devise classes for the students who remained. Michael Elliot was brought in to give lectures. Finally, the decision was taken to close the School early, and students were sent home.

As an interesting postscript and alternate version, with no mention of voice strain or tensions, the following is from Gwynneth Thurburn and Vera Sargent's 1967 History of Central:

John Blatchley insisted on the importation of a group of people with whom he felt he could happily associate. Gwynneth Thurburn had qualms about certain aspects of his plans, but she held that it had always to be borne in mind that students' training should not be disrupted more than necessary and that nothing could be satisfactorily judged in a three-year programme until it had run for three years. Although radical changes had taken place in part of the training, some of it retained the basic principles upon which it was founded. This latter part was in the hands of dedicated staff who were not happy

PETER GALE STAGE '62

66 Blatchley gave the impression he thought us all a pretty sorry, middle-class, uninteresting bunch. I think a lot of us left feeling a bit short-changed. In fact, I was from a lower working-class family from Slough and felt very out of my depth. I had never been to a dinner party in my life, didn't even know what an omelette was, and here were the likes of Lynn Redgrave and Gary Bond, delightful and talented students, regaling us with stories about meeting Olivier and Gielgud the previous evening at friends' houses.

The best things about Blatchley's new approach from my point of view were the classes given by Litz Pisk. Her astounding command and economy of movement remains vivid in my memory even today. People often forget that Central was established as a school of speech as well as drama, speech coming first. Gwynneth Thurburn's voice training, conducted mainly by Marjorie Phillips and then later Cicely Berry, was based on excellent common sense and stood me in good stead throughout my career, but I remember two rather pointless classes Miss Thurburn gave us herself. One involved repeating the waltz step interminably to no obvious purpose. The other featured a lecture (bafflingly) about John Milton's organ, which she informed us could still be viewed, was not very big but worked well. Our barely suppressed, juvenile guffaws initially puzzled Miss T, but the following week she had the generosity of spirit to acknowledge her innocent mistake.

I won the Ibsen Prize (given by Associated-Rediffusion) and the Gold Medal (I shared the latter with Angela Morant). Neither prize proved to be of any practical use to me. The Ibsen Prize was a cheque for £400, but when I proudly informed my local authority of it, their response was to cut my grant immediately, leaving me, in fact, £25 short. The £400 cheque was passed straight over my head to Central.

I heard someone talking on the radio the other day about how one had to learn to 'speak posh' in the early '60s. That is certainly true but things were radically changing and fast. Of course, one needed to do the standard repertoire of dramas, the drawing room comedies and thrillers, but the Royal Court was blazing a trail with new writing by authors from poorer backgrounds... **99**

with all of the new arrangements. When, at the end of three years Gwynneth Thurburn decided (with strong support of most of the Staff) that the whole was not working satisfactorily, she asked John Blatchley to review the programme. This he refused to do and in consequence he, and two members of staff who had come with him, left to set up their own training school.

A *Guardian* obituary for Malmgren on 13 June 2002 gives yet another viewpoint:

A casual encounter on a bank holiday evening led to him [Malmgren] being introduced to Harold Lang, a maverick advocate of the work of Stanislavski. Lang coerced almost everyone he knew into attending Malmgren's movement classes – students were to include Sean Connery, Diane Cilento, Natasha Parry, Patricia Neal, Gillian Lynne, Anthony Hopkins, Brian Bedford, Elizabeth Fielding, and the directors Peter Brook, Tony Richardson, Bill Gaskill, Michael Blakemore, Seth Holt and Alexander Mackendrick.

In 1960, Lang's influence once again proved decisive. Invited to join the staff of the Central School of Speech and Drama by John Blatchley, Lang made his acceptance of the offer dependent on the appointment of Malmgren as director of movement. Here at last the doors to European theatre were thrown wide.

Fascinated by rumours reaching them from students on the acting course, other students expressed dissatisfaction at their own syllabuses. The management lost its head, and sacked Malmgren on the trumped-up charge of creating 'neck tensions'.

Within days seven other teachers, including Lang and Blatchley, had left to be followed by three quarters of the students. A call to Olivier to save the day was firmly, if politely, rejected, and the Drama Centre London was born. The following year, Olivier invited Malmgren to undertake movement training of all National Theatre actors.

The 1963 Central split has as many opinions and viewpoints as there were people involved, but what seems clear over forty years later is that it was a difficult time for students and staff alike. Clearer still is the long list of talented actors who in the ensuing years have trained both at Central and at the London Drama Centre.

• • •

ADDITIONAL CENTRAL FACTS

1960
- Ex-student Marjorie Anderson presents a BBC Radio's *Woman's Hour* feature on Central called 'In Training'.
- Pat Ostler is appointed Bursar.
- ITN shows a short feature film on Stage students.

1961
- Southern Television donates £500 towards a series of three lectures on Television, which are given in the autumn: Christopher Fry introduces Dame Edith Evans and her lecture, 'The Actress and Television' ('The camera is the man behind it! Get on good terms with the head cameraman and lighting engineer.'); Michel Saint-Denis gives his speech, 'The Theatre and Television'; and BBC Producer, Rudolph Cartier, lectures on 'The Television and the Producers'.

1962
- Alone among the leading London drama schools, Central gives its 'A' Stage students the experience of working in a rep-type play, with a rep director, and with limited rehearsal in their final year. Some consider this a valuable experience; others see it as an apprenticeship in bad habits.
- Thurburn points out to the Governors that staff are often lost because an adequate salary cannot be paid. The Board again tries to bring the pay scale nearer to general standards.
- Clifford Turner is seriously ill, and gives only private tutorials and the occasional class. (He passes away in 1964.)
- The installation of a new Tannoy system gives 'increased training facilities to the Technical students'.

1962–3 • E Martin Browne casts students from 'A' Stage for two plays at Coventry Cathedral.

• Enrolment is 266. Thirteen students drop out, and the proportion of students receiving grants from their local authorities is: Teacher Course: 90%; Speech Therapy Course: 85%; and Stage Course: 62%. Of the Stage students not in receipt of grants, 47% are in their first year.

1963–78 • Under Peter Streuli, Stage Management is known as the Technical Course.

1963 • Fees are raised to £240.

• A Students' Ball is held on the river in May.

• Walter Hudd dies suddenly.

• Harold Lang takes a job in Malaya, and is gone for the spring and summer terms.

• 'B' and 'C' Stage record crowd scenes for John Blatchley's production of *Julius Caesar* for the Royal Shakespeare Theatre, Stratford-upon-Avon.

11

1963–1967

AS A GRAND START to the 1963–4 academic year, John Gielgud gave the Inaugural Address in the Embassy Theatre. A significant number of Stage students had left Central to join the new London Drama Centre, but enrolment for the Speech Therapy and the Teacher Departments had increased, so total enrolment was barely down from the previous year. No one knew what to expect at the beginning of the new year, but the Governors felt that the Stage Department should be rebuilt 'from within' and so had decided that an appointment to the post of Director would not take place immediately. Besides, at the beginning of 1963–4, both the Speech Therapy and the Teacher Department were under relatively new leadership, and the staff as well as the students needed time to settle.

In the autumn of 1962, Betty Fitch had resigned as Director of the Speech Therapy Department, and early in 1963 Margaret Greene was hired to replace her. Greene immediately set to work on restructuring the course in order to satisfy new syllabus requirements from the College of Speech Therapists.

The Teacher Department was also going through major changes. Director of the Department, A F Alington, submitted his resignation in the spring of 1963, and in July, Clarissa Bell was appointed as his replacement. For the next nine years, she would lead the course to further excellence. Teacher-students had long needed a performing space of their own, and during Bell's first summer, a lease was secured from Hampstead Borough Council for land opposite the Embassy Theatre on Eton Avenue. A temporary Studio was quickly built, and it was opened in time for the second week of the 1963 autumn term. Six years later, in 1969, a 'temporary' workshop would be erected behind the 'temporary' Studio. The Teacher Department had always taken their plays into Primary and Junior Schools; they could now also perform for Secondary School children in their new Studio. In 1964, staff and students also formed the Link Drama Group to tour plays to Secondary Modern and Grammar School children.

Another major change within the Teacher Department in the summer of 1963 was the resignation of Joan Cox (Staff 1957–63) as Head of Movement. Christine (Chrissie) Hearne (Staff 1963–84) took her place, bringing with her the training she had received from Litz Pisk at the Old Vic School.

1963 First National Theatre production of *Hamlet* at Old Vic directed by Laurence Olivier and starring Peter O'Toole

1964 Nelson Mandela is sentenced to life imprisonment on Robben Island

Brendan Behan and Sean O'Casey die

1965 First TIE Company forms at Belgrade Theatre, Coventry

Modernist poet T S Eliot dies

Dr Martin Luther King leads Alabama civil rights march

1966 Myra Hindley and Ian Brady sentenced to life for Moors Murders

Abortion and homosexuality legalised by Sexual Offences Bill

1967 Variety Artistes' Federation merges with Equity

First human heart transplant by Dr Barnard in Cape Town

Litz Pisk had a number of connections with Central. She had taught with John Blatchley at the Old Vic School, and occasionally gave movement classes for him part-time at Central between 1960 and 1963. After Blatchley and Malmgren left, Thurburn asked Pisk to become full-time Head of Movement on the Stage Course. Pisk, however, was by this time teaching pottery at the Camberwell School of Art and needed to give them at least a term's notice, so she asked her colleague and ex-student, George Hall, if he could fill in for her at Central until she was available. Hall joined the Central staff as movement tutor in the autumn of 1963 – for one term.

• • •

In spite of the trauma of the previous summer's split, within weeks of the beginning of the new academic year, Central's Stage Course was ticking along with the day-to-day events of any busy drama school. Students were forbidden to go to the pub during class hours – or to the betting shop ever. Then, as it became clear that nothing could be done to prevent students from using the betting shop, Vera Sargent was instructed merely to keep a list of the names of the students who did gamble – so that she would know to whom *not* to lend money! Girls were forbidden to wear stilettos in the School – especially the JD Wing – and smoking was restricted in certain rooms, unless approved by the tutor. More glamorously, Patricia Neal, Victor Spinetti, Vanessa Redgrave, Dorothy Tutin, John Dexter, Dame Edith Evans, Michael Elliot and Tyrone Guthrie all gave seminars and lectures to the students. In spite of this rally by supporters of the School, Virginia Snyders remembers that autumn of 1963:

> Because the students had come to the conclusion that acting was about getting the right 'numbers' for their speeches or something, they sort of lost touch with themselves. I don't think you can act without taking yourself onstage as well. So I did some very weird improvisations. I got John Cross [Gulliver] to fall off the edge of the stage in a faint and stay fainted. I think they all thought I was being very ineffectual – 'Oh dear, I think he's fainted'. They went into a panic. It got them to see how they really felt – the things that made them happiest, that frightened them. Finally they began to get back to who they were and began to bring that onstage.

Lionel (Hawes) Guyett (Stage '64) also remembers that autumn:

> I know the staff were aware we were a fairly damaged group, and they looked after us very well, but we were seriously damaged as far as acting goes. Anyway, [in my third year] we began to be liberated. They'd say, 'Very good, but…' and 'What about if…' and suddenly most of us began to sparkle. George [Hall] was wonderful. He talked to us about confidence, about music, about commercial theatre, about lightness and shade, about the business. He began to liberate us. …I'm eternally grateful to George. He made it fun.

Sara Kestelman (Stage '65), was in her second year that autumn:

> I remember the first class we had with George. I mean, we'd had classes with these very austere people who didn't laugh. Christopher Fettes does not laugh, and Yat was quite hard going. It was very,

SYBIL (MARION) LINES
STAGE '70

" I was recently chatting with a young drama student, chuckling about the end of each term when I was a student at Central. When I said that we were all so terrified of our critiques that we got each other to write down what was said in case we passed out, the student asked if that was because we hated our teachers? I laughed, 'We adored our teachers!' I remember George Hall on our first day, 'We will teach you everything we know. Please don't spend your energy arguing against what we are offering. Accept that it is your good that we want. In your life you will meet many other ways of teaching acting, and they should all be considered and used when you need them.' What a difference from the jealous Guru-mentality of some. What he gave grounded me not only during the three years at Central, but also for life. **"**

very serious this training. Suddenly into the building comes this cherubic-faced man with these twinkly eyes, in tights, with a little tambourine drum. It was a shock! What is he going to do – with his drum and tights? Then he started to introduce a lot of singing, some of his Victorian songs – we all know 'Joshua' – and they were fun. There was a bit of me that was thinking, 'Why are we learning these music hall songs; why aren't we studying Ibsen?' I suppose all of us were measuring whether we had lost out, whether we had made the right choice. George brought in this joyous 'bubble', and it was a surprise. Actually it was the most wonderful injection of energy and fresh air, but I'm not sure all of us realised that for a while.

At the end of his 'one' term that autumn of 1963, Hall was invited to remain as a full-time tutor. The next spring, he gave mask classes, and though singing had always been minimally taught as part of the voice training, he also began giving classes in musical notation and musical theatre. Later that spring of 1964, the Governors appointed George Hall the full-time Director of the Stage Course.

• • •

Speech therapy students spent a lot of their first year in JD Wing classrooms, with occasional outside observations in schools, hospitals and infant schools. Lectures were provided by full- and part-time staff from the Speech Therapy Department, and supplemented by visiting specialist lecturers in audiology, orthodontics, plastic surgery, and diseases of the ear, nose and throat. In their second year, students observed clinics in St Thomas's, St Mary's, Paddington and St Bartholomew's Hospitals. By their third year, clinic work became more concentrated, and students went out three or four times a week for three-hour sessions. When Teacher and Stage (this included Stage Management) students' fees were increased by £60 per year at the beginning of 1965–6, Speech Therapy students were excluded from the rise, as the Governors felt their course did not make the same demands on staff and space in their second and third year of training, with so much time spent in clinics. Students who successfully passed exams given at the end of their second and third years could become Licentiates of the College of Speech Therapists – and therefore qualified to practise.

There was little crossover between Speech Therapists and those from other courses in the School. Even social interaction was minimal, owing to the heavy academic and clinical demands placed on Speech Therapy students. In spite of this, or perhaps because of it, in May 1966 a voluntary voice and movement limber was instituted each morning at 9 am in the Studio. It was open to all students from all courses. There is no record of how many attended – or for how long these classes continued.

• • •

On 20 June 1966, Central celebrated its Diamond Jubilee, and all three departments contributed to the Open Day of classes. For three hours in the afternoon, exhibitions were presented on a rotating schedule – with stage managerial precision – and over 250 guests visited the School. Litz Pisk's first-year Stage students showed animal study exercises in a church hall; second-year Teachers presented 'Period Study' – a song, dance and mime pageant of theatrical fashion – in the Studio. The Speech Therapists' offering was reviewed in the *Times Educational Supplement*: '…Perhaps the most exciting, because more revealing, exhibits were in the static displays. The Speech Therapy room was packed with testimony, as hopeful as it was painful, to the slow progress made by handicapped children.'

In the Embassy, 'A' Stage students in their third year offered a range of presentations to demonstrate different skills – from a *Romeo and Juliet* sword fight to a song from Gilbert and Sullivan to a scene from *The Changeling*. In an innovative departure from the usual classical offerings, four songs from *Guys and Dolls* were sung by an assortment of students from all years. That evening, a performance of Kurt Weill's *Down in the Valley* given by 'A' Stage students was attended by the Mayor and Mayoress of Camden, HRH Princess Marina, the Duchess of Kent, and invited guests.

LOUISE (CORDINGLY) REYNOLDS STAGE MANAGEMENT '67

❝ I suppose everyone is aware of Bruce Robinson [Stage '67] and the film *Withnail and I*. Well, I remember Vivien Mackerell very well – the actor on whom Withnail was based, and he was exactly as the film portrayed him. I was on the Stage Management course (with Jason Barnes) when they were all on the 'A' Stage course – Bruce, Vivien, Mickey Feast, David Dundas (Lord David Dundas), David Horowitz, etc. We had to give them their rehearsal calls – and they were a very difficult lot to round up! I remember doing *The Hostage* with them and on the last night our Stage Manager, Sheila Horborth, substituted the awful mixture of gravy browning and Andrews Liver salts for real bottles of Guinness and the actors, who had been trained in pouring out the bottles from a great height so that they would froth, were now dealing with cascades of escaping foam.

And we had terrific fun with *Dandy Dick*, which was directed by Peter Streuli. We took it up to the exquisite little Georgian theatre in Richmond, and half of us were lucky enough to be invited to stay with David Dundas at his parents' stately home 'Aske' in Richmond. It was quite magical, exploring the huge grounds with peacocks, and then the games of Murder in the Dark (a euphemism of course) in those historic and romantic darkened corridors. David then drove us back to London in his open-top Cobra, causing much envy amongst his fellow actors.

Best of all was the George Hall production of the musical *Girofle/Girofla*. It was a stunning success. I was on Wardrobe for the production…and I remember Jason (Barnes) coming up to our tiny stuffy dressing rooms when I was trying to get the actors and actresses into their costumes and giving me a huge hug. Delighted as I was, I was also rather startled and asked him what I'd done to deserve it? He said that he remembered that in one of our early lessons on Stage Management technique we had been taught to 'go and give the wardrobe staff a hug as they can feel very left out'… ❞

The Diamond Jubilee would have been a perfect time for Gwynneth Thurburn to retire. In its first 60 years, Central had had only two Principals – Elsie Fogerty and Gwynneth Thurburn – and both women had been experts and leaders in all three of the fields of study offered by the School. When at the beginning of 1965–6 Thurburn announced her retirement, to coincide with the Diamond Jubilee celebrations, the Governors began their search to replace the irreplaceable. By the summer of 1966, they had still not found a suitable successor, and Thurburn agreed to stay for another year. One would have hoped her last year as Principal could have been an easy one, but in 1966–7, Central faced another major challenge – this time in the Teacher Department.

• • •

In 1963, the Ministry of Education had begun to believe that students needed training in educational theory instead of being totally devoted to their specialised subject. This was a complete turnaround from their instructions of the previous decade but, to comply, the balance of the Central Teacher Course was adjusted to allocate more time to the study of educational ideas and methods. Then, the Ministry approved a BEd degree for teacher-students at other institutions, and Central graduates were instantly put at a professional disadvantage. Future salaries would most likely be higher for those who held a degree, and a Central Diploma became less attractive than the new BEd being offered elsewhere. In January 1964, Department Director Clarissa Bell and School Governor William Stone had consulted John Allen (then H M Inspector of Schools with responsibility for drama) about elevating the academic status of the Central Diploma, and in 1965, Thurburn had met with the Secretary of the Council for National Academic Awards (CNAA) regarding the possibility of obtaining a heightened award for teacher graduates to equal the new BEd – without actually becoming a BEd. The Secretary had given little encouragement for this idea. Training for teachers was changing, and Central would have to restructure its course – or lose it altogether.

In 1966, Gwynneth Thurburn was 67 years old, and her last ten years at Central had been fraught – first with the worries of finding, funding and building new premises for the School, then with the walkout of nearly two-thirds of her Stage students in 1963. The diminishment of the Teacher Course must have weighed heavily. In the spring of 1966, she visited the University of Bristol and the University of Manchester to confer with members of their drama departments. Her findings were simple: no English university offered Central's unique combination of Speech and Drama. With Speech, Drama and English studied in isolation at most institutions, Central presented its traditional and distinctive integration of the subjects to the Department of Education as a course of study that was not only unique, but would 'make technical study of the voice and speech part of a larger study in different modes of communication, in literature, in formal verse and prose speaking, in drama.'

Central had always searched for a balance between the practical and the theoretical, but the School now had to convince the CNAA that its existing course easily equalled the supposedly more rigorous academic standards of a degree course. Early in 1967, Clarissa Bell submitted an application and trial syllabus to the CNAA and awaited their approval. It would be a long wait.

• • •

The early 1960s may have been worrisome for Gwynneth Thurburn, but they were an exciting and vibrant period for Central. Margaret Greene reorganised the Speech Therapy course to conform to the requirements of the College of Speech Therapists' new examinations, and Clarissa Bell began to restructure the Teacher Course to elevate its academic qualification. When George Hall became Director of the Stage Course in 1964, he, too, made significant changes: some gradual, most immediate.

Hall was born in Edinburgh on 5 February 1925. At 18, he was called up for national service and, after four years in the Air Force, he entered Michel Saint-Denis' Old Vic School as a stage management student. He transferred to the acting course for his final

LITZ PISK, 1909 (VIENNA) – 1997 (ST IVES, CORNWALL)

Obituary by George Hall for The Independent

None who worked with the movement teacher Litz Pisk, either as actor or student, will ever forget the sheer theatrical impact of her own movement, at once dynamic and sculptural.

Amazement at such physical creativity was often mixed with despair at the thought of ever achieving anything comparable, but the despair was usually short-lived, for the purpose of the demonstration was not to dazzle but to inspire. However clumsy and uncoordinated we were, she convinced us that we too had it in us to become more alive physically, more transformable and expressive.

Her way of working had nothing to do with striving for a preconceived ideal physique; instead she was concerned to free the individual body she saw before her from all its constricting habits and limitations. Initially this process might involve a certain amount of chaos, welcomed by her as a first step on the road to what she called 'a second simplicity'. When you could stand before her relaxed and balanced you were ready to allow your imagination to shape your body.

Born in Vienna in 1909 – the curious first name Litz is a form of Alice, *Alice in Wonderland* (*Alitzia in Wunderland*) being her father's favourite book – Litz first showed a natural talent for movement when her parents, worried by the curvature of her spine, sent her to Isadora Duncan's sister Elizabeth for correctional help. This talent for movement was matched by the facility she had already revealed for drawing, her subject matter invariably the human body in motion.

Unable to decide which line to follow, she continued to study both subjects and realised that the one sphere in which they could be united was the theatre – she would be a designer of costumes, sets and movement. Fiercely determined, she somehow enrolled at the State School of Arts and Crafts, although at 15 she was under age. She studied under Max Reinhardt's designer, Oskar Strnad, who described his subject as 'stage architecture', and his preoccupation with defining space by using the simplest means was to remain a great influence.

Although she had a successful career in Vienna both as a movement teacher and a designer – she was responsible for the sets and costumes for the Viennese premiere of *The Rise and Fall of the City Mahagonny*, working with Bertolt Brecht, Kurt Weill and Lotte Lenya – she came to England in 1933 and settled here a year or two later. Within days of arriving, she was engaged to do theatrical caricatures for the *Evening Standard* and the *News Chronicle*. Shortly afterwards, she started to teach movement at RADA – until then they had studied ballet and deportment – but although Sir Kenneth Barnes, the Principal, rather surprisingly welcomed this innovation, he drew the line at improvisation, whereupon a group of young rebels, headed by Harold Lang, Alan Badel and Miriam Brickman, persuaded her to run an unofficial extra-curricular class, whose public performances caused quite a stir in theatrical circles.

So it was a logical step for Michel St-Denis, George Devine and Glen Byam Shaw to invite her to join them when they opened their radical, but alas, short-lived Old Vic Theatre School after the Second World War. Despite the brevity of its existence, the school had a profound effect on theatre training throughout the English-speaking world. Since Litz Pisk's work played a central part in its success, her reputation grew and her approach to movement influenced many who followed.

[continued...

After the Vic School, Pisk had a spell at Bath Academy of Art, followed by a period as a student (and later a teacher) of pottery at Camberwell School of Art. But she continued to teach movement in Britain and Sweden, and worked on several productions in the theatre and on television.

Then came a decade at the Central School of Speech and Drama (as head of movement from 1964) until her retirement in 1970, the third of her immensely influential periods in theatre training... Litz Pisk remained active when she retired with her friend Barbara Coombe to their cottage in Cornwall. There were exhibitions of her drawings in London and in the West Country, and in 1975 she published *The Actor and His Movement* – she was working on a second book at her death.

Her students will always remember the heavily accented, nearly inaudible speech, the elegant hair that survived the most strenuous movement (in spite of a scattering of hairpins), the moments of pained sadness at our inadequacies which made us try that bit harder, and above all, the quality Michael Elliott so memorably described as 'a contagious seriousness that can create an atmosphere of deep concentration as if by magic, with a glance of the hooded eyes and a half-lost mumble'.

two years, and left in 1951. In his first year as a professional, he toured in variety as half of an act called 'Country Cousins': 'We were heavily padded and played very old men – with huge wigs, and makeup – and we sang a song I wrote called "Manure".' He acted in rep, wrote music for plays and television, and spent two years with BBC Light Entertainment.

In Manchester in 1954, Hall and a number of other ex-students from the Old Vic School presented a season of plays as the Piccolo Theatre Company. Under the leadership of Michael Elliott and Caspar Wrede, this group was the core of what would become the Manchester Royal Exchange Theatre Company. They re-grouped as the 59 Theatre Company in 1959, to produce the hugely successful *Brandt* at the Lyric Theatre Hammersmith, and when Elliott took over the Old Vic Theatre in its last year before becoming the temporary home of the National Theatre, Hall became resident composer and voice coach. Litz Pisk taught movement.

Hall looked back on his 1963 arrival at Central:

I had had very strong notions about training ever since my days at the Old Vic School. I thought a lot about it – all the time, in fact. And although I was aware of a huge debt to the Vic training – the clarity of thought, the idealism, the sheer inspiration of Michel Saint-Denis and his staff – I reacted against the severity of the criticisms and the rather stern atmosphere, which I found inhibiting. I was against the idea that there was one right way to work, and I strongly believed that a respect for a variety of approaches – plus sympathy and encouragement, and as much fun as possible – would lead to the best results. And so it was both my huge respect for the Vic's training and my reaction against it that I brought to my own work as a teacher at Toynbee Hall and then at Central.

What I found when I arrived at Swiss Cottage rather lowered my self-esteem. I had thought the Vic School superb as far as movement was concerned, thanks to Litz, but less impressive when it came to voice and speech, and I had spent years trying to put together in my head how I thought these subjects should be taught. I thought I'd come up with some pretty original ideas, only to find they were quite commonplace in Thurbie's regime, where the teaching of voice and speech and an approach to text were on a level I'd never encountered before.

JOANNA MOORE-SMITH
STAGE '66

66 Who can forget Litz Pisk, our innovative movement teacher? Although she must have been in her sixties, she was incredibly supple and put us through all kinds of amazing exercises to prepare us for the stage. There was George Hall, with his creative singing and music classes, and Cicely Berry, our speech teacher, who I can remember making me crawl under chairs whilst speaking Shakespeare, to sound more natural! 99

Inspired by both students and colleagues, in the autumn of 1964, Hall and Pisk began an experimental exploration of how movement affects the voice – the very thing that had fascinated Fogerty and Dr Hulbert in 1906. Hall spoke of this work:

Litz and I thought, 'All this voice teaching is very good, but it's very static. What happens if you make these sounds rushing about?' So we started working on this show. You just have to talk to anyone who was in that show – Sue Lefton, David Horovitz, Wendy Allnutt, anyone involved – and they'll tell you what an extraordinary experience it was. A year's work for a fifty-minute show! It was agonizingly difficult to create. It had a lot of singing, a fair amount of screaming, and a great deal of inspired Litz-type movement. Don Lawson did a remarkable drum score for it. We were thrilled with the result, but we never had the slightest desire to repeat the experience.

Movement and Sound gave three performances in May 1965. A year later, in June 1966 the students re-formed as Group 66 and re-rehearsed the show, which was then filmed by Hal Burton under the title *Explorations*. It was shown on the BBC that autumn and was introduced by Vanessa Redgrave in conversation with Litz Pisk.

As well as exploring exciting new pathways within the training, during his early years as Director of the course, Hall also changed the presentation of the public third-year students' shows:

The acting was often fine, but the shows were unbelievably dreary to look at and the theatre was far from inviting. There were three performances of each show, two evenings and a matinee. There was no bar, and the programme was a bit of typewritten paper. It was time to change all that. We started giving five performances of each show; we employed box office staff and charged for admission. The Stage Management

PRIZES BECOME HARDSHIP FUND

In 1964, George Hall discontinued the Prizes given to Central students. Some prizes came with a small monetary award, and in this case the money from these accounts was transferred to a newly formed Student Hardship Fund. The Sylvia Strutt Memorial Prize, set up in 1933, awarded a complete Shakespeare for the best performance in a Shakespeare. There was a Fogerty Prize for the best all round performance, and a Hazel Thompson Prize for the most 'resource' in characterisation throughout the year. The William Poel Memorial Prize was given for the 'best rhetorical delivery of stage speech', the Laurence Olivier Award for best performance by a man, and the Sybil Thorndike Prize was for the best performance by a girl. The Gold Medal was awarded to the best all round actor and/or actress.

students designed ambitious programmes, and from 1966 we ran a bar. The wonderful thing was that Thurbie and Sarge were so encouraging. Show evenings started to have a real buzz.

The first show for which we charged was *An Italian Straw Hat*, and we decided to launch the new arrangements by running for a whole week. I remember hiring a barrel organ and giving balloons to children – both to make a splash on the corner of Eton Avenue as well as to draw the attention of the local population to the fact they had a theatre on their doorstep. I don't know if the barrel organ had any effect, but I had a great time.

The Old Vic School was wonderful on the design front. It was the first place that had design, direction, technical work and acting taught under the same roof. So it was a shock to me to find that at Central there were no proper sets. There were just a collection of neutral flats in battleship grey, which were shuffled about in different shapes. There was an extensive wardrobe with a skilled staff, but there had never been a designer to co-ordinate sets and costumes. They never had any designers. It was essentially amateur. When I'd been at Central for a year, I was asked to do a show. My fee was £100, and I gladly paid half my salary to Clare Jeffery, who'd been a fellow student at the Vic School, to design the set. Thurbie and Sarge were thrilled when they saw the result, so I was able to persuade them to employ Claire, and with her great talent and great tact she made the shows look professional. She was later joined by David Lewis, who was very good at over-riding all objections, and consequently raised the design standards even higher.

There were other changes, both large and small. Student shows were taken to Averham, Bury St Edmunds, Richmond (Yorks), Ashford (Kent) and Welwyn Garden City. Hall proposed that from September 1967 students no longer be known as 'A', 'B', or 'C', but by their course and the year of their completion, e.g. Teacher '70, Speech Therapy '70, etc. Perhaps most difficult to believe now – almost forty years later and with all of the dedicated musical theatre courses now available – with Hall's final-year production of *Guys and Dolls* in June 1969, Central became the first major London *acting* school to

GWYNNETH THURBURN (1899–1993)

As had Fogerty before her, Thurburn advised and tutored many actors privately for films and plays. As well as her old student, Laurence Olivier, she worked with many others, including: Robert Flemyng, Robert Helpmann, Clive Brook, Vivien Leigh, Wendy Hiller, Margaret Rawlings, Moira Shearer, Kay Hammond and Irene Worth. Dame Edith Evans, a devout Christian Scientist, one day presented herself to Thurburn with a sore throat. Thurburn was aware that Evans' beliefs ruled out medication, and tentatively asked of the Dame: 'Would you be prepared to gargle?'

Thurburn once said…

66 Central is the product of a shotgun marriage between Elsie Fogerty and Michel Saint-Denis. 99

66 I think – and I am now talking to the students among you – your responsibility is to yourself. You know your own disciplines: your talents will be finding their own way out…you are the core of your own being, your voice is your own medium, you communicate. 99

66 It was always vital that if we were going to keep going, we should not waste a penny's worth of electricity or a piece of paper, a habit that has become ingrained in me. If we had not kept to Queen Victoria's remark, 'We are not interested in the possibility of defeat', we should probably not be here today. 99

66 People are their voices. To cure a person of a boring voice you have to cure them of being a bore first. 99

66 An actor's training has changed during the last few years, and so has a teacher's, and the growing recognition of drama in schools has meant the emphasis going on practical drama, rather than on voice alone. The old system of peripatetic teachers, with qualifications solely in speech, is now finished. It was just after the war when drama suddenly became interesting to the education authorities and, for a time, speech was left behind, but this is now coming back and the demand for teachers qualified in speech and drama will eventually increase. 99

66 There is something, I believe, uniting everybody in this School – actors, teachers, speech therapists. For me it certainly is the voice, being the centre of all communication. 99

present a Broadway-style musical for the public. The cast included Lynda Bellingham, David Robb, Robin Nedwell and Nickolas Grace.

Another change to the actors' training came in the form of a new fencing master. For many years, William Harmer-Brown had taught both fencing and acrobatics, but in the autumn of 1965, Hall brought in Bill Hobbs (Stage '59) to teach the weekly fencing class to second-year Stage students. Hobbs recounts a conversation with Vera Sargent: '…When "testing" the School's attitude to Stage Combat, I asked why fencing was on the curriculum. The reply I received was a gem, and I think said a great deal – showing the difference between then and now. It was "for grace and deportment" – sounding, I think you'll agree, more like a young ladies' finishing school than a drama school.'

At the age of fourteen, Hobbs had been the youngest competitor to reach the finals of the New South Wales Open Foil Championships, and shortly afterwards he had come to train on the Stage Course in Central's last year at the Albert Hall, spending his second- and third-years at the Embassy Theatre. His early acting career at the Old Vic with Olivier's National Theatre Company instigated his second career – internationally renowned fight arranger for stage, film and television. He puts fencing and acrobatics for performance in its historical perspective:

> There was no such thing then as teaching stage combat. What you had was mostly military people or fencing masters who taught fencing or acrobatics, but who knew nothing about the drama. Stunt men were taxi drivers, brave chaps. At that time, things started changing in the theatre – in the late 1950s. Nowadays, Equity has a stunt register of those who have got their six skills; but when I started most of those who did the work in films were villains who got their skills in the bar. That's all changed. They were much more interesting then! More villains and laughs around in film at that time.
>
> Stage combat started a bit later. There were a couple of people – B H Barry, Paddy Craig – but most of it was done by actors who'd done a bit of fencing. It hadn't become specialised. B H Barry was very accomplished – I have great respect for B H – I think, in a way, he was the first to specialise in that area.

There was another major alteration that significantly affected not only the training, but also the general atmosphere for actors on the Stage Course. On the Teaching, Speech Therapy and Stage Management Courses, students were judged term-by-term on examination results. If they didn't keep up with their studies, they were asked to leave. On the Stage Course, the criteria were far more subjective. At the end of each term of the first year (known as trial terms) and then again at the end of the second year, acting students were evaluated by their tutors, and if it was felt they lacked ability or application, they were not invited to return. John Jones (Stage '63) remembers: 'When my year started, there were 45 of us, and when we finished there were 19. Twenty-six had been 'weeded out', including in my view, some of the best in the year.'

Dropping students meant fewer fees, and had a directly negative impact on the financial health of the School. In her role as Company Secretary, Registrar Vera Sargent was in charge of balancing the books, and as Hall says, 'Every time the staff thought someone should go, it must have been a blow to the heart for Sarge, but there was never any compromise.' Hall discontinued the policy that had been in effect since Central had started, and once a student was accepted, very few were ever forced to leave. By recalling all initially successful candidates, auditions became more thorough. Fewer students were accepted, but fewer mistakes were made. Hall remembered Thurburn's reaction to his changes: 'I must say that her openness about every change I proposed was extraordinary. She was a great, great woman in that tradition of English women of her period – intellectually rigorous, dedicated, idealistic, and quite unshockable.'

• • •

Thurburn's life had revolved around Central since 1919, and she was ready to retire. The search continued to find someone to replace her, and – after forty applications and a number of interviews – the Governors offered the position to Geoffrey Axworthy in December 1966. Starting at a salary of £3000 per year, he would also be provided with rent- and rate-free accommodation. The School purchased a house at 8 Lyndale Avenue for £13,300 to be used as his residence.

A retirement party for Gwynneth Thurburn took place on 18 June 1967, and Thurburn was presented with a cheque, a gold watch and a leather album containing the names of all those who had contributed. The two-hour show at the Mermaid Theatre commemorated Thurburn's long history with the School, and included speeches, scenes and songs from past and present students. Judi Dench and Richard Gale did a scene from *The Importance of Being Earnest*. There were sketches by Harold Pinter, and contributions from Virginia McKenna, Joss Ackland, Elspeth March and Wendy Craig. Students sang songs from *Guys and Dolls*.

Thurburn remained on the Board of Governors, becoming a Vice President of the School in 1971. Vera Sargent retired from Central in 1968, and the two women moved to a cottage in Suffolk – embracing a whole new life and a whole new set of friends. Thurburn's health declined, indeed it was never robust after she retired, but she enjoyed another 25 years of gardening, fine embroidery, cricket, her cats and her friends before she passed away on 20 March 1993.

Geoffrey Axworthy took over as Central's third Principal on 1 July 1967.

• • •

ADDITIONAL CENTRAL FACTS

1964   • Two third-year speech therapy students win working scholarships to Pittsburgh
University in the USA, to study for an MSc in Speech Pathology.

      • Investigations instituted to determine the cause of cracks in the west wall of the
Embassy Theatre.

      • The academic year starts with 117 on the Theatre Course (both acting and
technical), 103 on the Teacher Course (including the one-year course) and 47 on
the Speech Therapy Course, for a total of 267.

      • David Terence joins the staff of the Stage Course.

1965   • January: Chairman of the Board of Governors, John Davis, steps down and is
replaced by Sir Joseph Lockwood. Davis becomes a Vice President.

      • Cis Berry directs a successful student presentation of music and poetry called *Rouse
Me*. Requests for the show come in from Nottingham, Colchester, Ipswich and
Cambridge. The show is also performed at the March Annual General Meeting and
is included that year in the Hampstead Festival of Arts.

      • The centenary of Fogerty's birth on 16 December is marked on *Woman's Hour*
with a special feature called 'A Speech Pioneer', and includes contributions by
Dame Peggy Ashcroft, Dame Sybil Thorndike, Sir Laurence Olivier and Gwynneth
Thurburn. Marjorie Anderson, also one of Fogerty's ex-students, is the presenter.

1966   • Teacher and speech therapy students give a wine and cheese party and recital in
the new Studio to raise money for the College of Speech Therapists' 21st Birthday
Appeal.

1966–7 • For the first time, two Technical students are selected at the end of 1966–7 to
remain for a third year of advanced study in aspects of production and radio work.

1967   • Central's first collaboration with design students at the Wimbledon School of Art
takes place, with second-year actors presenting songs and scenes in the round at
Wimbledon.

12

1967–1970

BORN IN PLYMOUTH on 10 August 1923, Geoffrey John Axworthy earned an MA in English from Oxford and taught for four years in Baghdad before joining the English University College, Ibadan, Nigeria in 1956 as a lecturer in English. Axworthy was founder and Director of Drama of the University of Ibadan School of Drama. He enjoyed both creating live theatre and encouraging young actors and new writers, and later merged the Drama Department with a student dramatic society to create a Travelling Theatre to tour Nigeria with a collapsible stage on the back of a trailer. In 1992, Jon Holliday wrote this tribute to Axworthy for the *South Wales Echo*: 'He took his work seriously, but never himself. A gentle humour threaded through all his conversations. …Shy, quietly spoken, he could be exasperating, but he was never malicious or bitchy, never lost his temper, possessing that rare quality so necessary to anyone involved in the Arts in Wales, the ability to work with committees.'

When Axworthy took over as Principal, Central was respected internationally, yet it continued to struggle to survive financially. The 1963 Employment Act had set down government guidelines requiring that salaries remain in line with the Burnham (and when Central officially became a 'training college' in 1972, the Pelham) Scale of pay, and so expenditure increased. Student enrolment had hovered at around 265 for the previous few years, so fee income had remained the same. Central continually had to find 'creative' ways to save money. This was Vera Sargent's genius.

By the time 'Sarge' retired in 1968, she had worked for 38 years at Central – 30 of those as Registrar and Company Secretary. In 1966, Hazel Hill became Assistant Registrar, and took over Sargent's position as Company Secretary. Neil Gibson replaced Hill in both those positions the next year. When Sargent retired in 1968, Barbara Coombes became Registrar, and it was at this point that Company Secretary Gibson pointed out an interesting, and very 'Central', reality. Only half of the staff were on any sort of salary scale – Burnham or otherwise – and very few had any kind of contract. Sarge had always just paid people what she thought was 'right'. John Jones (Staff 1966–88) recollects: 'Sarge kept Lyle [Watson] and I on starvation wages for about three years. Having worked there, and very hard I might add, I'd say to Sarge, "Could I be promoted yet?" She'd just say, "Try me next year."' Virginia Snyders adds: 'People often underestimate how much Sarge

1968 Martin Luther King and Robert Kennedy
        killed
        Russian tanks roll into Prague
        Lord Chamberlain's censorship abolished
1969 Conference of Drama Schools founded
        Men walk on the moon
1970 Laurence Olivier is created a Life Peer
        Gay Liberation Front holds first public
        demonstration in UK
        Equity's Living Wage campaign assures
        £18 per week in provincial theatre

was responsible for what was achieved by Thurb, but they did run it a bit like a church tea party. Typical of the way they thought was their reasoning for how people were paid: it was all about how much they needed the money. It wasn't about men or women, or age and experience – it was about people's private means.'

After Sarge retired, staff began to receive pay that at least attempted to conform to government pay scales, and expenditure increased further. The only way for Central to increase its income, was to raise student fees. In 1968–9, Acting and Teacher-students' fees went up to £425 per year, while the Speech Therapy and Technical (Stage Management) Courses remained unchanged. In 1970, fees were raised again – by £25 per year from January 1970, and another £25 per year from September of 1970. Entrance test fees were raised to £5. School fees were now equal to those of similar teacher training institutions – New College and Rose Bruford – and could not realistically be raised higher.

• • •

Geoffrey Axworthy spent a great deal of time in his first two months as Principal observing classes, and he concluded: Central was facing a severe shortage of suitable facilities. This was not news; Central had always needed more accommodation. However, even though space at the Albert Hall had been limited, at least its maintenance had been someone else's problem. Now, not only was there a shortage of space, but the space available was in need of repair, upkeep and improvements, and this expensive headache was now entirely Central's responsibility.

At the urging of George Hall, in 1968 a forestage was added in the Embassy Theatre at a cost of £250, but the theatre's problems went deeper than lack of stage space: the old building was subsiding. Cracks had begun to appear in 1964, and by autumn 1969, it was deemed cheaper to purchase, rather than rent, scaffolding to shore up the cracked back wall of the stage. No one mentioned the cost of repairing it; there was *definitely* no money for that. The JD Wing already (again) needed structural repairs, and in the spring of 1970, Camden Council notified the School that the Studio on Eton Avenue, built in 1963, would have to be removed. Within two months, the School's solicitors had permission from the Council to rent land behind Central on Buckland Crescent to build a replacement Studio. Central was running hard to stay in the same place.

In 1969, Camden Council finally received word from the Ministry of Transport on a proposed road improvement scheme for Swiss Cottage. Camden would be allowed to take over the land on the corner of College Crescent and Eton Avenue, and they notified Central's Board of Governors that the western triangle of land to the left of the theatre would finally become available for Central's use – but there was a catch. Camden wanted to build a Civic Centre, and Central was invited to use only a *part* of this site. The offer was not ideal, but the Governors instructed the School's architect to come up with a proposal that would provide enough classrooms and facilities for Central's needs, and discussions began on finances. When the Governors were finally shown Camden's plans for a Civic Centre – which included a permanent repertory theatre, a huge concert hall, and annexes for exhibitions and smaller gatherings – they recognised the Council's plans not only as too expensive but also as totally insufficient for Central's needs. The School's hopes for expansion were dashed. The Governors recognised that the Embassy Theatre had been a great home, but they now reluctantly began to search for alternative premises.

ELSIE FOGERTY MEMORIAL LECTURE

In 1966, the Speech Therapy Department instituted the Elsie Fogerty Memorial Lecture, and its first offering, 'Voodoo and Brainwashing', was given by Dr Sargent. In 1967, Lady Stocks gave 'The Emotional Association of Words'. Joan van Thal gave the Lecture, 'Emergence of Speech Therapy', in 1968. In 1969, Stanley Ellis presented 'Attitudes to Accents', and in 1970, Betty (Fitch) Byers Brown gave 'The Practice and Prediction of Speech Skills'. Byers Brown spoke again in 1971, and from here, the list of lectures is incomplete, with no record of speeches from 1972 to 1974. In 1975, Professor A C Gimson was invited to speak, and in 1976, Dr Eric Briault, Director of the ILEA, lectured on 'Speech and the Inner City Child'. In 1978, Gwynneth Thurburn gave her speech 'Why Central?' and the next year, Mary Warnock spoke on 'Learning to Communicate'. Francis Cammaerts, Principal of Rolle College, gave the Lecture in 1980.

• • •

Meanwhile, the educational life of the School faced its own challenges. All of Central's courses were considered of the very highest standard, but now the Speech Therapy and the Teacher Courses were both being pushed towards achieving new academic qualifications.

Margaret Greene had been part-time Director of the Speech Therapy Department since 1963, and was used to adhering to the strict academic guidelines of the College of Speech Therapists. She herself was a Fellow of the CST, and as author of the seminal textbook, *The Voice and Its Disorders* (1959), she was recognised internationally for her research. She was also a practising therapist of considerable standing, and had been an examiner for the first degree in Speech Therapy, which was awarded by Newcastle University in 1967. There is no question that Greene and the Speech Therapy Course at Central were held in high regard, but now there was a very real danger that, with an eye towards their future employment, students would choose a degree qualification over a Central Diploma. The University of Manchester had followed Newcastle's lead with their BSc in Speech and Language Therapy, and no one knew how much longer the College of Speech Therapists would consider Central's qualification worthy of a CST Licentiate.

Equally, the Teacher Course was under pressure. Under Thurburn, in 1967, Central had applied to the CNAA for a new Teacher Course qualification (not a BEd) to equal the BEd degrees being offered elsewhere. In January 1968, the CNAA had asked for a redraft of the proposal, but by the following September, Axworthy suggested that no more time should be wasted on this application. He believed that the only way Central could survive was to offer degrees in both Teacher Training and Speech Therapy. He convinced the Governors that Central must offer academic qualifications in order to assure students they would be both eligible for mandatory grants from their Local Education Authorities and highly employable after their graduation. Drastic alterations to the Speech Therapy and Teacher Courses would have to be made.

• • •

In December 1969, having set in motion this important shift in the Central mindset, Axworthy gave notice of his intention to resign in August 1970, citing his wish 'to engage more actively in creative work in the theatre than the duties of his present post permitted'. The job of Principal at Central was gradually becoming more about the ebb and flow of government educational policies than about the subjects it offered to its students. Without the personal commitment to the School possessed by Fogerty and Thurburn, Axworthy had no reason to stay, and he left Central in 1970 to become the Director of Drama at University College, Cardiff, and the founding Artistic Director of the new Sherman Theatre. His practical and artistic talents created and served one of the most successful of Britain's provincial repertory companies.

The Governors advertised for prospective replacements but, after a number of interviews, they could find no one suitable, and in September 1970, the Board invited Central Governor, William Stone, to take over until a new Principal could be found. Stone was offered a salary in line with the Pelham Scale, an allowance for a car and annual expenses of £300.

• • •

ADDITIONAL CENTRAL FACTS

1967 • Sir Joseph Lockwood organises a student recording of *Black Beauty* for EMI, and £41 in royalties go to the School.

• Ex-student, Maria Garde, leaves £50 to Central in her will.

• Jane Cowell (Teacher '53), daughter of Marjorie Webb (Teacher '28), starts as part-time voice tutor on the Stage Course.

1968 • HRH Princess Marina, Duchess of Kent, Central's Royal Patron since 1935, passes away. Her daughter, HRH Princess Alexandra, becomes Central's new Royal Patron.

• Autumn: Sir Joseph Lockwood resigns his Chairmanship, and is replaced by Board Member Norman Collins of Associated Rediffusion (A-R) Television. Lockwood remains on the Board, and in 1969, is made a Vice President.

• Neil Gibson, Company Secretary, reports £152 income from letting the Embassy Theatre during the summer vacation.

1969 • A small hut is erected behind the Studio for use as workshop.

• Five Silver Cups, previously awarded annually, are sold. The £69 is spent on books for the library and the refurbishment of Central's two skeletons.

• Betty (Fitch) Byers Brown is appointed to the Board of Governors.

1970 • Barbara Coombes resigns as Registrar and is replaced by Jenepher Hawkins.

• Beryl Shorthouse retires after 25 years as School secretary.

13

1970–1972

WILLIAM GEORGE STONE was born on 20 July 1903. After graduating from University College London, he spent his early career teaching in a number of different institutions, and while lecturing at Southampton, acquired his MA in Education. He soon became Deputy Director of Education for Warwickshire, and in 1947 took over as Chief Education Officer in Brighton, where he remained Director for the next 22 years. Largely as a result of his tenacity and resourcefulness, Sussex University was approved by the relevant government bodies and established in 1959.

Though not professionally trained in either discipline, Stone had a deep interest in both art and drama. An amateur painter, he exhibited in local art shows (he once had a picture accepted for the Royal Academy Summer Exhibition), and he directed a number of plays for local dramatic societies. He was President of the National Association of Art Institutions, served on the National Advisory Council for Art Education and was a Governor of the Royal College of Art.

When in 1961 Central had amended its Articles of Association to allow various government educational bodies to appoint representatives, Stone had been invited to join Central's Board as a representative from the Association of Education Committees. In 1969, he retired as Chief Education Officer in Brighton, so when asked to step in as Principal of Central, he accepted the position – but only for one year. He assured the Academic Board that he was unlikely to suggest major changes, and he would merely work towards safeguarding existing proposals. He then proceeded to devote himself entirely to solving Central's academic and financial difficulties. Stone's experience with the bureaucracies of governmental departments had always been helpful to the Board of Governors. Now, he would guide Central as it began to explore new educational qualifications for its Teacher and Speech Therapy students.

• • •

Central had always had an uneasy relationship with the country's Local Education Authorities when it came to student grants. Both Speech Therapy and Stage (Acting) students received grants only at the discretion of their Local Authorities, and while some LEAs were eager to provide grants to successful applicants, others refused outright.

Occasionally an Acting student already accepted at Central would have to audition for his or her LEA three or four times – only in the end to be turned down. Often, students were asked to complete a full year of training without financial help, with their LEA grant dependent on a progress report from the School at the end of their first year.

However, as long as the Department of Education and Science (DES) accredited the Teacher Course, their students' grants were

COURSE ACCEPTANCES

In 1970–1, 35 Acting students were accepted out of 383 candidates. 17 Technical students were accepted out of 62 applicants. 13 ACSD students were accepted out of 16 applicants. 50 Teacher students were accepted out of 151 applicants. 21 Speech Therapy students were accepted out of 56 applicants.

mandatory. Then, in 1969, the DES indicated that it would cease giving 'Qualified Teacher Status' to graduates of *specialist* teacher-training institutions – those, like Central, who trained their students first and foremost in their specialist subject. To maintain mandatory grants for its students, Central had to amend the Teacher Course to comply with DES guidelines. Early in the summer of 1970, Central opened negotiations with Sidney Webb College, which was then part of the University of London Institute of Education. To satisfy DES requirements, Central would merge the experience and prestige of its own specialised training in speech and drama (which was becoming increasingly attractive to students) with Sidney Webb's approved course in education. At the same time, the School would explore the possibility of offering a BEd.

By autumn 1971, the DES had agreed the general terms for collaboration between the two institutions. Central and Sidney Webb could offer a three-year course, with students registered for a University of London Certificate in Education, but if students achieved a high enough standard in the Certificate exams, they could stay a fourth year and take a University of London BEd. Students remained based at Central, but were also registered at Sidney Webb College; they were taught by staff from both institutions and could use the facilities of both. This new course started in 1972, and was designed to prepare students to become teachers of English, speech and drama. As a result of this collaboration, Central was admitted to the University's Institute of Education as a constituent college, thereby guaranteeing fee awards from the LEAs. It would take a few more years before Central could find a way to guarantee awards for its Stage and Speech Therapy students.

• • •

Just as the Inner London Education Authority (ILEA) awarded fees for its students, so the ILEA Further and Higher Education Sub-Committee awarded grants to the educational institutions themselves. Over the years, Central had made a number of requests for support to the ILEA. On some occasions the School was awarded small amounts for specific

1970	The Beatles dissolve partnership in court
1971	Charles Manson convicted of Tate murders
	British currency becomes decimalised
1972	Israeli Olympic compound stormed by Arab guerrillas
	Sir John Betjeman becomes Poet Laureate
	First Miners' Strike

purposes, but just as often, its applications were turned down. Stone now pushed Central's relationship with the ILEA further.

Since its relocation to the Embassy, Central's survival had been a never-ending carousel: to increase income, the School increased enrolment; when enrolment increased, the School needed more space and more staff; the added expense of additional space and staff salaries brought with it the need for more students. Stone recognised that the only way off this economic merry-go-round was financial security, and he saw the ILEA as the brass ring.

Stone applied to the ILEA for grant-aided status. Should Central be accepted, the School would remain a registered charity, and even though it might have to give up some of its independence, in return it would receive not only an annual grant of government money for day-to-day overhead, but it would also get financial help for maintenance as well as for the expansion of the physical premises. Armed with Central's accounts and its strategies for future academic improvement, Stone and a delegation of Governors met with the Chairman of the Further and Higher Education Sub-Committee of the ILEA to put their case.

In the midst of negotiations with the ILEA and the DES, Stone's term as Principal came to an end. He agreed to stay on for one more year.

• • •

While Central awaited an answer from the ILEA, the Governors continued their search for more space. The Axworthy residence was sold for nearly £15,000, and the proceeds were used to rent Camden Council land behind the School on Buckland Crescent and build the 40' x 40' Studio One, which opened in autumn 1971. Central was also allowed to rent back the old Eton Avenue Studio (now Studio Two) until Camden Council started work on its new Civic Centre. This rental arrangement continued for the next seven years, and Camden's Civic Centre plans were never realised.

Since the Stage Management Course had been created, the Acting Course was variously referred to as either the Acting Course or the Stage Course. In 1963, Peter Streuli became Head of what was now renamed the Technical Course. The Acting Course became the Stage Course, and both the Stage and the Technical Courses came under the heading of the Theatre Department. Over the next few years, these titles and names would change again. And again. And again.

Whatever it was called, the two-year Technical Course was intended for those who wanted to work in the theatre other than as actors or designers, and it was billed as

JODI MYERS TECHNICAL '72

❝ I had a great time at Central – the training was invaluable. Peter Streuli and Frank Gearing were excellent – if idiosyncratic and contrasting – teachers, as was June Wooldridge who taught sound. On reflection Streuli and Gearing came from a style of theatre that was beginning to change significantly by 1970 – they were none the worse for that but there was scant recognition of emerging ways of making work, and I remember Frank not being encouraging about the possibility of me working in TIE.

I suppose amongst the most important lessons I learnt at Central was being prepared to work very long hours and taking responsibility – in fact, in one way Central was tougher than the business turned out to be (not that working in the theatre has ever been easy!), but it was a magnificent apprenticeship. I haven't worked in stage management since 1974 but I have continued to use many of the skills I first developed at Central throughout a career which has encompassed marketing, working at the Arts Council, managing venues, commissioning and presenting work and consultancy. The stage management training was a fantastic discipline and on top of that we got to experience in a small way some of the things the actors were having to take on, which made for greater understanding of the pressure they were under and how work is made.

The other thing Central taught me was the importance of teamwork. One of my most vivid memories of that time was being sent on a tour of one-night stands in the southwest and we were pretty much on our own. The tour was full of incidents. In one barn of a theatre there were more people on stage than in the audience, and we had to work out whether to cancel or not (the show went on, though it was tough keeping up morale).

Then there was the summer research project into European theatre – everyone else got Germany, France, Spain, Holland etc and I got bloody Iceland. Iceland! There was one theatre there at the time, and I became something of an expert on it. The only thing I can remember now from that blooming Icelandic theatre project is that there once were man-size penguins in Iceland... **❞**

providing experience for those who wanted to become stage managers, producers, directors, or specialists in stage lighting, sound, stage management or television. Out of this course has come a wide range of successful practitioners over the years, including the producer Cameron Mackintosh, the director Deborah Warner and the musical director Jae Alexander, to name but a few. As with other Central courses, Technical students were required to take classes in voice (with tutorials) and movement, reading, music, make-up and dance. Unlike the actors, they studied the history of costume and staging, and had classes in lighting and sound; workshops in scenery and props; classes in Routine and Organisation, and Plans. They studied plays, had production seminars, did 'exercises' in the theatre, made models, did period research, built scenery and worked in the wardrobe department. They studied design and electrics, and they learned how to do lighting plots, make prompt books and do scale drawings. In their second and final year, they were assigned to third-year Stage students' productions as stage managers, wardrobe, lighting, props or crew. In light of all of this application and dedication, it seems only fair that Technical students were finally given above-ground classrooms and allowed out of the basement for a bit of fresh air. Technical Course headquarters had long been located in Rooms X and Y in the basement of the Embassy building, directly beneath the main office. Now, a temporary building was erected behind the JD Wing to house two Technical Course classrooms. This new building also provided a larger room for the expanding library, as well as a new reading room.

One of the newly vacated basement rooms in the Embassy was now allocated to maintenance, and the other was offered to the Advanced Certificate in Speech and Drama (ACSD). This was eventually considered unsuitable for these more mature students, and they were allotted a far more 'grown-up' dressing room in the Eton Avenue Studio Two.

• • •

The ACSD Course had started with nine students in the autumn of 1968 as a replacement for the Certificate in Diction and Drama. It, too, was a one-year course for experienced teachers who wanted either to lecture in speech and drama in colleges of education, to work as local education authority organisers of drama or as heads of departments in large secondary schools, or to become leaders of drama groups in youth clubs and colleges of further education. Up to 15 students could be enrolled each year.

The ACSD was in two parts – practice and theory – and placed an emphasis on the voice. In three terms, students received two, three or four hours of voice work per week, and the group had seven hours of voice tutorials each term. There were poetry and prose classes for two hours per week, and one hour per week ear training for all three terms. Students had acting study in their first term, presented a drama project in the second term, and did a playwriting production in the third. There were classes in movement and educational drama in all three terms, with dance (two terms) and singing (one term). Tumbling, recording, studio work, design, make-up and programme work were offered for one term each. On top of this, they were allowed to go to classes on the three-year Teacher Course 'when they were free'. In the final part of the course, there were two hours per week of Special Study: forums and seminars. Students selected one or two areas in the field of speech and drama in education, and within five months of the end of the course, reports were due on their chosen topics.

• • •

With the ACSD, Technical, Stage, Teacher and Speech Therapist Courses fully enrolled, Central's premises were functioning at more than capacity, yet the School was still running at a deficit. Fees were again raised for 1971:

Stage and Teacher: up £50 to £525 per year
Speech Therapy: up £10 to £375 per year
Technical: up £25 to £450 per year

For extra income, the School also began to rent its premises during the summer holidays. A three-week summer course for American teachers and university students was given during the 1969 and 1970 summer vacations. In 1971, Choate School, a private high school in Connecticut, USA, used Central Stage staff to teach its three-week course, and the USA Association for Cultural Exchange employed staff from the Teacher Course for a one-week school. William Stone suggested that the Governors consider organising a short summer school for teachers of Speech and Drama. Someone passing Elsie Fogerty's portrait reported a smile and an amused shrug.

STUDENT HARDSHIP FUND

Many Central students were regularly short of money. When there were unexpected expenses for required orthodontics, contact lenses or special medical treatments, students could apply to an unofficial hardship fund, which had been set up in 1964 by George Hall from the proceeds of the former prizes and bursaries. This fund was occasionally enhanced by donations and bequests, and in 1970, Joan van Thal left £438 to the School in her will, which was included in this fund. In 1971, the Governors officially approved the Student Hardship Fund, and the Chairman immediately donated £100. In 1973, this Fund stood at over £4000.

• • •

Late in 1971, the ILEA finally came back with an offer of support for Central, and the School's fortunes changed forever. An ILEA representative attended a December Board Meeting and outlined for the Governors what changes would have to be made should Central accept grant-aided status. First, the representative assured the Board that there were no plans to merge the School with any other institutions, but should this issue arise, the Governors would be 'consulted'. Second, the School would need ILEA approval should it want to launch a new course. Third, although existing rights would remain with the Governors, ILEA representatives would attend all meetings. Fourth, fees would be lowered significantly – they would drop to £70 per year for private students from Britain, and to £250 per year for overseas students. Fifth, should any new building works seem necessary, they would have to fit into the ILEA programme, and approval would take at least five years after the submission of proposals. The Governors saw this as an answer to Central's incessant financial woes, and they unanimously accepted grant-aided status. In 1972, Central officially came under the wing of the Inner London Education Authority.

As the years passed, this liaison would prove both terrific and terrible, but in those early days it was a financial banquet. Although the School's independence was reduced, Central still retained more autonomy than that of 'grant-maintained' institutions. The School was finally free from total dependence on student fees, and now its economic security – in the form of grants and budgets – would come directly from the ILEA. For the first time, staff were paid well, with salaries immediately raised 10% and set to remain in line with other ILEA schools in the future. Department budgets were finally sufficient,

PARIS ECOLE NATIONALE SUPERIEURE DES ARTS ET TECHNIQUES DU THEATRE

In May 1971, final year Stage students performed *A Day in the Death of Joe Egg* at the Paris Ecole Nationale Supérieure des Arts et Techniques du Théatre. In reciprocation, the following February 1972, the Paris Ecole Nationale Supérieure des Arts et Techniques du Théatre gave a performance of *L'Ecole des Femmes* at the Embassy Theatre.

repairs and new equipment were more easily obtained, and within two months, the library had stocked £1500 worth of new books. George Hall said of those transitional years: 'Until that moment, we used to call it "threadbare college". It was so broke that the office staff were told to write on both sides of every piece of paper. You got old bits of paper – show reports or minutes of a meeting – with your month's salary, and when you looked to see how much you'd earned and how much tax they'd taken off, if you looked at the wrong side you'd read, "This show overran by ten minutes." Carbon paper was used and re-used until it had to be retired, and we all went about switching off lights. Then the ILEA became our provider, and we had a slightly over-enthusiastic accountant who told us, "The ILEA will only respect you if you spend your budget to the full." Suddenly we had everything we asked for.'

In February 1972, the Labour-controlled ILEA applied for a 7% budget increase for 1973, which was higher than the Greater London Council's 4% and the Government's target of 4.2%. Within the ILEA's £189 million proposed budget was a £100,000 award for Central. In June 1972, expansion plans were drawn up by School architects and presented to the Governors, and the ILEA indicated that it would help with capital outlay for new buildings. It might even be prepared to consider financing them sooner than the five years originally indicated.

Central began receiving money on 1 September 1972, but, in preparation for the changes and in order to allocate the numbers and grades of the teaching staff and their predicted salaries, courses had been graded throughout the previous spring according to the Burnham Further Education scale. Teaching and administrative staff were given new contracts of employment and full-time staff became eligible for pensions. £30,000 was requested to purchase and upgrade theatre sound and lighting equipment. A part-time Audio Visual Aids (AVA) Technician was appointed and more money was requested for the future purchase of Video Tape Recording (VTR) and projection equipment.

At the end of 1971–2, Central's account balances were in deficit once again, but no one was worried. In the past, this would have meant an increase in fees for the coming year, but now the School could depend on the ILEA to come up with the shortfall. It looked like the School's financial troubles were finally over. Central was hooked to the gravy train.

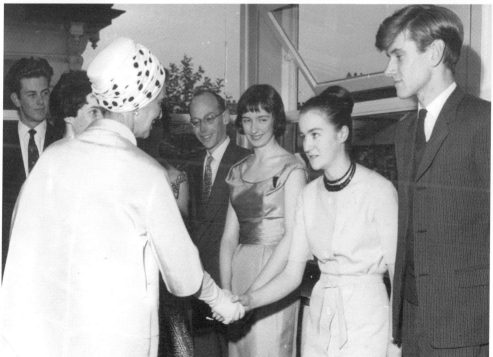

TOP: Redecorated Embassy Theatre from the balcony. A production was staged for the camera. On stage, left: Hugh Rose, Fiona Walker, Noelle Finch (sitting); right: Julie Christie, Jonathan Burn, Kate Lansbury. Foreground (backs of heads): Clare Fox, Louisa Browne, Tim Byford. In the stalls: Trevor Banham. BOTTOM: At the opening of the John Davis Wing, HRH Princess Marina, Duchess of Kent, shakes hands with the Student President (24 May 1961). Left to right, background: Roger Mutton, Councillor, Clare Fox, Student President, Robert Grange.

TOP LEFT: Aileen Wyse Dance (1930). TOP RIGHT: Gwynneth Thurburn, portrait by Patrick Phillips (1960).
BOTTOM: Students at the zoo for animal study (1960). From left to right: Donald Van Der Maaten (Holland),
Jon Lord (of Deep Purple), Roger Timms, David Roberts.
OPPOSITE TOP LEFT: *Monitor* Programme, 'The Class', shown on the BBC at 10 pm, 9 April 1961: Robert Grange.
TOP RIGHT: *Monitor* Programme. Left to right: Jennifer Samuels (Tudor), Sandra Freeman, Robert Grange and
Christopher Timothy at the back. MIDDLE LEFT: *Monitor* Programme. Left to right, back: Jennifer Samuels (Tudor),
Sandra Freeman, Robert Grange, Angela Down; front: Katherine Barker, Bridget Arestion. MIDDLE RIGHT: *Monitor*
Programme. Left to right: Jennifer Samuels (Tudor), Sandra Freeman, Robert Grange, Angela Down.
BOTTOM: Embassy Theatre from the corner of Eton Avenue and Finchley Road, before the Swiss Cottage road scheme.

TOP: Student Maggie Lambert at the fruit and vegetable stall on Eton Avenue opposite Central.
BOTTOM: Corner of Eton Avenue and Finchley Road before the Swiss Cottage road scheme.

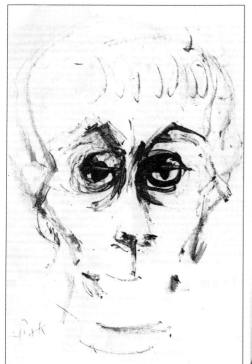

TOP LEFT: Sketch of Gwynneth Thurburn by Litz Pisk. TOP RIGHT: Geoffrey Axworthy (*courtesy of Brian Tarr*).
BOTTOM: Litz Pisk teaching movement in Room D.

TOP: Vera Sargent, Central Registrar and Company Secretary, with David Roscoe and Christine Drummond, President and Secretary of the Students' Association (1960s). BOTTOM LEFT: William Stone, Principal 1970–2. BOTTOM RIGHT: Portrait of John Allen, Principal 1972–8, painted by Paul Wyeth (1975).

TOP LEFT: Ishbel Fox in the wardrobe department at the Embassy Theatre for Restoration costume fitting.
TOP RIGHT: Front of Embassy Theatre before renovation.
BOTTOM LEFT: George Kitson, Principal 1978–87 (courtesy of Alex Riddett).
BOTTOM RIGHT: Jane Cowell, conducting fellow Central Teachers '53 in a cabaret sketch at Kensington Town Hall.

TOP: Teaching staff from the Speech Therapy Department, early 1980s (left to right, back: Malcolm Stockley, Susie Summers, Ed Conduit, unknown, Andy Spencer; front: Kay Mogford, Hazel Dewart, Elaine Hodkinson, Kay Coombes, Margo Drew). BOTTOM: Central's 75th Birthday Celebration, 1981. Left to right: George Kitson, Norman Collins, HRH Princess Alexandra, Sir Laurence Olivier.

TOP: HRH Princess Alexandra and Chairman of the Board of Governors, Norman Collins, cut Central's birthday cake, watched by Gwynneth Thurburn and George Kitson (1981). BOTTOM: Tamsin Olivier and Adam Price in second-year Ibsen, *Rosmerholm* (Spring 1984).

70 ROEBUCK HOUSE
PALACE STREET
LONDON SWIE 5BE
01-828 4256

11th November 1981

George Hall, Esq.,
Embassy Theatre
Eton Avenue
London N.W.3.

My dear George:

       I cannot let another minute go by
without telling you what a wonderful show your people
put up last night. I have never before seen any
acting students persuade you that they were no longer
students - or ever even had been. They were
professional to the topmost degree and one could only
sit and admire the authoritative confidence and pure
information that they imparted to the audience.

       Truthfully, I was so thrilled by it
and find it hard now to express my deep admiration for
your so remarkable teaching. I hope you were pleased
to see your students rise to that teaching so nobly
and with such admirable sang-froid.

       Joanie sends love and wishes very much
that she could have been with you.

              Yours sincerely, ever,

                    Laurence Olivier

TOP LEFT: Letter to George Hall about the late-night show, *Sweet and Sour*, presented by Michael Chance, Peter Risafi, Martyn Ellis, Eryl Maynard, Emma Watson and Zanna Hamilton for the 75th Birthday Celebration.
TOP RIGHT: HRH Princess Alexandra and Sir Laurence Olivier at Central's 75th Birthday (1981).
BOTTOM: Robert Fowler, Principal 1987–2000.

TOP: Embassy Theatre Extension (1994). BOTTOM: Drama, Applied Theatre and Education students present *The Odyssey* at The Minack Theatre in Cornwall (2003). (*Photo by Keith Orton*)

TOP: Jocelyn Herbert, theatre designer, and HRH Princess Alexandra at Opening of the new Library and Learning Resources Centre on 18 November 1997. A part of Jocelyn Herbert's design archive is on display.
BOTTOM: Library and Learning Resources Centre. HRH Princess Alexandra and Peter Collett look on as a student demonstrates audio-visual equipment (1997).

Front of Embassy Theatre after refurbishment (2002).

TOP: Street view of West Block from Finchley Road (2005). (*Photo by Mike Benwell*)
BOTTOM: Sky view of West Block (2005). (*Photo by Mike Benwell*)

TOP LEFT: Gary Crossley, Principal 2000–07. (*Photo by Fatima Namdar*) REMAINING PHOTOGRAPHS: Centenary Celebration at Old Vic Theatre, 4 June 2006. (*Photos by John Rasmussen*) TOP RIGHT: Cicely Berry and Lynda Bellingham. BOTTOM LEFT: Rufus Sewell and Wendy Craig. BOTTOM RIGHT: 'Tribute to the Foyer' from Centenary Event. Left to right: Lolly Susi, Harriet Thorpe, Jennifer Saunders; foreground: Emma Watson.

TOP: Graham Norton and James Nesbitt.
BOTTOM: Teachers '53.

• • •

Before this transfer to the ILEA, in the spring of 1972, Clarissa Bell announced her retirement as Director of the Teacher Department. An inspiring teacher and valuable leader during the joint Central/Sydney Webb degree applications, Bell had been at the School during one of its most difficult and most exciting times. She had put the Teacher Course on its path, and her successor, Audrey Laski, would pick up where she left off. Bell would remain connected and loyal to the School, and she was elected to the Board of Governors the next year.

At the end of 1971–2, William Stone also stepped down. He, too, was immediately re-elected as a Governor and would serve on the Board until 1974. In his two years as Principal, Stone's most important contribution was an act that forever changed Central's future: he had navigated Central towards the ILEA and achieved grant-aided status. It was thought this surely would assure Central's future financial security.

Stone's successor, John Allen, was appointed Principal in July 1972.

• • •

ADDITIONAL CENTRAL FACTS

1971   • Joan Washington joins the staff of the Teacher Course as voice tutor.

         • The student notice board in the foyer of the theatre is designated for Teachers
           and Speech Therapists. The Stage Course students are given a notice board in the
           corridor to the backstage stairs.

         • A one-way viewing mirror is installed between Rooms 3 and 4 in the JD Wing to
           enable speech therapy students to observe patients while being treated and to
           provide at least minimal on-premises clinical experience.

14

1972–1978

BORN ON 30 MARCH 1912, John Piers Allen was educated at Aldenham School and St John's College, Cambridge. While still an undergraduate, he made his London acting debut in James Bridie's *The Anatomist*, which was directed by Tyrone Guthrie and starred Flora Robson. He continued acting from 1931 to 1936, during which time he worked with the Old Vic (1933–5) and the avant-garde Group Theatre at the Westminster Theatre. From 1936, he directed productions for both the Unity and the Scala Theatres, and in 1938–9, he worked on the staff of Michel Saint-Denis' London Theatre Studio. Allen was a peace-loving Quaker, but having spent three months in Germany with relatives in the 1930s, he had seen first hand the inhumanities of Hitler's regime. When war broke out in 1939, he was one of the first to enlist, serving as an Engineer Lieutenant in motor torpedo boats and taking part in the D-Day landings.

After the war, Allen became the administrator and producer of Glyndebourne Children's Theatre, and in 1951 he became a scriptwriter and producer for BBC Schools Broadcasting and the Third Programme. He was a frequent delegate to ITI/UNESCO Conferences on Children's Theatre. When appointed H M Inspector for the Department of Education and Science (DES) in 1961, he was given national responsibility for drama.

Allen was the author and editor of a number of books on theatre and drama, and during his time as Principal of Central, he served as Chairman of the newly formed Conference of Drama Schools. He was also a member both of the Dance and Drama Panel of the Council for National Academic Awards (CNAA) and of the London University Special Advisory Committee in Drama. In Allen, Central had found not only a great Principal with a wide range of interests, abilities and experience, but also an open and easy-going leader with a commitment to the arts.

From his first Academic Board Meeting in September 1972, John Allen – like others before him – expressed his great concern about Central's lack of space. Almost immediately the ILEA promised they would acquire the land adjacent to the theatre and apply for money from the DES for construction of a new building. The new Principal, the Governors and the Central staff collectively exhaled.

The ILEA urged Central to take advantage of the Authority's many resources in the London area, and Allen and George Hall visited the Slade School of Art to discuss possible collaboration with their Theatre Design Department. The Royal College of Art approached Central to use Stage students for their Film and Television unit, and early in 1973, the London College of Fashion sent two members of their hairdressing department to help with the third-year Stage productions, *One Flew Over the Cuckoo's Nest* and *The Voysey Inheritance*. The London College of Printing offered to design posters for Central productions. In the spring and summer terms of 1974, Theatre Design Department students from the Central School of Art and Design worked on two Central third-year Stage productions at the Jeannetta Cochrane Theatre: *Girofle-Girofla* and *Flint*.

By March 1973, cable was being laid for an ILEA Educational TV network, and £1000 of VTR equipment was on order. One basement room was assigned to the Audio-Visual 'department', while the other remained allocated for the school caretaker and maintenance.

Besides providing resources, the ILEA also made demands and laid down rules. Early in the involvement with Central, dissatisfaction had been expressed with the security arrangements. Accommodation for a school-keeper was considered urgent, but the only flat in the building was occupied by Ishbel MacGlashan Fox (Stage '31). Fox had had a successful career as an actress, but returned to the School as wardrobe mistress when it was still at the Hall. When Fox's husband passed away in 1958, Thurburn suggested she and her daughter, Clare, move into the flat at the Embassy. (Clare, Stage Management '62, was the only student ever to have lived – legally – at the Embassy while studying on a course.) Fox's tenancy was protected by the terms of her employment, but in 1973, she was given a small sum as compensation in return for vacating, and a school-keeper was hired to live on site as 24-hour security. Even this didn't prove a reliable safety precaution, and finally a night-watchman was hired. The flat was remodelled in 1977 to become Rooms F, G, H and J – for small classes and tutorials – and this space is now used for offices and storage.

Another ILEA requirement was that Central hire a qualified librarian. In the days of Fogerty, the library had consisted of a few volumes of 'recitations', but since then the library had grown and shed its skin a number of times. It was first housed at 52 Hyde Park Gate, later in the foyer, and then on the third floor of the JD Wing. As Central enrolment increased and academic demands on students grew, a further temporary building had been put up behind the JD Wing in 1971–2. Joan Jeffery was hired as librarian in March 1973, given an increased operating budget by the ILEA, and by the end of that year was able to keep the library open five full days a week. By 1974, the library was (again) already too small, and Central Governors personally paid for a prefabricated hut to be erected beside the JD Wing for use as an extra reading room. Within three years, library stock had more than doubled, and shelf space was exhausted. Central would soon be under pressure from degree and course validating bodies. It was in need of a new and larger library.

• • •

1973	Fuel shortage results in three-day working week
1974	Richard Nixon is first US President to resign
	Michael Baryshnikov defects to West in Toronto
1975	National Council for Drama Training established
	Civil War in Beirut
	Fall of Saigon
1976	National Theatre moves to South Bank complex
	James Callaghan becomes Prime Minister
1977	Red Rum wins its third Grand National
	Country celebrates the Queen's Silver Jubilee year
	Elvis Presley, Maria Callas and Bing Crosby die
1978	Argentina wins World Cup at home

Coinciding with John Allen's appointment, Audrey Laski became Director of the Teacher Department in the summer of 1972. Born in 1932 and educated at Colwyn Bay Grammar School, she went to Cambridge on a scholarship and received a first in English. Before arriving at Central, she had been a teacher at the Sheffield High School for Girls, Deputy Head of Peckham Girls School, and had written three novels: *Venus in Transit*, *The Keeper* and *The Dominant Fifth*.

Laski was nothing if not unique. Even a casual observer would have to describe her as an eccentric dresser – her wardrobe included a bright yellow fake fur coat, black leather biker gear, a silver 'space look' and a surfeit of extreme accessories. Colleagues, friends and past students remember her as sharp, intellectual, concise, firm and fair. She was certainly unforgettable.

When Laski became Department Director, Central's University of London Diploma in Dramatic Art was finally discontinued after almost fifty years. This signalled a decade of change. Central's new joint three-year Certificate in Education and four-year BEd with Sidney Webb College satisfied DES requirements by allowing generous time for the education syllabus without diminishing the excellence of Central's drama specialisation. However, almost immediately Sidney Webb entered negotiations with the Polytechnic of Central London (PCL), and these discussions eventually led to Sidney Webb's annexation to PCL as a constituent School of Education. Central quickly had to decide if it would continue its joint accreditation with Sidney Webb through the University of London Institute of Education (and risk annexation of its course by PCL) or apply for separate accreditation from the CNAA.

Meanwhile, Laski developed a new BEd – one that students could take starting from their first year, rather than only being able to opt in for a fourth year after acquiring their three-year Certificate. As the new BEd took shape, it became apparent it wasn't viable for students sitting for a three-year Certificate to be taught in the same classes as those studying for a four-year degree, so in January 1975, Central announced that the three-year Certificate would be phased out. That next September, the three-year Central Certificate with Sydney Webb became validated as a four-year Council of National Academic Awards (CNAA) degree.

After all this, by September 1976 there was widespread anxiety about the future of all teacher training. The DES wanted to limit the numbers of teachers by reducing candidates at entry level, and therefore, the ILEA required a reduction in enrolment for the Sidney Webb/Central Joint BEd. The threat of further cuts to the budget was implicit. As a result, the intake for Central's Teacher Course was lowered from 27 in 1975 to 25 in 1976. In 1977, enrolment was reduced to 20. Staffing was reduced accordingly.

Undeterred, Laski went ahead with a proposal to the CNAA for the new four-year BEd in conjunction with Sidney Webb, which was now a part of the Polytechnic of Central London (PCL). Early in 1977, a CNAA panel visited the School. In preparation for the inspection, the medical room was checked to see that the number of medical boxes was sufficient, the saw in the workshop was ordered to remain quiet, and no frying was allowed in the canteen. These precautions seem to have worked, and with only minor amendments, the CNAA panel validated this new joint four-year BEd with Sidney Webb to start in 1977.

VIVIENNE 'VINKI' GREY
STAGE '31

The small ex-library off the foyer became the office of the Stage Course secretary, Vinki Grey. To those who knew her when they were students, Mrs Grey had always seemed ancient, and the 'story in the foyer' was that she had once been Samuel Beckett's lover. (It seems she merely went to school with him when they were very, very young – but perhaps they held hands?) As Vivienne Grey, she trained on the acting course at Central in the same class as Ishbel Fox. She later appeared in *Cavalcade* in the West End and played in repertory theatres across England. Through her work in Scotland for the Wilson Barrett and Brandon Thomas Repertory Company, Grey soon became the worldwide licensing secretary for Brandon Thomas's 1892 comedy, *Charley's Aunt*. Grey returned to Central in the early 1960s, and worked in her little office off the foyer for almost twenty years.

Laski next opened discussions with the Polytechnic of North London (PNL), and submitted a proposal to the CNAA for a joint four-year course with them to start in September 1978. Confusingly, by 1978 the third-year students were working on a three-year Certificate with the Sidney Webb School (PCL), the second-year students were working on the new four-year BEd degree with the Sidney Webb School (PCL), and the first-year students were working on a revised four-year BEd degree with the Polytechnic of North London (PNL). Between 1972 and 1978, pressure on the Teacher Department for these course validations was considerable, but they were not the only strain on the Department.

The Regional Advisory Council (RAC) had approved Central's application to start a new three-year Advanced Course in 1974, which would be run along the lines of the ACSD course but only be part-time – and therefore take three years to complete. David Herbert was appointed to run both the new three-year part-time course and the existing one-year full-time ACSD in 1975.

In 1974, negotiations had also begun with Westfield College to offer a joint BA in Languages and Drama. Drama degree courses were growing in popularity, and the Drama and the Modern Languages Departments at Westfield wanted to establish both a separate degree in drama as well as a three-year degree offering drama jointly with a language. They wanted Central's expertise to add the practical element to these courses. Voice classes would provide the practical and theoretical study of the basis of speech; movement work would include a practical approach for the study of texts in terms of theatrical realisation; acting study would involve practical work on scenes, and an investigation of actor-audience relationships; Theatrical Representation would allow study of theatrical conditions in different historical periods; and all four areas would be integrated with each other and with the selection of plays chosen for study by Westfield. Plans for the Westfield Joint Honours Degree in Drama and a Language (University of London degree) were completed and approved in 1975, and in early 1976, recruitment for the first 12 students began.

• • •

While the changes in education during this period were indeed frantic, the world of speech therapy was also far from calm. From 1969 to 1972, Lord Randolph Quirk, a renowned linguist and expert on the English language, had led a government Committee of Inquiry into Speech Therapy Services. The 1972 Quirk Report formed the cornerstone of the UK's speech therapy services, and among other things, it emphasised that for speech therapy to survive, the profession first had to establish 'academic distinction' – in other words, a degree. Secondly, it would have to increase the number of students studying the subject. Over the next few years, compliance with Quirk's suggestions would involve Central's Speech Therapy Department in a great deal of additional work and require a full-time Director.

Jennifer Warner had trained at Central and joined the staff as a lecturer in Speech Pathology in 1960. She had taken over as part-time Director of the Speech Therapy Course from Margaret Greene in 1969, but with the impending increase in administrative work, it was apparent that the traditionally part-time Director's position would ultimately require a full-time commitment. With a thriving private practice to consider, Warner resigned as Director in the summer of 1973, though she would later return on a part-time teaching basis. As the ILEA now funded Central staff salaries, it was possible to appoint a full-time Director of the Speech Therapy Department for the first time. Elaine Hodkinson remembers: 'When John Allen phoned to tell me that I'd got the post, he told me he was keen to have someone who understood drama, who was interested in what the Stage Course was about. That was significant. I'd always worked as a clinician, but with my background in drama, I fitted in with the drama side. John encouraged the "three-legged stool" – the three departments were a professional trio. There was never any dispute or acrimony between departments. They always worked well together and supported and understood each other's work and needs.'

Hodkinson had trained as an actress at the Royal Welsh College of Music and Drama, and her educational drama work there with handicapped children led her to train in Speech Therapy at the Oldrey Fleming College in London. She later worked as a specialist in voice disorders at the National Hospital for Nervous Diseases, the Whittington Hospital and the Royal National Ear, Nose and Throat Hospital, the New End and the Royal Northern Hospitals. Throughout her career, she worked with an extensive range of patients in Paediatrics; Neurology and Neurosurgery; Geriatrics; and Ear, Nose and Throat. She had been a clinical lecturer at Oldrey Fleming, had supervised students in clinics, and had taught part-time at Central since 1972. She would now lead Central's Speech Therapy Department towards its first degree.

As universities began to offer degrees in Speech Therapy, it became clear that Central could only compete if it, too, developed a BSc. It was impossible to predict if employers would give preference to degree-holding graduates over diploma-holders (comparisons would not be relevant until Colleges started producing more graduates), but it was a reality that speech therapy students on diploma courses such as Central's could still only obtain discretionary grants from their Local Education Authority (LEA). To attract students and help guarantee LEA grants, Central needed to develop the three-year Diploma of the Licentiateship of the College of Speech Therapists (LCST) into a three-year (and later a four-year Honours) BSc. Whether it would develop through the CNAA or the London University was still in question.

In 1973, Hodkinson met with the ILEA-aided Polytechnic of Central London (PCL) to develop a programme to submit to the CNAA, and in 1974, the three London schools offering speech therapy (Central, Chelsea College and University College) met with a validation committee from London University to discuss a degree in Speech Sciences. London University was reluctant to form further relationships with other institutions and difficulties arose over the registration of external students for a university course. In 1975, the University rejected a BSc Speech Sciences degree, but indicated that it would be open to further discussions in the future.

Meanwhile, at the urging of the DES and the ILEA, the Speech Therapy Department's September 1975 intake increased from 20 to 30 students, and even though preference was often given to Central for clinical spaces, it became more difficult to find practical placements for students. Then, in 1976, the CST introduced a new and more demanding syllabus. As a result, even when the Area Speech Therapist, Lena Rustin (Speech Therapy '50), arranged a full-time clinic for the Central students in the Borough of Camden, the academic strain on students and staff meant practical clinic visits had to be kept to a minimum. During this time, Central continued to pursue London University about a possible Speech Therapy degree course, at the same time as pushing forward with PCL and PNL for a first stage degree submission to the CNAA.

• • •

Just as the Quirk Report had impacted on speech therapy provision, external forces now also influenced the Stage Course. In 1971, British Actors' Equity agreed new rules with the Theatre Managers' Association and Repertory Theatres that set an annual national entry limit of thirty new members. Each July, the Directors of the three Departments at Central had always proudly reported to the Governors on the employment status of their recent graduates. In the summer of 1964, George Hall's report to the Governors had recounted 21 out of 23 students with jobs – within weeks of finishing the course. In July 1971, he reported only 12 of 17 men and three of 12 women with work, and in June 1973 he pointed out to the Governors that due to Equity's restricted membership quota, it was becoming more and more difficult for actors to obtain their first jobs. Chairman of the Board, Norman Collins, agreed to meet with the Principals of RADA, LAMDA and Central and to take this issue up with Equity. Early in 1974, the Conference of Drama Schools decided to lobby the Council of Equity on their policy of restricted entry, but by 1978, only one third of all Stage students had work by the autumn after leaving. A decade later, Stage Course success became calculated by how many graduates had agents.

Another significant event to impact on the Stage Course occurred in 1971. The Gulbenkian Foundation set up a committee of inquiry into training for the theatre and the economics of drama schools, and their resulting report – *Going on the Stage, A Report to the Calouste Foundation on Professional Training for Drama* – came out strongly in favour of drama schools being the best method of training for the professional theatre. The report not only urged both Equity and Theatrical Managers to take more responsibility for actor training, but also concluded that the DES and LEAs should provide more funding for this training. When the committee's report was published, the CNAA waded into the discussion, saying they might be 'interested' in offering a BA degree to acting students if the DES would support training more generously.

Central staff immediately, and robustly, voiced the conviction that it would be improper for the CNAA to be involved in training actors. Allen, who had been a member of the Gulbenkian committee, agreed. He told the Academic Board in March 1974 that, while the Teacher and Speech Therapy Courses were developing in the direction of degrees, he was anxious that the School generally should not become degree dominated, and he thought it essential that the Stage and Technical Courses not be tied to rigid academic standards. Central should maintain its policy of accepting Theatre Department students without laying down academic requirements.

In 1976, largely as a result of the 1974 Gulbenkian Inquiry, the National Council for Drama Training (NCDT) was established to give voice to its constituent member drama schools. The next year, Allen and the Principals of LAMDA, RADA and the Webber Douglas Academy of Dramatic Art, and the Vice Principal of Rose Bruford College wrote a letter to *The Times* about the inequity of discretionary awards for non-degree courses:

> Traditional concepts of university education leading to non-vocational degrees are as valid as ever, but there is support of degree courses with mandatory grants against discretionary awards that are widely associated with vocational courses.
>
> Why should learning to study the plays of Shakespeare and to write about them critically be considered an educational activity more worthy of official support than learning to stage the plays of Shakespeare and to recreate them artistically? The one activity subsumes the other. The actor does not put his mind to bed when he acts King Lear: the English graduate does not suppress affective impulses when he studies the play.
>
> We do not oppose the degree course in English studies or in fine arts: we question the favoured position of degree courses in general and the devaluation of so-called vocational, practical and non-academic courses.

In 1978, an Accreditation Panel was set up within the National Council for Drama Training (NCDT) that consisted of theatre managers, agents, actors and others with experience in drama. Its aim was to set standards and take responsibility for accrediting drama schools, and they hoped this could assure student grants for all successful applicants. John Allen was appointed Chairman.

External pressures also brought about another significant change to the Stage Course during this period. There are no records of how many Afro-Asian students had trained at Central, but that number was surely very low in the early years of the School. In 1975, a paragraph in the *Guardian*'s 'London Diary' was devoted to what was then Central's policy of offering 'coloured actors' a seven-term, not a nine-term, training – due to the restricted number of parts in public shows for Afro-Asian characters. Possibly in response to this criticism – and certainly not before time – Central concluded that in future it would be possible to offer more scope to such students and invited them to remain for the full nine terms.

• • •

For the first two years of the Central/ILEA partnership, there were benefits to Central that must have seemed like winning the lottery. Each year the ILEA awarded the School a more and more generous Block Grant budget. In addition to budgetary abundance, from the very beginning of the grant-aided relationship, the ILEA was keen to include Central in its building programme. To assist with planning, they asked the Directors of Departments to identify space requirements based on the organisation of the courses and the projected student numbers for the next five years. As a result, in 1972 on Central's behalf the ILEA requested a grant for £50,000 from the DES. In July 1974, a £30,000 grant was awarded, and Central went ahead with long-overdue improvements to Embassy Theatre electrics, lighting and sound. Additionally, an ILEA student medical service at St Katherine's House, Albany Street, became available to Central students from the summer of 1973. Affordable living accommodation for new students had always been a concern to the Governors, and in 1974 the ILEA decided to buy a house for use as a student hostel, and a search for suitable accommodation began. Repairs were undertaken on the JD Wing, but the safety rule remained in force: 'no strenuous activity in classrooms allowed'.

Most importantly, since 1956 the School had been trying to gain title to the site surrounding the Eton College-owned Embassy Theatre. In February 1974, as part of the Swiss Cottage Development Scheme, Camden Council agreed to give the School 11,000 square feet of land running from Buckland Crescent to Eton Avenue. This piece of land would become known as the 'Bank Site', named after a branch of the National Westminster Bank that was erected there as a temporary building. The Council also agreed to grant permission for a four-storey building to provide 44,000 square feet of classroom, studio and office accommodation. Negotiations were opened to agree terms. Spirits were high.

Then, just when it looked as though Central was finally going to get the space it needed, the government announced national cuts in educational building programmes. By September 1974, the ILEA could offer no money for expansion, and plans to build on the Bank Site were postponed indefinitely. ILEA plans for the purchase of a student hostel were dismissed – instead, a handbook was printed with the phone numbers of rental agents.

Gradually, Central began to see cutbacks in all areas. In 1974, the ILEA issued instructions that the School should make certain economies. Company Secretary Neil Gibson asked staff to see that the heat did not go above 63°F and when classrooms were vacated, please, please, turn off the lights. Cuts would not affect salaries or repairs to the buildings, but in response to the serious financial state of the country, the ILEA immediately cut 6½ % on postage, stationery, telephone and office expenses. Cuts would increase to 10% by the next year. In early 1975, heating hours were reduced by an hour a day, from 7:30 am to 9:30 pm. Gibson instructed staff that in future all stationery had to be requisitioned from the Assistant Registrar, and discretion was to be exercised in the use of headed paper and envelopes. In a throwback to the days of Thurb and Sarge, scrap paper was to be used whenever possible. All mail was to be sent second class, and staff were reminded that a short phone call was cheaper than sending a letter. There was to be 'no electricity wastage'. Staff were again asked to *please* remember, 'Turn off the lights!' The Central/ILEA financial honeymoon was officially over.

In the beginning, the ILEA had provided a direct budget to each Department Director – now more often referred to as the 'Head' of a Department. Heads of Departments had full discretion to move money from one budget heading to another, as long as they didn't spend more (or strangely, less) than they had been allotted. George Hall watched the situation worsen over the next decade: 'Accounting became bureaucratic, and you weren't allowed to switch things from one heading to another. If you saved £500 on production costs, you weren't allowed to spend it on teaching, and if someone wasn't able to turn up for two weeks to teach fights, you couldn't say, "Good – I can hire another wig." I was always sure that with more freedom I could have made the money go further.'

Along with concern over budget cutbacks, the Governors became worried that if no building were erected on the Bank Site, however temporary, Camden Council might withdraw their consent for Central to use this space. In spite of this, owing to lack of funds the ILEA turned down a proposal to erect a temporary building for use as a Speech Therapy clinic.

ILEA cutbacks were causing general frustration, but the space limitations were

> ### KAREN (BRADLEY) HAMMOND TECHNICAL '75
>
> **"** I remember queuing for lunches at Gerry and Marianne's canteen with my then boyfriend, Richard Walker, and his best mate, Kevin Whately. They kept us all amused doing their 'finger in the ear singing'. Carrie Fisher arrived on the Acting Course whilst I was there and used to float into the canteen in billowing chiffon outfits, continually smoking very long American cigarettes and drinking Cola-Cola straight out of the glass bottle. This was totally bizarre in the mid-'70s. We all used to watch bemused, and in awe of her. Then she used to finish the day and be collected by her chauffeur to go back to The Dorchester where she stayed whilst at Central. She didn't complete the course, as she left to do *Star Wars*. **"**

now more serious than ever. Central was being forced to expand its courses to become degrees, and yet was being severely limited by the space available to teach these courses. With building projects curtailed, Central had to hire more outside accommodation for classes and rehearsals. In 1975, enrolment for the School stood at 296. Present classroom accommodation was considered by the CNAA as inadequate for degree course requirements, and both the Teacher and Speech Therapy Departments stressed to the Governors that if their degree applications to the CNAA were to be successful, they needed to show evidence of more tutorial space and small seminar rooms. The Stage Department was placing greater demands on Studio Two, and more Stage productions also meant that ACSD use of the dressing room in Studio Two was now untenable. Audio Visual Aids had extended to take over the other basement room. Additional room was required for Technical students' lockers. Storage space under Studio One on Buckland Crescent was cleared for use as a teaching space, and the Lecture Theatre, previously the Upper Circle of the Embassy Theatre, was converted into a multi-purpose teaching area by levelling the raked floor, and creating two teaching rooms.

Studio Two on Eton Avenue had long been considered only a temporary building so, by way of a replacement, the DES indicated in September 1975 that it would be willing

tnnt
nubr 17

ENRLBK

to build a new studio on the triangular site next to the Embassy. Although it wouldn't be as grand as the four-storey 44,000 square feet promised by the ILEA for the Bank Site, Central jumped at the chance of any new facility. The £250,000 purchase of the triangular site from the Greater London Council (GLC) was tediously slow, but by November 1976, the GLC had allocated the land for educational use. The GLC/ILEA architects took staff suggestions, the Camden Officers accepted the plans, and permission to begin work on the new £87,200 studio was granted in January 1977. Meanwhile, the School would continue to use Studio Two until the end of 1977–8. George Hall proposed the new theatre be called the Embassy Studio, and the official Opening, attended by HRH Princess Alexandra took place on 21 November 1978. Six students from Stage '79, directed by Hall, presented their revue, *Take Six*, and Governors, members of the ILEA, Officers of Camden, student representatives and staff attended a post-show reception held in Room D.

• • •

After ten years as Assistant Registrar and Company Secretary, Neil Gibson retired in March 1977 at the age of 65. In 1933–4, Gibson had studied at the Embassy School of Acting under Eileen Thorndike and had worked as an actor (West End, television and rep), a director (rep and tours) and a teacher (Corona, university and adult education). This was certainly not a background that made him an obvious choice for his job at Central. He spoke French and Spanish, could fence and ride horses, and could do a cockney and a Welsh accent. None of these talents marked him as the perfect person to hound staff to turn off lights and use scrap paper. However, he had been a good choice for the School at a time when it needed someone who 'understood'. When the ILEA notified Central it was now large enough to warrant a Vice Principal, John Allen suggested Gibson be upgraded to this position from January until his retirement in March 1977. Along with Gibson's promotion to Vice Principal came a reorganisation of the Company Secretary's job to separate finance and administration. Eric Newsome had taken over from Anne Herbert as Registrar in 1976, and when Gibson retired, Newsome was appointed Administrative Officer. This new position combined the duties of Registrar of Academics with the administrative duties of the Company Secretary. Frederick Wentworth-Bowyer was appointed Company Secretary (financial) and Finance Officer from April 1977.

• • •

While Central's educational and financial politics continued behind the scenes, Gerry and Marianne Romaine fed the students. Their café on the opposite side of Finchley Road had been a student favourite since Central arrived at the Embassy Theatre in 1957, and when the Swiss Cottage Road alterations came about in 1961, the Romaines took over catering at Central. Marianne ran the small coffee bar off the foyer, which offered tea and coffee, snacks and cold food from 9 am to 5 pm – and when Stage students left at the

ANDREW VISNEVSKI STAGE '76

❝ It had all been going so well. The end of my second year on the Acting Course was approaching. We'd finished our colourful spring collaboration with the Wimbledon School of Design and had worn fabulous, although sometimes impractical costumes; our struggles with the complexities of *The Winter's Tale* for the third term showings were also over. My wish to assimilate culturally was being realised and I could see myself as an English actor-in-the-making, I was happy in the training, had made friends for life and had experienced my first love affair (pretending to hide the love bites by wearing a flimsy silk scarf round my neck) and its dissolution.

However, at the interview with the full panel of staff, like a bolt out of the blue came the suggestion that I should perhaps consider leaving the course and was there anything else I was planning to do? I had been deemed 'stylistically incompatible' by general consensus. I thought I had entered a nightmare: anything else I was planning to do? For four years I had longed to return to London and train for the British Theatre and I had journeyed across Europe and stuck it out in foreign universities to be able to do so, not to mention selling grilled hamburgers and fried chicken and chips at Mother Kelly's on the Finchley Road during night shifts! My world collapsed – I could not belong…

I doggedly returned to stay out my third year at Central. Miracle of miracles, I could not have been happier: the casting I was given was very wisely chosen by George Hall, ranging from Humpage in John Whiting's *Penny For A Song*, sitting up in a tree with a copper pot on my head and bell in hand awaiting Napoleon's invasion, to the calculating policeman Shauva in David Terence's revolutionary production of Brecht's *The Caucasian Chalk Circle*, designed by Clare Jeffery. Oddballs? Yes, but so very rewarding. And allowing me to find my own voice in the theatre. George and his team could not miss my cultural 'otherness', but had the courage to make me aware of it and to teach me how to own it. I realised that perhaps it was not a tragedy to be different – to be a 'pepper in a can of beans' as one friend described it… It did not make life any easier, but I suspect that the 'stylistic incompatibility', so painful to me when it was pointed out, has been the sole reason for whatever success I may have achieved in the thirty years since receiving my Diploma. **❞**

end of their training, it became a rite of passage to present Marianne with their photo to hang on the coffee bar walls. Gerry ran the canteen upstairs, serving hot food from noon to 2 pm. In the spring of 1973, students complained to the School's management, demanding a more varied menu and more fresh food. When this was brought up with Gerry, he raised his objections and no more was said. The Governors recognised that, should the Romaines resign, Central would have to run the catering itself, and this would present significant difficulties. For the time being, the meals remained unchanged. In 1976, however, the Romaines' relationship with Central was reorganised, and they were hired directly by the School. At the end of each month they submitted their accounts, and Central made up any deficits – which meant that from that time, the School became responsible for the menu. Complaints, of course, continued. In 1976, a student coffee bar in the upstairs canteen was opened between 5 and 7 pm weekdays. Originally run by Marianne's assistant, Peggy, this was soon taken over by the Student Union, who also ran a coffee bar on show nights.

Gerry Romaine, School caterer for 27 years, is still remembered for his dry humour and his love of the greyhounds he raced each weekend – Russell Keith Grant (Stage '80) gave perhaps the most profound advice to first-year students, Stage '81: 'Never eat Gerry's mince on a Monday.' Gerry died on 25 December 1988, leaving his wife, the colourful Marianne. Marianne is fondly remembered by generations of students for her occasional mangling of the English language, and only years later did anyone think to question whether her malapropisms were the fruit of her tenuous grasp of English or of her brutal sense of humour.

● ● ●

In 1975, to conform to ILEA rulings, the Governors passed a resolution that all staff and administrators had to retire at 65, though they could be temporarily re-engaged each term until the age of 70. This, of course, included the Principal. Governors could serve until the age of 70, but would have to be re-elected annually after that.

Early in 1977, the Governors were notified that Principal John Allen would be 65 in March. Allen consented to stay through 1977–8, and the Governors agreed that during this year he would also undertake an assignment for the Council of Europe to survey the state of drama across the continent, looking into the state support for theatre in certain Common Market countries. Five years later saw the publication of Allen's book, A History of the Theatre in Europe. He was awarded an OBE in 1978, and though retired from Central, continued to lecture on Theatre History at Westfield College for the next five years.

In 1978, the Governors and the ILEA Education Committee approved the appointment of George Kitson to the post of Principal.

● ● ●

ADDITIONAL CENTRAL FACTS

1972 • The Academic Board addresses the problem of publicity, and for the first time, Clare Jeffery and David Lewis designed posters to be displayed in front of the Embassy and on the walls by the two Studios.

1973–4 • George Hall presents the first two late-night shows, *Afters* and *Buckshot and Bows*.

1974 • July: Anne Herbert replaces Jenepher Hawkins as Registrar.

  • John Allen suggests that the Board of Governors should include more members from Speech Therapy and the professional theatre.

1975 • Clive Brook bequeaths £1000 to the Central School.

  • The DES increases fees for the Teacher Course to £140 per year (£340 overseas students) and to £100 per year for all other courses (£320 overseas students). All students under the age of 18 are trained for free.

  • January: The Student Union is granted an extension to 2 am for parties, if they promise to play only quiet music after midnight and warn Central's neighbours in advance.

  • December: June Wooldridge leaves the Technical Course staff.

1976 • Julia Wilson-Dickson, daughter of Livvy Wilson-Dickson (Olive Rudder, Stage '32), joins the voice staff on a part-time basis.

  • Dame Edith Evans dies on 14 October. A Central Governor since 1954, she had been made Vice President in 1961.

15

1978–1987

GEORGE KITSON WAS BORN on 18 May 1922 and educated at the Royal Belfast Academic Institute. He came to England at 18, joined the RAF as a navigator, and after the war, graduated and received a postgraduate degree in child development from the University of London. After teaching at a number of schools, including Dartington Hall in 1949–50 (when Ballet Joos and Laban were in residence), he went into teacher training and was made Principal at Man College, Northampton. After becoming Vice Principal at the Philippa Fawcet and Furzedown College in Streatham, he was in charge when the college closed due to the widespread cuts in government funds for teacher training. His next college was closed by the same cuts, and as Kitson said later, 'After having closed down two colleges, you can imagine what they thought when I arrived at Central!'

Kitson remembered those early days at Central: 'The financial situation was healthy, but the whole thing was still rather haphazard. When I arrived, visiting lecturers were paid over the counter. They just went up and said how many hours they'd done, and were handed cash.'

In 1978, Teacher-students Jennifer Saunders and Gill Hudspith interviewed Kitson for an autumn 1978 student newspaper:

JENNY Is it difficult working in a smaller, more specialised college?

GEORGE …It may not be quite so difficult in another smaller college, but this one is quite unique because it's deeply rooted in tradition… It's all a bit hazy and one has to pick up the nuances and the qualitative aspect of the whole thing rather than the more detailed organization. Things aren't on the surface as you find in a highly organised college. There are a lot of things that aren't said, and much of the organisation is assumed and you can't really anticipate anything because it's something completely different.

JENNY How do you see your role as Principal?

GEORGE This kind of community, whether it's concerned with education or not, involves people; and I think that unless individuals are able to interact effectively, the thing breaks down. Maybe I would look upon it as a major part of my role to try and clear any blocks in the relationship, blocks in communication – facilitating the opportunities that people feel they should gain from an experience of this kind.

JENNY Do you intend, or would you like, to take some classes with students?

GEORGE I have taken one or two already. I've spent my life in teacher education. When I was in Leicester I worked within the Leicester Institute of Education at the University and I contributed there in the field of Social Psychology, group dynamics and so forth. That may not be quite so necessary in this kind of college, but one can contribute there in the Education Department. I've also worked with a Speech Therapy course in Leicester, so there's an area there within child psychology – child development – where I might be able to contribute. Perhaps, if someone got terribly excited about Irish Drama I might be able to contribute in that way, but my field is rather limited. Maybe one day someone might ask me to produce a play, which would excite me enormously; but I would be very hesitant because there are so many professional, and excellent, producers around.

JENNY Are there any things in Central that you would like to see changed?

GEORGE …I think really one can only underline those things already known, and that is the lack of space in these awful buildings. But in a way, if you give people more space, in some ways you could affect the whole atmosphere of the place. Some of the charm of Central is that people have great difficulty in finding space to work, and they are thrown together. I think space would allow more development and more interaction, but it would destroy the particular atmosphere that is here.

GILL Do you feel the lack of interaction between Departments?

GEORGE I think it's quite out of character to create artificial links. There are many natural growing points where links could be made, and I'm sure nothing but good could come of them. With much less timetable pressure in the future – should the new buildings come about – then this will be more possible.

JENNY Do you think small specialist colleges like Central have a future? Or will they have to adapt to fit in with larger institutions?

GEORGE I think they have a great future – the value of this small type of college (and it isn't a mono-technic, it's a polytechnic with a number of courses, isn't it) – there is a place for this kind of intimate establishment where relationships are important. After all, the whole of the four areas we work within depend on the development of good relationships. The bigger the institution, the more anonymous one becomes.'

As had his predecessors, Kitson had identified the lack of student, staff and administrative space as his immediate challenge. However, where he was prophetic was in his recognition

1978 Jonestown massacre in Guyana
First test tube baby born

1979 Unofficial strikes in protest against 5% pay rise limit disrupt the country
Margaret Thatcher becomes Prime Minister
Comedy Store opens in West End

1980 SAS storm Iranian Embassy in London and rescue 19 surviving hostages
Reagan defeats Carter to become US President

1981 Prince Charles and Lady Diana Spencer marry
Summer riots occur in cities across Britain
First London International Festival of Theatre (LIFT)
Greenham Common Peace Camp forms

1982 Argentina invades Falkland Islands
Israel invades Lebanon
Channel Four is launched

1983 14-mile human chain of protest at Greenham Common
Margaret Thatcher is re-elected

1984 AIDS virus is discovered
Miners Strike
IRA bombs Tory Conference in Brighton
National Theatre Studio founded
British and American Equity enter 'exchange' agreement

1985 Gorbachev becomes Soviet leader
Over forty soccer fans die in Bradford City football ground fire
Greater London Council abolished

1986 Challenger Space Shuttle explodes on take-off
Chernobyl nuclear reactor goes into meltdown

1987 Andy Warhol dies during an operation
British Theatre Museum opens

that an expansion of Central's premises would lead to the alteration of Central's atmosphere.

• • •

Central enrolment had dropped from its high of 296 full-time students in 1975 to only 273 in 1978, and the ILEA pressured Central to accept more students. For a number of years, the variety of courses offered by Central had changed very little, and in the spring of 1980, Kitson encouraged Margaret Braund to develop a new one-year full-time Postgraduate Specialist Advanced Diploma in Voice (ADVS).

Braund (Teacher '43) had been associated with Central since she had won a Pivot Scholarship in 1940, and she was now on the staff of the Teacher Department. She brought in Cis Berry and Sally Grace to help formulate a structure and advise on what might be required for a new one-year course to teach voice and 'work in areas where effective verbal communication is important'. When the Regional Advisory Committee (RAC) of the DES turned down an initial proposal with a suggestion that the course run part-time, Braund urged the Principal to re-apply. In the autumn of 1980, the RAC finally recognised the unique character of the course, but when a proposal was submitted to the CNAA, they could not be persuaded to approve the course as a degree. In spite of this, in 1982 Central went ahead with the Advanced Diploma in Voice Studies (ADVS) Course as an internal award. The ADVS Course would not be awarded degree status for another decade.

During the 1970s, the Stage Course changed little, and the staff remained fairly constant. George Hall remained Director and principal lecturer. Barbara Caister, who had assisted and then taken over from Litz Pisk in 1970, taught movement and related courses. In 1972, Alan Marston was brought in to teach movement part-time on all courses. Jane Cowell, Bardy Thomas, and Julia Wilson-Dickson (all Central graduates), and Geraldine Alford (who had taught at the Old Vic School with Saint-Denis) taught voice and related subjects. John Jones (Stage '63), Lyall Watson and David Terence taught acting and were staff directors. Bill Hobbs (Stage '59) taught fencing; B H Barry taught stage fighting. Karen Rabinovitz taught tap and jazz, which was added to the curriculum in 1976.

During the 1970s, alterations on the Technical Course were more profound. Changes in key positions included the retirement of Frank Gearing in 1978, who was replaced by Douglas Cornelissen. When Peter Streuli retired in 1981 after

> ## CENTRAL NAME CHANGE
>
> At a Governors' Meeting in November 1929, it had been suggested that The Central School of Speech-Training and Dramatic Art become known as The Central School of Speech and Drama. Someone promised to look into it. In July 1952, it was again suggested the name be changed, but the decision was taken to first use up the stocks of printed letterheads and envelopes. Generally, though not officially, from that time the School took on its new moniker. Then, in April 1978, the Governors resolved that the name of the School finally and *officially* be changed, and the Department of Trade agreed to the 'new' name: The Central School of Speech and Drama.

21 years at Central (18 of those as principal lecturer and Director of the Technical Course), Douglas Cornelissen was made Head of the course. Late in the 1970s, believing stage managers to be in need of an official body to look after training standards, Kitson was instrumental in persuading the National Council for Drama Training (NCDT) to incorporate stage management. The NCDT accredited the Technical Course in 1982. Kitson also saw the need for a stage management qualification, and in the spring of 1980, Cornelissen submitted a syllabus to the Technical Education Council (TEC). The TEC approved a 1982 start, and the first stage managers to receive a B/TEC (Business/Technical Education Council) Higher Diploma left in summer 1984. TEC immediately validated the course for a further three years.

Teacher Department staff had remained fairly constant for the first years of Audrey Laski's directorship. Margaret Braund, Christine Hearne, David Herbert, John Roberts, Alan Allkins, Gerard Benson, Simon Cooper, David Lewis, Helen Wynter and Joan Washington all taught either full- or part-time. Clare Jeffery moved from the Theatre Department to the Teacher Department in 1978, and David Lewis joined the Theatre Department from the Teacher Department in 1979.

However, if the Teacher Department staff remained constant, the course surely didn't. The 1970s had seen a tangle of degree proposals and CNAA validation applications for Central and its two partners – Sidney Webb (at PCL) and the Polytechnic of North London (PNL). During her entire tenure, Laski juggled one-year, three-year, four-year and Honours degree validations. In 1978, an application for the Central/PNL joint BEd

AIMEE BIRD TRAVASSOS-VALDEZ

In 1962, Aimee 'Birdie' Valdez came to Central as Housekeeper and Box Office Manager.

66 When I was first there, they had all the shows in the afternoon. Sarge and Thurb brought their clothes from home and would go up and change, then go down to greet the agents. When it went to evening shows, they would do the same thing. I started making the agents coffee and sandwiches, because they'd have come directly from work, so relationships evolved.

There were poster showcases outside the theatre, and we had two boards made to put posters along the fence. A lot of the shops put posters up. When George [Hall] was there, we had more people than could ever get in. There were lines of people. **99**

Birdie Valdez retired as full-time Housekeeper in 1980, and continued as part-time Box Office Manager until 1983.

to become an Honours degree was pending approval from the CNAA, but without expanded library facilities, administration, teaching and study space, the CNAA was unwilling to approve this latest application. The BEd Honours degree would not go ahead until 1982.

The Speech Therapy Department also went through changes in the 1970s. When Elaine Hodkinson became full-time Department Director in 1973, the three-year Speech Therapy Course prepared students for examination for the Licentiateship of the College of Speech Therapists. As a result, examination requirements dictated course provision. Hodkinson, Carol Miller, Renata Whurr, Jessica Coles and 17 other part-time and visiting lecturers taught: Anatomy and Physiology; Child Development; Human Communication; Acoustic, Physiological and Psychological Aspects of Speech; Language and Voice; Phonetics; Psychology; Disorders of Articulation and Language in Childhood; Audiology; Paediatrics; Disorders of Voice and Fluency in Childhood – and Learning Disorders and Education; Psychology and Psychological Medicine; Neurology; Laryngology; Disorders of Voice, Articulation, and Language in Adults; Disorders of Articulation and Language in Children associated with neurological and emotional problems; and Social Studies. Staff from other departments at Central taught additional subjects, which included classes in movement and voice. Throughout their training, speech therapy students regularly visited clinics for observation and treatment of patients.

From 1975 to 1978, Carol Miller acted as assistant to Hodkinson, and two new part-time staff members were also hired. In 1976, four new part-time staff were added. By 1977, there were also two psychologists on the full-time staff (John Allen, Hazel Dewart), plus nine part-time staff and nineteen visiting lecturers. In 1978, Kay Coombes, Helen Wynter (phonetics) and Andrew Spencer (linguistics) became full-time lecturers, and in 1979, six new part-time and visiting lecturer positions were added. Hodkinson remembers: 'We ended up with ten full-time staff by the time I left [in 1988], so we were expensive.

Pressure was put on us by the validating bodies – the RCSLT, the CNAA and PCL – for a full-time phonetician, which changed the balance of the degree from therapy. We became expensive because we developed into a degree.'

Hodkinson had been exploring various avenues for a Speech Therapy degree with a range of partners since 1973, but whomever it partnered with, Central could not gain CNAA degree approval without first gaining approval for the course from the College of Speech Therapists (CST). In the autumn of 1979, Central and PCL submitted a joint Speech Therapy degree application to the CST. When the CST expressed concern that there were too few staff, more full- and part-time lecturers were hired immediately. However, there was a more difficult complaint to address, and it had been heard before. It had affected Central's applications for both the ADVS and the BEd Honours degrees – the School's deficiency in accommodation. Unless Central could guarantee this problem would be solved by the start of the new Speech Therapy degree in 1981, the CST would not support the planned application to the CNAA.

DAVID BECKWITH-MACY
STAGE '79

❝ One of my more vivid memories of Central involves John Jones, who apparently decided that, as an American, I needed some Method-style assistance in a key scene of *Camino Real*. My character was being arrested by a couple of Mexican cops and John directed us to struggle briefly, then I was to run offstage. Not just offstage, but out into the foyer, past the café, up the stairs and into the balcony, where the cops would beat me senseless and drag me back down to the stage. We blocked the scene and then ran it. John said, 'Yes, well. Almost. Do it again.' So we did: offstage, up the stairs, into the balcony, beating, and back down to the stage. John said, 'Very nearly very nice. Do it again.' And we did, over and over and over and over, until John finally said, 'OK, good. That's fine.' The cops were soaked in sweat and I think I lost ten pounds that rehearsal. I sometimes tell this story to a cast if they start complaining about a 'hard' rehearsal. They usually get the message: get to work or I'll go 'John Jones' on you!**❞**

The problem Central faced was both complicated and simple: to gain CNAA approval for the proposed 1981 Speech Therapy BSc, the 1982 BEd (Hons), and for the 1982 postgraduate ADVS, Central needed more classrooms, library/study space and administrative offices. Central's existing facilities had been mended and rebuilt and mended again. Cracks in the outside theatre walls had been patched, and load was reduced on the theatre's lighting rig to protect the precarious roof, but a recent architectural survey of the Embassy Theatre had projected its life span at only 30 years. Students and alumni might have seen a certain 'charm' in the run-down, threadbare nature of the buildings, but the CNAA did not agree.

In spite of this urgent need for more accommodation, the ILEA suspended plans for the construction of any additional permanent buildings, and instead offered an alternative solution: keep the School together but split the Courses amongst two or more different sites. Chairman Norman Collins and George Kitson requested a meeting with the ILEA to put Central's case: without new building *on site*, the pending CNAA validation proposals would fail, and without an increase in students resulting from these new courses, the current budget could not keep Central alive. Grudgingly (but immediately) the ILEA agreed that temporary accommodation could be put up on adjacent land, and they granted £100,000 for 'minor works'. A promise was made for a new library/classroom building to be completed by the autumn of 1981 – in time for the first of the new courses to start.

With this promise from the ILEA, in January 1981, the CST gave permission for Central's BSc degree application to go to the CNAA, and in April, the CNAA approved the course for an autumn 1981 start. When two months later construction on the new library/classroom building was delayed while the GLC and the ILEA debated ownership of the land, the CNAA rescinded degree approval. At risk of losing the new BSc, Hodkinson frantically explored the ILEA's original proposal for a split-site solution. PCL offered accommodation, and though this was far from ideal – students would have to spend four days per week at PCL in Regent Street for the first year – Central assured the CNAA once again that the new building would be ready for the second year of their degree. The CNAA granted a temporary one-year validation to allow an autumn 1981 start for the new BSc.

The ILEA/GLC land ownership disagreement was finally resolved, and construction was confirmed to start in November 1981. It didn't. The GLC architect confirmed that building would definitely start in January 1982. It didn't. In February, Kitson wrote to the Chairman of the Development sub-committee of the ILEA, explaining that any further postponement would have grave implications for Central. Accommodation was grossly insufficient – there was no space for student activities, private study or staff office space – and the CNAA viewed these inadequacies as very serious. If the CNAA rescinded any of Central's degrees and further recruitment was of necessity to cease, it would be disastrous to such a small institution as Central. The School needed to know if it could assure the CNAA that there would be a new library and classrooms for a 1982 intake to the BEd (Hons) and the BSc degrees. Could Kitson and Central assume the building was still going forward? ...There was no response.

With building not even started by March 1982, the possibility of completion by autumn 1982 was fast becoming unlikely. A fallback measure of occupying alternative accommodation at PCL for the second year of the speech therapy intake was discussed, but new students accepted for the BEd, BSc and the ADVS were notified that their acceptance was 'conditional on CNAA acceptance'. With delays and broken promises, by now the School's credibility with the CNAA was seriously in question.

Finally, Central received an explanation for the most recent delay. National Westminster Bank had raised planning objections with the GLC, who had agreed to rebuild their Swiss Cottage branch when the Camden Civic site was developed. No one knew if plans for this Civic Centre would ever be revived, but as Central was not proposing *permanent* development of the site, National Westminster Bank finally agreed that Central's temporary building could go ahead. The Borough of Camden and GLC Planning Committee consent was expected shortly, and building could begin. It didn't.

Construction finally began in November 1982, a year after it had been due to be completed. The new Seminar Wing and Library was opened on 29 June 1983, and named after the late Chairman of the Governors, Norman Collins. The old library behind the JD Wing was transformed into a Student Union, and office space was created with internal reconstruction of the old Student Common Room (between the stairs and Rooms A and B) in the Embassy Building. The CNAA immediately approved the BEd Honours and the BSc. The ADVS would have to wait until 1993 for external validation.

The ADVS Course had its first intake in the autumn of 1982 under Course Tutor Helen Wynter, and two months later, it was already attracting overseas enquiries. In spite of only awarding an internal qualification, within a very short time the course became recognised as one of the world's best specialist training courses in voice, and it was the only one of its kind in Great Britain.

The first Speech Therapy BSc and BSc Honours students graduated in

JANE COWELL (1931–88)

Bridget (Evans) Davies, Jane Cowell's classmate on the Teacher Course, wrote:

Jane was a student at Central from 1950 to 1953. While there she 'urg'd her height' and played Helena, as had her mother when she was a student in the 1920s. Her first job was at Malvern Girls' College and later she taught at Sherborne School for Girls. She went as part-time tutor to Central in 1968 and became a full-time Voice Coach on the Stage Course in 1982. She was married to Gordon Pemble in 1970, and they have a son Matthew and a daughter Amy.

Jane was unmistakably English. In a photo taken at a Cabaret for a Central Ball in Kensington Town Hall, she is conducting a choir of the Women's Institute (played by her fellow 1950 intake on the Teacher Course) in a rendition of 'Nymphs and Shepherds'. She is wrapped in a sheet and naturally we all longed for it to fall down; it didn't, but even if it had, it would have become yet one more in a long stream of 'Jane scrapes'. It was no surprise for example that she managed, with Jocelyn Emberton, to get herself locked out of her flat in her nightdress on the morning of an interview. And no one ever told the stories of her mishaps as hilariously as Jane herself did. 'My dear,' she would begin and then follow with gales of laughter.

Her students will no doubt remember her quick flashes of rage – usually brought on by the stupidity of mechanical objects. Her fights with her tape recorder were legendary and caused George Hall to dub her 'The Lady Bracknell of the Four-Letter Word'. They will also remember her beautiful natural voice. I can never forget her 'Ode on Melancholy', her chosen piece in our final year.

Her death came very quickly and devastated her family, Central and her countless friends: 'our luminous Jane', as one described her.

1985. The three-year Teacher Course became a four-year course in 1985 – as a result, there are no Teacher '85 graduates. Instead, 1985–6 was the first fourth year offered, and in the summer of 1986, the Teacher Department graduated students with Central's first four-year BEd. The same year, Central had to re-submit for validation for a new joint course with Avery Hill College/Thames Polytechnic, as the DES had closed the Teacher Training Course at PNL.

In 1986, another important new course was also brought to Central. The Sesame Institute (UK) had held its first short training course exploring the use of art in therapy in 1964. The Institute set up a full-time course in 1976, and in 1985, the Sesame Institute began a one-year advanced diploma course at Kingsway Princeton College offering a foundation in movement and drama in therapy. In autumn 1986, the Sesame Course moved to Central, bringing with it national funding and 14 full-time students. Patricia Watts became Course Leader of the Central School Sesame Joint Certificate in Use of Drama and Movement in Therapy.

• • •

When Central's first Speech Therapy BSc began in 1981, there were still two years of Speech Therapy diploma students in training. Over the next few years, there were continual degree submissions, an increase in the number of students and staff, persistent constraints on accommodation, and numerous Departmental problems to overcome. One of the more disturbing of these 'problems' occurred in 1985, and it would preoccupy the Department for the next 18 months.

The trouble stemmed from an ongoing balancing act between practical and academic training, an issue that had been a consideration within the Department from the beginning of the degree applications. The spring 1980 four-year BSc Honours degree submission had been initially rejected by the CNAA, and only later approved when resubmitted with academic subjects more centrally integrated into the course. In the spring of 1985, the CST had re-accredited the BSc Degree course (though again pointing out the need for a clinic to give students more practical training), and in July of that year, most of the first group of Speech Therapy BSc and Honours degree students graduated. However, four Speech Therapy students failed the *practical* component of the Speech and Language Pathology and Therapy final examinations, and were therefore deemed to have failed the whole course. By the end of that month, all four students had lodged appeals with the School's Academic Board.

Earlier, when at the insistence of the CNAA Kitson had reorganised the Academic Board into a more formal body, some had protested that, as a small institution, Central was better suited to settle its problems informally. However, if Central were to offer degrees approved by the CNAA, it had to ensure the maintenance of academic standards, and this, among other things, meant providing an adequate back-up structure for complaints

DAVID CAREY HEAD OF ADVANCED VOICE COURSE 1986–2003

David Carey was born in Reading and brought up in Edinburgh. His mother was the ex-Central teacher and actress, Elna Graham (Teacher '39). He trained as a Speech and Drama teacher at the Royal Scottish Academy of Music and Dramatic Art, gained a degree in English Language and Linguistics from Edinburgh University, and taught for five years at Queen Margaret College in Edinburgh, before starting as Cis Berry's assistant at the Royal Shakespeare Company in 1983. He spoke of his years as Head of the ADVS Course:

66 During my years as Head of the Course, it went from an Advanced Diploma to a Postgraduate Diploma, which meant it went from being internally validated to externally validated by the Open University Validation Service (OUVS). Eventually we added a part-time MA component, and then integrated it into the course so that now it is a full-time one-year MA.

When I inherited the course from Helen Wynter, the syllabus was: anatomy, phonetics, practical voice, movement (an hour a week), dialects, and teacher practice. Initially I consolidated that as a syllabus, but it began evolving. I expanded the connection between phonetics and dialects, so there was more of a through line, and also expanded the movement work. Helen Wynter [who ran the course for its first four years] had started putting in Alexander Technique and I did more of that. Also, I introduced applied communication skills and beefed up the practical voice and text side of things, alongside physiology and anatomy. I spent the first four or five years developing the course this way, largely in response to how I saw the students engaging with the work. The course isn't one thing for one kind of person. Someone may want to do dialects, or voice coach in theatre, or the corporate world, or mix and match all of that...whatever was possible in a year.

Central was entering the university arena, and it made sense to add on the MA platform; it became apparent it would serve students better to have that part of the course integrated from the start. This led to a slight restructuring so that most of the practical class teaching took place in the first two terms to allow students to undertake their more independent work in the third term. I tried to preserve practical work as much as possible. I reduced anatomy and phonetics taught hours, but not in a way that reduced their knowledge and understanding of the subjects. There were projects and other requirements, which meant the students were applying their understanding more....

The Postgraduate course used to be 14 [students], now the MA is 24 – in my final year it was 20. That had been raised from 16 over three or four years. 99

and appeals. The total number of members of the Academic Board had been increased from 20 to 27, and a number of new sub-Committees had been set up. One of these was the Appeals Committee. When the Speech Therapy appeals were lodged in July 1985, they first went to Kitson for consideration, but because of the summer vacation, it proved impossible to gather a quorum of staff and students for the Appeals Committee. By the time the Academic Board finally dealt with the appeals in late September, there was unanimous agreement that the four students should be allowed to resit their exams.

Instead, the students went to the Board of Examiners, asking them to reconsider their decision that a failure on the practical side of the exams meant a failure of the total course. The Examiners referred the matter to the CNAA. The CNAA referred it back to the Board of Examiners, suggesting a list of steps to follow. By early 1986, the Board of Examiners had met four times, reached no decision, and was still unable to produce a precise definition of where it stood, saying it was 'dealing with a matter of principle'. Meanwhile, the students in question obtained legal counsel, and Central was forced to do the same.

The Board of Examiners finally referred the matter back to Central's Academic Board with the 'matter of principle' defined: 'Notwithstanding any possible ambiguity in the Regulations for the BSc Honours in Speech Therapy, students are required to pass the practical part of the examination in Speech and Language Pathology and Therapy before they can be recommended for a degree.' The Academic Board accepted the clarification of the regulation and upheld the decision to fail the four students, again offering them the opportunity to resit their examinations. The students instead took their complaint to the High Court. In an anticlimax, judgment was given in favour of Central on a technicality, and the School was awarded costs.

The CNAA and Central held to their decision to allow the four students either to resit the practical part of the exam that would qualify them for an ordinary degree and a licence to practise, or to resit all of their fourth-year exams and be eligible for an Honours degree. Either way, the students would not be grant-aided. Two students accepted this offer and both passed the resit for the BSc ordinary degree.

While the appeals had been pending, the Chairman and Governors received letters from parents and students complaining about aspects of the appeal and about the teaching within the Speech Therapy Department. Concurrently, two members of the Speech Therapy staff initiated grievance procedures, and some members of staff protested to the CST with allegations regarding the management of the School. Once the students' appeals had been exhausted within the School, a Governors' Committee of Inquiry was set up to deal with additional letters of complaint and to consider whether they required further action. This Committee also appointed an outside expert to clarify the Speech Therapy Course structure, regulations and examination requirements, as well as to help in preparing for the next CNAA degree submission in 1987. As a result of these cases, a more streamlined appeals system was instituted whereby issues could be addressed and decisions made more quickly. The Academic Board set up formal Course Committees for all courses.

The shortcomings in the appeals procedure later identified by the Committee of Inquiry may well have applied to all Departments, but there were problems specific to Speech Therapy. The educational debate between clinical and academic training had developed into conflict between staff members, and between staff and students. Hodkinson recalls: 'It was a professional practical degree. All the degrees in Britain were like that at that time – there was only one where you could opt out of being a clinician. In our department, there were one or two academics who didn't want it to be like that.'

As well as the Governors' Committee investigation, the ILEA also conducted a review, and their findings pointed out an extraordinary set of circumstances in existence at the School: 60% of Central's courses were undergoing validation at the same time, and therefore pressure on staff was enormous. The ILEA recognised, as had Kitson in his early student interview, that although Central was a small institution, no one could take communication within the School for granted. Therefore, the ILEA suggested changes in the School structure. The roles of Personal Tutor, Year Tutor, Course Leader and Head of Department, and their relationship to the Principal and Deputy, were re-defined. More interaction between departments was created with cooperative teaching, cross-course study units, and liaison tutors from each department, and the composition, roles and working methods of the Academic Board Committees were also examined. Central was no longer a Gwynneth Thurburn/ Vera Sargent 'tea-party'. It was becoming an establishment of official procedure prescribed by government, the Board and the ILEA. Although this meant the School was becoming less of a family and more of a business, it also meant Central was becoming more openly accountable to its 'customers' – the students.

RENEE HOSKING

Renee Hosking was born in London in 1930 and attended Skinners' Company's Grammar School for Girls from 1941. The School was evacuated for a time to Welwyn Garden City during the war, but returned to its North London base in 1943. In 1946, Hosking did a one-year secretarial course at City of London College, after which she worked first at a merchant bank, and later a publishing company. She met her husband, John, when they were both appearing in an amateur production at the Unity Theatre. Married in 1960, she had four children, and by 1975 was looking for a part-time job. She said in 2005: 'Going to the School changed my life. It gave me such a sense of an exciting world. It was wonderful. It also, incidentally, changed the life of my eldest son, Mark, who whilst working in the Maintenance Department met a Teacher '91 student (Sheron Pusey) who is now my daughter-in-law.' After ceasing as Registrar in 1996, she held a part-time post as Academic Support Officer before retiring in 2002. Even today she can be found on site at Swiss Cottage, helping the friends and colleagues she has made in her over 27 years of association with Central.

• • •

Late in 1978, Frederick Wentworth-Bowyer resigned from his position as Company Secretary and Finance Officer, and Registrar Eric Newsome temporarily took over his duties. A new administrative structure was proposed, and Eric Newsome's temporary post became permanent. No new Finance Officer was appointed, and the duties of Finance Officer, Company Secretary and Administrative Registrar were amalgamated. Renee

Hosking had been secretary to both the previous Registrar, Anne Herbert, and to Eric Newsome. In 1979, she became Registrar.

Shortly after Newsome took over from Wentworth-Bower, he discovered a loss of £30,000 from the School investments. Sold investments inadvertently had not been reinvested, but instead placed in the School's general account and subsequently spent on School running costs and expenses. Kitson introduced annual departmental budgets, and a Finance Committee was formed of the Heads of Departments and the Head Librarian. Strict budgeting was enforced. Within a year the deficit was reduced from £30,000 to £9000.

Mismanagement of the Central's investments was only the beginning of the financial problems. Once again, it became evident that either income had to be increased or expenditure would have to be decreased. ILEA Block Grants were partially based on student numbers and expected fees, and an ideal recruitment target to ensure adequate funding was 300 students. When 1979–80 enrolment once again dropped – to 266 – it affected Central's Block Grant provision. Permanent staff jobs were at risk, and part-time teaching hours were restricted. Increased enrolment on either Stage or Technical Courses could lead to problems with NCDT accreditation, and Speech Therapy was struggling to start a BSc and find clinical placements for the already increased numbers. Only recruitment to the Teacher BEd degree could accommodate additional numbers. Audrey Laski frantically developed degrees and looked for academic partners – to increase enrolment and, therefore, income.

• • •

There had been a great deal of overspending in the previous years – some of this due to building improvements required by the 1978 Health and Safety Act and some due to an insufficient budget. In 1980, the ILEA warned Central that it had to remain within its allocated funding, or face the consequences. Although no time was ever a good one financially for Central, this warning could not have come at a worse time. Eton College proposed an increase from £800 per year to £40,000 per year for the remaining 18 years of the lease on the Embassy Theatre site, and although Eton eventually agreed to only £15,000 per year, with one rent review to take place after nine years, this was still a huge increase. Camden Council also raised their rent for the Studio One site to £7250.

An ILEA audit team was critical of aspects of the School's financial administration, and in autumn 1980 the School's auditors, Price Waterhouse, examined Central's finances and suggested procedures to strengthen financial and budgetary controls. For reasons unrelated to his role in Central's financial management, Eric Newsome resigned on 31 December 1980, and in early 1981 Stephen Tapster was appointed Company Secretary. A new financial structure was put in place that immediately resulted in even less flexibility for Department Heads and course budgets. For example, while there was an overall surplus in the School's total budget, when the Speech Therapy Department had problems financing visiting lecturers, Central couldn't use spare money from the budget for that purpose – it was not permitted to exceed the salaries grant for approved staff numbers because the 'underspend' had not come under the Salary budget line. The old days of Fogerty using her private teaching fees to supplement Central's income (or the more recent days of Departments helping each other out with overspends) were well and truly over.

While Central went through financial difficulties, its students reaped both the rewards and the penalties arising from government policies. Margaret Thatcher had been Prime Minister since spring 1979. In an effort to cut public spending, the Government announced that, starting in autumn 1981, overseas students (not including those from the EEC) should pay full-cost fees. A formal protest from the Governors was signed by Lord Olivier, President of the School, and presented to the Parliamentary Under-Secretary of State. That was the end of that. When early in 1981 the two Theatre Courses, Stage and Technical, were graded as being 'workshop- or laboratory-based', overseas student fees increased from the expected £1380 to £1890. The next year, home and EEC student fees were reduced from £900 to £480 per year, and overseas student fees went up from £2649 to £3400 per year. There was pessimism regarding the likelihood of recruitment of overseas students to the ACSD Course, and a general feeling that the increase would limit the range of overseas students applying to all courses.

Early in 1982, Central's budget was again squeezed when the ILEA reported a £4 million

ERIC BRANDENBURG
STAGE '82

" I got on a plane to England in '79, and ended up living in a bed-sit in West Hampstead with a bed on four stacks of bricks and daylight showing through holes in the wallpaper. (How could that be? It couldn't be simply the 'outside' on the other side of the wallpaper could it? I still wonder.) I was saved by some friends going to Webber Douglas who'd lost a roommate, and it was a big step up, and very chaste, sharing the living room of a basement apartment with a guy, while the two girls got the bedroom. The living room had a huge picture of a mountain glade covering one wall. I suppose it did make the place feel bigger.

Stage '82 was from Wales, Scotland, the home counties, London, Oxford, Cambridge, Yale, high school, trade school, no school, Brooklyn, LA, Connecticut, Belfast, Glasgow and other places: 28 people who didn't get along all that well much of the time but ended up very fond of one another in the end, while still not understanding each other even remotely. I remember staring at the lot of us smoking in the alley behind the Embassy Theatre in the third year, waiting to go on as 'dust balls' with bare branches (a design conceit) in *Peer Gynt* and wondering what on earth was going to become of us, when one confided in an offhand way that he'd proposed to another member of our year. Just after they were married, we stood around the piano singing, 'Why am I always the bridesmaid, never the blushing bride?', which we'd learned in George's Music Hall Class, and feeling very together in our love for them. **"**

deficit for its own financial year and deferred part of Central's monthly grant payments for February and March. The ILEA 'hoped' to make it up in the next financial year. Central was again asked to reduce its expenditure, but *without affecting the quality of education*. In spite of these budgetary restraints, four months later Dr Tim W Leggatt (son of successful actress, Alison Leggatt, Stage '29) was appointed to a newly created post – Deputy Principal. Money for a new salaried position had been approved and earmarked within Central's budget for a year, but had been initially unfilled due to lack of office space. When building began on the new library and classrooms, an office became available, and the position was filled. This presented an obvious dichotomy – between increasingly tight budgetary restrictions for course delivery and the creation of an expensive new administrative position. It was just the kind of government logic that left Central observers scratching their heads.

• • •

In the 1970s and early-1980s, besides Central's course changes and accommodation headaches, there were larger political issues that would affect the School's long term future. As the government sought an affordable way to educate its populace, pervasive changes in Higher Education policies in the United Kingdom began to take place, and when the DES proposed a range of serious reorganisations and cutbacks, some institutions did not survive. Central was considered a College of Higher Education and was therefore ruled by government educational policies. On the other hand, it was in a unique position in that it was also tied to the fate, and the funding, of the Inner London Education Authority. While the DES explored ways to cut all spending, the ILEA focused on streamlining existing funding through a relocation of resources – in other words, by reforming ILEA educational institutions. The concept of 'efficient amalgamation' brought the ILEA and the DES together. They both agreed that small institutions were not cost-effective, so they would be sacrificed. Central's prognosis was clear, and options for survival were limited. The School could do one of three things: increase enrolment to increase its income, amalgamate with another institution, or attempt independence. Each option came with it own problems.

An increase in enrolment meant that, as accommodation at the Embassy was already strained, either the Teacher or the Speech Therapy Courses – or both – might very well have to be relocated to other premises. More students would also require an increase in staff, which was unlikely to be in proportion to student numbers, and therefore the student-teacher ratio would surely suffer. The second option – to amalgamate with another institution – was the obvious favourite of both the ILEA and the DES. Central had shown that it could successfully collaborate with Polytechnics for the teacher-training part of its academic provision. However, Central had always seen education as only a branch of its overall work, and the School considered the interdependence of courses as their greatest strength. Not only would amalgamation in all likelihood mean the splitting up of the three courses, but also many of Central's potential partners for these course amalgamations were already at risk of closure themselves.

Central's third option – a return to total independence – was very appealing. It was also unrealistic. The previous decade of ILEA funding had not solved Central's intrinsic need for more space, and if the School were to revert to private, charitable, non-grant aided status, it would face the same financial problems it left behind in 1972: an ever-increasing need for higher fees (and therefore an expected drop in student numbers) and a lack of expansion capital. Without private, long-term funding in place, an independent Central would face the very real possibility of closure.

Late in 1981, Chairman Norman Collins, Principal Kitson and Company Secretary Stephen Tapster met with the Director of Education for the ILEA to clarify Central's position. Out of the blue, the ILEA Director assured them that Central would not need to amalgamate with any other institution, and there was no cause for concern for the future or for the funding of the School. In addition, the next spring the ILEA Director – by then also the Secretary Designate of the newly formed Local Authority for Higher Education – told Central that with the amalgamations and 're-organisation' of other institutions, there would soon be redundant secondary schools available for Central's use. However, though Central would remain intact, it should expect no new permanent accommodation to be built at the Embassy site. Even though a split-site solution had never seemed ideal, considering the alternatives, Central was relieved. The reprieve, however, was short-lived. The ILEA was also at the mercy of government policies.

By the end of 1982, the DES projected economies for public institutions of ten percent across the board. Courses offered at Central were small and unique, and a ten percent cut in expenditure could not be accomplished without cutting staff – possibly even cutting courses – and Central could not absorb this kind of financial restriction. Once again the School was at risk. However, Central was not alone. With the loss of its Science Department, Westfield College had lost one-third of its students, and – in an unexpected about-turn – the ILEA once again proposed amalgamation, this time with Westfield as a potential partner. The ILEA maintained that its pressure on Central to merge with Westfield stemmed directly from the national policy on Higher Education that favoured broadly based (more and varied courses) above narrowly based (specialist) institutions. Smaller institutions were less flexible and less cost-effective, and amalgamation would increase student enrolment and justify increased funding. Westfield and Central had a successful history with its joint BA in Drama and a Language, and a partnership would mean augmented premises and accommodation – including residential student housing. Laurence Harbottle, the new Chairman of the Board of Governors at Central, was not impressed.

When Norman Collins retired as Chairman in the spring of 1983, Laurence Harbottle, who had been a Governor since 1975, was unanimously elected to take his place. Harbottle was a solicitor with his own firm, Harbottle & Lewis, which dealt extensively with charities and matters relating to the arts – primarily within the areas of theatre, television and film – and he knew his way around committees, bureaucracy and government. He possessed shrewd insight and an uncanny ability to define and clarify both problems and solutions.

Wary of the merger with Westfield College, Harbottle sought answers on a number of matters. Foremost among these was that Central needed assurance that it would retain its theatres. The Embassy Theatre site was certainly not perfect. The condition of the buildings was a major concern, and in 1984, the theatre had only 14 years and Studio One only four years remaining on their respective leases – but in spite of these drawbacks, the site had irreplaceable facilities. Westfield had nothing comparable. When the ILEA indicated that Central would only keep the Embassy theatres for a short period and that no finances were available to build a theatre complex at Westfield, it became apparent that no matter how keen Westfield might be to retain Central's identity, success was doubtful. As had happened to other small colleges in the recent past, Central might gradually be absorbed into the larger institution and within a few years cease to exist as a separate entity.

Without assurance that the University was prepared to guarantee a long-term future for Central, the Governors were reluctant to continue negotiations. Kitson calmed student unrest with reassurances that the talks with Westfield were 'exploratory', but even early in 1984, the ILEA was pessimistic about any long-term future of the School without amalgamation. Central had financial problems, and as a consequence of rate capping, it was likely there would be further budgetary reductions to their ILEA Block Grant. Central's future was insecure, to say the least.

Believing that Central would have to become part of a larger operation or face 'dismemberment' – that is, the reallocation of each of Central's courses to separate larger institutions – the ILEA brushed aside the reservations of Harbottle, the Board and the Central management. Then, they changed tack again. The ILEA assured Central that they would maintain the Embassy Theatre and Studio, and they emphasised their commitment to preserving the name and integrity of the School and keeping its departments and teaching intact. There was only one little problem. The Speech Therapy Department was linked to PCL for science course provision, and as Westfield's science department was now non-existent – and no PCL teaching support would be allowed to continue once a merger with Westfield had occurred – the Speech Therapy Department was at risk. This was not good enough. The Central Board was committed to keeping the School intact. Governors agreed to carry on merger negotiations, but they also continued to explore other contingencies.

In spite of ongoing negotiations between Westfield and Central, Westfield was a federal college of the University of London, and there was no guarantee that the University would agree to a merger. Nevertheless, under pressure from the ILEA, Central addressed the academic considerations inherent in such an amalgamation. Kitson was particularly worried about University examination procedures, feeling that the CNAA had so far allowed Central freedom in its courses – suiting them to the needs of the professions, whereas University regulations could often distort them.

The Governors felt the Stage, Technical, Advanced Certificate in Speech and Drama (ACSD) and Advanced Diploma in Voice Studies (ADVS) Course particularly needed to stay clear of the university system. Central's Speech Therapy degree differed from Speech Sciences in universities by its emphasis on practical work, and if it were to enter the university system, the College of Speech Therapists would support the degree only as long as changes didn't affect the clinical and practical content. The Teacher Department was also at risk. The previous autumn (1983), the CNAA Institutional Review of the School had been successful for the Teacher Courses, and the CNAA had been approving of Central's relationships with PCL and PNL. A merger with Westfield would threaten both of these associations.

A final decision to merge would have to be made by the end of 1984 to ensure 1986 admissions, and the Statement of Intent of amalgamation with Westfield went to London University's Joint Planning Committee in June 1984. If assurances on the integrity of the courses and finances could be obtained from them, the Governors and Harbottle might be prepared to shift their position from pessimism to cautious optimism. The ILEA hoped the Westfield relationship would come to a satisfactory solution, but if this became impossible and no new partner could be found, it was very clear on what it would do. If the merger were refused, the ILEA would dismember the Central School.

When in autumn 1984 London University ruled against a merger between Central and Westfield College, what earlier might have seemed like a pardon was now clearly recognised merely as a stay of execution. Central was soberly aware of the ILEA's threats of 'dismemberment' and realised it must find another possible partner. The School immediately explored an extension of the existing relationship with PCL, but no one knew where the government's educational policies would next turn, and very possibly PCL was under threat itself. It was experiencing savage cuts, and its 11:1 student to staff ratio was far higher than Central's 8:1. As a safety net, in July 1985 the Governors began looking for long-term independent financial support. If Central faced dismemberment, it would of necessity become an autonomous charitable institution.

Meanwhile, the Central Academic Board passed the following resolution:

The Academic Board of the Central School of Speech and Drama recognises the possible advantages of closer association with a larger institution. It recommends the opening of serious exploratory discussion with the Polytechnic of Central London. It asks for regular reporting back to the Academic Board and to Governors. *It resolves to maintain observer status in relation to the London Institute.*

• • •

This is the first mention in any Central document of the London Institute. The London Institute was being formed in 1985–6, and at its inception, would consist of seven constituent colleges – four Art and Design, and three Design. If Central were to join these ranks, it might retain its independence while also fulfilling the ILEA's wish for amalgamation. At a Governors Meeting in March 1986, the London Institute's Rector, John McKenzie, assured the Board that should Central join, it could retain its links with PCL and the PNL – there was no wall around the Institute. Central would have to change its status from grant-aided to grant-maintained, thereby sacrificing its charitable status, but most importantly, he stressed that if Central joined the Institute immediately as a *founder* member before the DES's National Advisory Board completed its next review – the School could enjoy 'certain advantages'. Pressure to act quickly was applied. It was a classic 'Step right up, one-day-only!' offer.

Central's Academic Board was in favour of immediately opening negotiations. After successfully avoiding a merger with the academically based Westfield, an amalgamation with a group of more practical and arts-based schools and colleges seemed an attractive prospect. The Governors, however, decided to consult other bodies and explore both the advantages and disadvantages of this new offer.

In the midst of this, due to the illness of his wife, in May 1986 George Kitson was given a year's sabbatical. Deputy Principal Dr Tim Leggatt had retired in 1984 to be replaced by Dr Stephen Hazell in 1985, and now Hazell was appointed Acting Principal. Immediately, he was faced with a number of problems. The PCL Academic Council warned that if Central joined the London Institute, PCL's relationship to the School would have to cease. Relationships with partner institutions, Westfield College and Thames Polytechnic, would also have to be redefined. There were issues to resolve with the Charity Commission. There were technical and managerial points to consider, such as the structure of both Central's and the Institute's Governors' and Academic Boards. There was a question of the legal status of Central within the Institute. Foremost in the minds of everyone, however, was the retention of Central's identity and special character.

Some Central Governors were in favour of taking advantage of McKenzie's offer without delay. After all, if the School committed itself in principle, it would have an immediate right to participate at least as an observer in ground-floor policy-forming committees. Other Governors warned against committing the School without sufficient information as to the responsibilities and the benefits of the liaison. In the early summer of 1986, a detailed discussion with the Institute was delayed until Central could complete preparations for re-validation of some of its courses. Central staff were under a great deal of pressure, and it was wisely decided to prioritise their energies. Nevertheless, there was concern that the delay might cause the London Institute to lose interest. John McKenzie's pressure tactic was working.

Then, in the autumn of 1986, the Governors' Board minutes reveal: 'The School's NAB (DES's National Advisory Board) numbers had been attached, without prior consultation, to those of the London Institute.' This meant the Institute was already including Central's enrolment as part of its overall funding projections for the Institute, and as the Central Governors had made no formal or informal commitment to the Institute, they were irate. They felt they were being railroaded.

In December 1986, Robert S Fowler was appointed as Principal Designate to take over prior to George Kitson's official retirement the next May. Initially, Fowler was optimistic about the London Institute liaison, and at his first Governors' meeting in December 1986 he told the Board he believed membership would be a 'great opportunity for the performing arts'. His position would change. Although he could not officially be made Principal, Fowler was formally appointed a Governor so that he could take over the tumultuous negotiations with John McKenzie and the London Institute.

• • •

In spite of the backstairs political upheaval, the artistic life of the students remained robust. In 1980, student late-night show, *Footnotes*, directed by George Hall, was performed at the London Drama and Film

ADAM PRICE STAGE '85

66 First, I am extremely proud to be associated with Central!

In my year were, to name a few, Teri Banham, Linus Roache, Lucy Jenkins, Tamsin Olivier, George Roth; also Devon Scott, Matthew (now Harry) Burton and Patrick Brennan. I shared the famous 11 St George's Terrace with the last three. The parties there were legendary.

I recently met up with another classmate, Hilary Tones, and we chatted about our Central days, and we both remembered this bizarre and slightly creepy happening in our second year. We were in Room D rehearsing Ibsen's *Rosmersholm*. Tony Falkingham was directing. I was playing Rosmer, Tamsin Olivier was playing Rebecca, and Hilary was playing Mrs Helseth. Needless to say, the play itself is full of 'ghosts' of the past, with particular emphasis on Rosmer's dead wife, Beata, who committed suicide 18 months earlier. In the middle of a scene, Hilary screamed and jumped so violently that we, of course, all stopped in our tracks. She turned as white as her blouse. A single drop of blood had landed on her wrist – it had 'spattered' as if it had fallen from height. Nobody in the room had an injury – least of all Hilary. Checks of nosebleeds and paper cuts, grazes and possible broken scabs proved fruitless. Tony took to the rehearsal floor in utter amazement, and we all automatically looked towards the ceiling expecting to see a patch of blood seeping through – nothing. To this day I remember a cold, hollow feeling combined with the frustration of there being no possible explanation. I think we immediately took a fifteen-minute tea break and told everyone who happened to be in Marianne's Café at the time. Ghostly goings on in Room D! **99**

Jubilee Dinner at the National Theatre, and in November 1981, Central presented a 75th Birthday Gala at the Embassy Theatre. Again, third-year Stage students presented a revue, highly praised in a personal note to Hall from Lord Olivier. In March 1982, due to the efforts of Stage student, Peter Arp, a third-year production of Caryl Churchill's *Cloud Nine* was taken to Kiel, Germany, for three performances. In May 1982, a second-year BEd student, Antony Grounds, had his play performed at the Lyric Theatre, Hammersmith.

The Student Union was also active during this period. In 1978, it started a wholefood co-operative, where students could order healthy food in bulk, such as inexpensive beans, grains, peanut butter. The Union also did its best to schedule social events in Studio One, and later the Embassy Studio, but timetabling and space constraints kept School-wide activities to a minimum. Nevertheless, in the 1980 spring term the Union organised a series of lunchtime seminars by Timothy West, Cicely Berry and Peggy Ashcroft. The Union also regularly organised student 'discos' and cabaret evenings, which included student contributions from all the courses: a punk-rock band with Teacher-student Julian Sands, songs from Stage student Betsy Brantley, and some of the first 'public' performances of comedy team, Teacher-students Dawn French and Jennifer Saunders.

• • •

In May 1987, after a year's sabbatical George Kitson officially stepped down, and Robert Fowler became Central's seventh Principal.

• • •

ADDITIONAL CENTRAL FACTS

1979
- The National Council for Drama Training (NCDT) panel visits Central for the first time and accredits the Acting Course for five years – the maximum allowed.
- Ishbel Fox retires in summer of 1979; Vinki Grey retires in summer of 1980. Together, they had over 100 years association with the Central School.

1980
- Daniel Bond replaces Tom Errington in Stage Management.

1981
- Pat Ostler retires in March, after 21 years as Bursar.
- The Beatrix Lehmann archive collection is formally accepted. A famous actress, Lehmann (1903–79) attended RADA, and was British Actors' Equity's first female President.
- Annual stipends begin for under-supported pre-ILEA pensioners.
- Dr Kathleen Dacre is appointed Course Tutor to Central's joint BA with Westfield College.

1982
- Stipends are raised to £500 per year for Gwynneth Thurburn, Vera Sargent and Beryl Shorthouse. The amount is minimally increased each year after 1982.

1984
- Margaret Braund, Barbara Caister and John Roberts retire.
- Chrissie Hearne passes away.
- Senior Administration Officer Stephen Tapster and Librarian Joan Jeffery retire.
- Angela Douglas is appointed Librarian, and Dr John Griffith becomes Secretary and Clerk to the Governors; Finance Officer James O'Reilly resigns and is replaced by Stephen Sageman. Bill Palmer of Media Resources retires. Ruth Posner replaces Barbara Caister, and Diana Cooper replaces Alan Marston as movement teachers.

1985
- Nickolas Grace becomes a Governor. Judi Dench is made Vice President.
- For the first time in the School's history, in July a Leavers' Ceremony is held, with Dr Jonathan Miller as speaker.
- The NCDT accredits the Acting Course for a further five years.
- George Hall traces acting students from previous ten years: 90% are still working in theatre.

1985–6
- Staff costs are approximately 73% of total budget: 53% academic and 20% administration and support staff.

1986
- Helen Wynter retires after 25 years at Central.

1986–7
- Staff costs are approximately 68% of total budget: 49.9% academic and 17.2% administration and support staff.
- Student Hardship Fund total: £9000.

1987
- Arthur Wish retires.

16

1987–2000

ROBERT STEWART FOWLER was born in Birkenhead on 1 February 1932 and graduated from Oxford in 1955. His interest in drama sprang from his own schooldays in amateur theatre and influenced his initial career as an English teacher. Fowler recalls: 'I went as Head of English to Forest Gate – a secondary modern 1890s school with a rooftop playground – and I started things there that had never been done before, like take the kids to plays at Stratford. Joan Littlewood was at Stratford then, and it was the days of plays like A *Taste of Honey* and *Fings Ain't Wot They Used T'Be*. I got to know them a little, developed what Central would call a totally amateur interest, but nevertheless, it was a background.'

Fowler went on to teach for six years at Bretton Hall, an arts-based teacher-training college, and aged 30, he moved to Sittingbourne College in Kent to become one of the youngest Deputy Principals in the country. He took over as Principal ten years later. National educational policies aimed at reducing the number of teachers affected many teacher-training colleges, and when Sittingbourne was notified of closure, Fowler left to join the Inspectorate. He very quickly became Senior Inspector for Drama:

> 'From the cradle to the grave' they called it – I was responsible for drama teaching
> in nursery schools and up to all colleges that had any kind of grant-aided students. It
> meant that for some years I got to know all of the drama schools, and so I got terrific
> insight into what worked, what didn't. What occurred to me was that I saw plays at
> schools and some of the actors were terrific. Some of them trained – but not many. One
> of the reasons was that their parents didn't want them – the schools didn't want them
> – to go to a place that couldn't give them a degree, a qualification.

Fowler valued the benefits of qualifications and, perhaps because of his background in education and the Inspectorate, there were concerns among some observers during his first years as Principal that he alone was responsible for pushing Central into Higher Education. The 'Fowler Years' were a time of substantial change, and although other specialist drama institutions have recently found their survival lay down the same path, at the time, a disapproving attitude towards Central began to percolate among sections of the profession. There was criticism, even anger, against Fowler for making alterations to the

Central that alumni had known and loved. To understand what happened during these critical years, one must first understand the challenges Central faced in 1987. One must also keep two separate issues clear – the events and the perceptions of those events.

• • •

Robert Fowler officially became Principal in May 1987. By that time, he had already spent five months as Principal Designate and was well aware of Central's two major historical obstacles: lack of space and lack of money. The School was in financial difficulties again – in 1987–8, it faced a projected deficit of over 25% of its total annual budget – and the ILEA was threatening to further decrease

WARDROBE THE CAT

Debbie Scully recalls an initial financial quandary:

" When I first came to do financial management, I found out we were spending £8000 a year on the cat, so I took the matter to the Finance and Special Purposes Committee. 'The cat's diabetic, visits the vet a lot, and has to eat special tinned food.' They said, 'You can't touch the cat!' 'Well, all right,' I said, 'but what would you have me do? Do you want me to put him on the payroll?' I think eventually Wardrobe went home with one of the staff. **"**

the School's Block Grant. To say income was not keeping up with expenditure would be a monumental understatement. Fowler spoke of his first years at Central:

When I joined the School, the Chief Inspector for the ILEA said, 'You won't be able to do it. There's the financial problem, but there's also a court case on in Speech Therapy. Then you've got Teacher Training, which is coming up for re-validation. You've got Stage Management who are still in a two-year course.' It did seem like a catalogue. Anyway, I didn't actually sack any academic members of staff, but one or two left. …It left the way open for me to make some appointments of people I thought would help me to put things right. They had to be experts.

So Debbie [Scully] and Linda [Cookson] were both appointed separately. Debbie came from a humble career – I say humble in the sense that she wasn't a top Registrar in a university. She was young, but she'd come through the very best kind of training. She knew all the ropes. She was probably the best interviewee that I've ever met – so completely calm, so collected as a young person. She came in as Senior Administrative Officer. Her job was to get the finance perfect… Linda Cookson was an Oxford graduate, and I appointed her as Academic Registrar and Senior Tutor – which is a university term, really a catch-all. Her job was to look after everything academic: accreditations (particularly the documents), the forms, and the submissions. That all had to be perfect. After ten years in the Inspectorate, I knew just what the civil service wanted. I knew what worked. The point is: we got that going as a team. …Debbie got the house, the books, in order; Linda trained the staff in what was expected of them in the new world of education.

1987 110 mph winds lash England
Underground fire at King's Cross station, London

1988 Soviet troop withdrawal from Afghanistan
Lockerbie air disaster

1989 The Berlin Wall comes down
Vaclav Havel becomes President of Czechoslovakia, Ceausescu is ousted in Romania, Emperor Hirohito of Japan dies

1990 First Gulf War begins
Poll tax riots

1991 Terry Waite freed

1992 Riots in LA over Rodney King beating

1993 First terrorist attack on World Trade Centre
Campaign by Equity maintains Schedule D tax status for actors

1994 Nelson Mandela becomes President of South Africa

1995 Equity replaces AGM with Annual Representative Conference

1996 Ella Fitzgerald dies

1997 Britain hands Hong Kong back to China
Princess Diana killed in car crash in Paris

1998 President Clinton impeached in USA

1999 Serbs withdraw from Kosovo

Fowler recalled his initial perceptions of Central:

...I had attended the Gala [November 1981 Gala Performance for Central's 75th Birthday] as an Inspector, and what appealed to me was that Olivier said even here – not many people necessarily would have realised how astute he was, but Laurence Olivier says in that Introduction: 'Despite the valiant support of the Inner London Education Authority we live in difficult times for higher education.' Interesting that Olivier used the term Higher Education. It was a term of abuse for a long time. Although there was a degree in Speech Therapy, and Teacher Training became a degree, Acting was only an internal Diploma when I arrived, and Stage Management was a Higher National two-year course. But Laurence Olivier was clearly talking about Higher Education: '...and the pressure on teacher and student alike is considerable. Scholarships, grants, student accommodation, teaching aids and equipment all present problems at this time and above all the School premises are getting old and need extension. These problems can be, indeed must be solved, if the School is to be assured as productive a future as that which lies in the past.' [from Gala Programme]

That I thought was enormously important, and that's what I took as my mission when I went to the School. My main focus: the School was falling down. The theatre was propped up with scaffolding, and the scaffolding was falling down – no one even knew how long the scaffolding had been there! At the same time a library had been built, a small outside library, and though it was modest, it was infinitely more than RADA ever had. I realise it is very difficult to sing one's own, one's own staff's, achievements if it looks as if you're damning what was there when you came and what went before – the historical things. I think one's always got to be cautious of that.

Along the way, a lot of 'what went before – the historical things' would disappear, and this at times caused great unease amongst alumni and staff alike. Yet Fowler and his management team took the School towards a more suitable physical state for a college of Central's stature and reputation. Hard decisions would have to be taken. It was a highly political route, and Fowler's personal style did not always make him friends.

• • •

The most serious and immediate challenge facing Fowler was Central's relationship with the embryonic London Institute. In December 1986, Central again had three clear choices for survival: it could cut all ties with the ILEA and attempt to survive once again as a private institution (seen as a last resort), it could form a stronger link with PCL (although PCL was itself possibly at risk of closure or amalgamation), or it could remain within the ILEA and join the London Institute. Government funding effectively controlled Polytechnics and Colleges by decreasing or increasing budgets, and institutions with higher enrolment and more diverse courses were in favour. As a federation of ILEA-funded arts-based colleges, the London Institute could improve funding for the small, specialised colleges such as Central, not only by showing increased enrolment but also by providing more diverse courses. The London Institute was enthusiastic about the addition of a drama college to its portfolio, and the ILEA was keen for Central to join this federation. Nevertheless, in spite of the ILEA's enthusiasm Central Governors were cautious. No one could predict what joining the London Institute would ultimately mean for Central.

Fowler had taken over negotiations with the Institute and its Rector, John McKenzie, in December 1986, and had been initially in favour of a liaison. However, as George Kitson, remembered, 'I think he and Bob [Fowler] didn't mesh,' and it didn't take long for Fowler's optimism to sour. There had already been one 'misunderstanding' prior to Fowler's entering the mix when, in the autumn of 1986, the Institute had prematurely attached Central's student numbers to their funding projections. Now for an unspecified reason, the Institute ruled that, unlike other heads of colleges, Central's Principal would not become an Assistant Rector of the Institute. The Central Governors stood firm: if Central were to join the Institute, it would be as an equal partner in every respect, and this must include the awarding of equal status to its Principal. Central would negotiate no further if not on this basis. The Institute hastily changed its position on the issue, and once more began to woo Central. Recalling this period in 2006, Fowler wrote:

> What would happen to Central if it were to be dragged to the altar for marriage
> with the Institute? Certainly we would have lost our independence. It was strongly
> rumoured that we would also lose our Swiss Cottage site which some saw as an
> attractive headquarters for the Institute. At that time, and as matters turned out, it
> seemed the most important of all priorities to retain our independence. It was also the
> most tricky to achieve... I was aware that a forthcoming White Paper would specifically
> give Central an alternative to tying the legal knot with the Institute. We had to hang
> on for that White Paper. The pressure of the courting by the Institute became intense.
> It was suggested in a taxi that I and the Rector of the Institute should divert there and
> then to the Department of Education, see the Minister, and confirm our intentions. I
> pleaded the metaphorical headache...

Although unwilling to make a final commitment, early in spring 1987 Central Governors entered into informal arrangements and agreed instead to become a *de facto* constituent college. To continue Fowler's metaphor, Central was 'engaged', though no legal vows had been taken. The earliest possible membership in the Institute was September, but John McKenzie continued to press Central for a decision, giving May 1987 as a deadline. Central stalled. The government White Paper on Education was imminent.

The 1987 White Paper reflected the political climate of Thatcher's Britain. The Act would 'encourage' educational institutions towards a more business-like structure with the promise of more funding. Whether one agreed with its politics was immaterial, because its relevance for Central's future was considerable. Any LEA grant-aided or grant-maintained institution – with enrolment of more than 350 and with over 55% of its full-time students in Higher Education – could establish itself as an independent Higher Education 'Corporation' and become an equal member of a new funding council, with equal access to its funding. Fowler said in 2005: 'I think there is one thing I don't think anyone could possibly have done other than me, and it was related to the experience I luckily had had. Central wouldn't exist now, as Central, if I hadn't been able to play this game, if you like – or make this piece of politics work. People who could shoot me for whatever else I did, don't know what was really important.' Fowler pressed the Board of Governors to rescind their previous 'engagement' with the Institute, which they did on 26 May 1987. Central now waited for the White Paper to become law.

When the 1987 White Paper became the 1988 Education Reform Act, it formally created two new and distinct funding bodies: the Universities Funding Council, and the Polytechnics and Colleges Funding Council (PCFC). Local Educational Authorities continued to exist, but the Inner London Education Authority (ILEA) was abolished. All ILEA assets and liabilities were transferred either to the existing Local Authorities (in Central's case, Camden) or to the new independent Higher Education 'Corporations'. Central joined the PCFC, and on 1 April 1989 – 'Vesting Day' – Central finally became the owner of the valuable freehold land along College Crescent known as the Bank Site.

The PCFC immediately laid down new conditions and procedures for its members. Since becoming dependent on the ILEA in 1972, Central had gradually learned to accommodate increasing requirements for public accountability – effectively becoming a small business. With the 1988 Act, however, Higher Education now effectively became Big Business. Central became a Corporation, and its Principal became the Chief Executive Officer (CEO). In retrospect, it is clear that for Central this was the point of no return. If Central had joined the London Institute, no one knows whether Central would have lost its independence and identity. Perhaps it could have remained a small institution and become an even more specialised conservatoire for practical training. On the other hand, in time Central's Principal might well have been reassigned to another college within the Institute, with Central's independent administration becoming a small, off-site office with little connection to the Embassy or to the Central students and their needs. From here on, what might have been no longer mattered. Central had resolved to enter the world of Higher Education, and it was now presented with a new and concrete set of problems. To receive funding from the PCFC in the Government's new arena of corporate accountability, Central would have to accept substantial changes in how it ran its affairs or face the consequence of restricted funding – possible closure.

One early PCFC requirement was a review of the composition of the School's Governing Body, and the Governors Meeting in March 1989 was the last of Central's existing Board. Many Governors were considered eligible to serve on the new Board, but those deemed not suitable – for whatever reason – were asked to join the newly formed Advisory Board. The required reformation of the Board was a fortuitous requirement for Fowler. Nickolas Grace (Stage '69) was a Governor from 1985–9: 'We were told we had to resign to be reappointed, but we were never reappointed. We were just told that we were on an Advisory Board. We stayed on it for a while, but had absolutely no influence. We were an Advisory Board whose advice was never taken. I resigned.' There were major changes about to take place. A new CEO needed a compatible Board.

Another far-reaching PCFC requirement was that the Governors and the administration present a Strategic Plan for the future of the School. At the time, there was a widely held perception that PCFC funding requirements for small colleges would eventually call for a minimum enrolment of 600 students to assure survival, and it became clear that Central would have to expand its accommodation and facilities. Hired by Fowler, Debbie Scully had come to Central from her position as Registrar at Southwark College of Further Education, and it would be her job, with the help of external advisors, to appraise the options and develop an Estates Master Plan. She recalls:

> We looked at all kinds of options – should we stay here, should we consider moving someplace else, in London, out of London? We concluded, happily, that the Swiss

---

BEATRICE LILLIE ARCHIVE

Beatrice Lillie (Lady Peel) died on 20 January 1989, leaving her Henley Estate, Peel Fold, to her lover, John Huck. Huck died the next day, but had expressed in a letter of intent that Peel Fold should pass to a charity for the advancement of education, with particular reference to Musical Theatre. At John Gielgud's suggestion, the executors named Central as the beneficiary, and in 1990, Central accepted the Henley Estate, Peel Fold – conservatively valued at £850,000.

A separate charity, 'The Beatrice Lillie International College of Comedy and Musical Theatre', was created from proceeds of the sale of Peel Fold, and it remains under the control of three Trustees: the Chairman of Governors, the Deputy Chairman and the Principal. Grants from the trust are to be used for Musical Theatre. As a specific example of its use, in 1999 a £13,000 grant from the Charity was used to buy pianos and sound equipment for the new postgraduate Musical Theatre Course.

GEORGE EDDY

In 1989, George Eddy received a British Empire Medal in recognition of his dedicated service to Central and its students. Through a recommendation from Gerry Romaine, George was hired by Central in the 1960s and remained School caretaker for over thirty years. He passed away in 1995.

Cottage site had sufficient capacity to meet our long-term needs. We probably needed to grow in size because of the infrastructure costs, but we knew that we didn't want to ever go beyond 1000 students, so we were working on the basis of how much accommodation we would need. At the time there were temporary buildings on the Bank Site, and there was the Norman Collins Block. Low-rise, with no capacity to build up, neither made good use of the site at all. We had the theatre, and although it needed refurbishment, structurally it was very fine. And so all of the investment appraisals concluded that to stay here was the right thing. We devised a master plan where we would upgrade accommodation and develop the site in sections as funds became available. In the early years of the PCFC, there were no major capital grants, but there were minor capital awards, which meant that one could bid for up to £1 million. Our first priority was to put up the Embassy Extension. But we needed to do that in three phases, to fit with the funding. We had an excellent case, as all of our accommodation was categorized as 'unfit for purpose'.

Phase One of the Embassy Extension provided a double height workshop and prop area, replacing the small scenic workshop from which sets had overflowed onto the Eton Avenue pavement for as long as anyone could remember. Planning permission was obtained to build a further three storeys, a separate award was received to reconstruct the student canteen and kitchen area, and another award was given to repair and decorate the front elevation of the Theatre. These PCFC awards were a blessing for the crumbling buildings. Neither independently nor within the London Institute could Central so quickly have acquired the money to make such essential improvements to the facilities. Nevertheless, while the PCFC's generosity with capital funding was a huge benefit, some of its other policies were less palatable. At the same time as the PCFC provided funds for massive building works, it provided a framework for increased salaries for senior management and instituted severe budget restrictions for course provision. This created the perception that Central was squandering money on its facilities and senior salaries at the expense of its students.

• • •

Many Higher Education Institutions were undergoing the same government cutbacks. At its most basic, the 1988 Act had addressed government concerns that the number of students entering Higher Education was too low and the cost per student was too high. Its solution was simple, but devious. Initial PCFC funding per student was generous, but the funding allocated for each student decreased by a certain percentage each year that enrolment did not increase. Therefore, the only way any Higher Education Institution could maintain funding (much less enhance it) was to recruit more students. So, colleges and polytechnics recruited aggressively, but with the knowledge that extra student numbers would not generate enough additional income to provide more staff. As a result, not only did institutions need to create more facilities to handle increased enrolment, but staff to student teaching ratios rose uncomfortably. As Debbie Scully confirms: 'The number of students would have to increase by two or three percent each year just to stand still. Throughout the institution, the only way we could survive was to change the staff to student ratios by that percentage each year. This was common throughout Higher Education.' Where Central was different from other Higher Education Institutions was that its practical training ideally needed to maintain low student numbers and small teaching groups. If Central were to keep the growth of student numbers on its practical training to a minimum but still increase overall enrolment, it had to add new courses. There had been few additions to Central's curriculum over the years, and for Fowler's first three years as Principal courses remained largely unaltered. Behind the scenes was a different story.

Fowler brought in Robert Freeburn to run new part-time In-Service Courses for those already in employment, and in 1991–2 the first evening and summer courses began under the umbrella of the Speech, Theatre, Education and Professional Up-Dating Unit (STEP-UP).

NICKOLAS GRACE STAGE '69

Nickolas Grace was born in West Kirby in 1947 and educated at King's Chester Public School. From 1972, and throughout his successful career in theatre, radio, television and film, Grace has often returned to Central to direct and teach. He served as a Governor from 1985–9, and received an Honorary Fellowship in 2003. As he explained in a 2005 interview:

66 Central training was always passed on, in through-lines that came from Benson and Fogerty to Thurburn and Olivier – from the Old Vic School and Saint-Denis through George Hall and Litz Pisk, who had worked with Brecht. These through-lines are terribly important. Whenever I taught at Central, I tried to point out to students how assimilated techniques are passed on. For example, Olivier once said to me: 'Darling, always breathe from here, from the diaphragm. Fogie used to teach me that. Just push the grand piano with your diaphragm. When she did it, it used to move three inches; when I did it, it didn't move at all!'

The School has always given a complete training, with its focus on movement, its focus on voice. Students try modern, and they try classical, and it all combines to make the course. The more information and layers students are given, the better the training. After all, just look at the list of students who came here: Olivier, Judi Dench, Vanessa Redgrave, Julie Christie, Harold Pinter, Rufus Sewell, Graham Norton, Jason Isaacs. It's a complete cross-section of extraordinary theatre practitioners, of theatre and film actors. 99

That same academic year, Central also opened its first new department for almost half a century – Design, Interpretative and Visual Arts (DIVA) – which in 1993 would be renamed the Production, Art and Design (PAD) Department. The architect and first Head of this new department, Anthony Dean, had joined the staff at Central in 1987 after nearly a decade of experience in the professional theatre. In 1990, he launched an Advanced Diploma in Stage Design for eight students, and the next year developed six new courses: a CNAA-accredited Master of Arts (MA) in Stage Design, and Advanced Diploma Courses in Costume Design, Lighting Design, Computer Aided Design (Theatre), Fine Art (Painting) and Prop Making.

Debbie Scully defends Central's rapid growth in this area against criticism that the new courses were created only to increase enrolment:

> I think we were reflecting changes in the industry. For example, we used to offer just a technical Stage Management Course. But there was certainly a demand for – jobs for – sound designers, costume designers, stage designers, scenic artists, scenic carpenters because – particularly for scenic artists and scenic carpenters – the apprenticeship model wasn't around any more. It was a dying trade for them. Those courses didn't exist anywhere, and there was a demand for them, and they were related to theatre and theatre production. Our feeling was that stage designers were trained in art schools, divorced from actors and theatre. The philosophy was to offer comprehensive training, alongside other practical disciplines, and to replicate theatre as closely as possible.

Dean was a strong personality, and pushed his new Department to the forefront, often winning space and resources from other departments and leaving students and staff from other courses feeling sidelined. Other departments sought to keep up – new MAs were validated in Arts Education (Drama) and in Performance Studies – but in 1992–3 Dean and his staff added ten new courses: Advanced Diploma in Creative Theatre (New Writing), Advanced Diploma in Creative Theatre (Directing), Advanced Diploma in Costume Design, Advanced Diploma in Lighting Design, Advanced Diploma in Puppetry (the only such course in the country), Advanced Diploma in Costume Cutting and Construction, Advanced Diploma in Scenic Construction, Advanced Diploma in Scenic Art, and a Foundation in Art and Design. The reputation of the Production, Art and Design (PAD) Department grew, and it was soon taking student work to international festivals, including the Fourth Meeting of European Theatre Schools and Academies in Romania, the International Festival of Regional Theatre in the Czech Republic, and the UK Schools' exhibition at the Prague Quadrennial. Puppetry performances were taken to the International Puppetry Festival in Charleville-Mezieres, France. Two Central students took part in an experimental theatre laboratory in Amsterdam as part of the International Theatre Schools Festival, and a joint theatre project was organised with staff and students of the Theatre Department of Carnegie Mellon University, USA. In addition, the department attracted staff of the highest quality – in 1993, scene painting tutor, Leslie Woolnough, and in 1998, puppetry tutor, Penny Francis, received MBEs – and by the end of the decade, PAD had achieved an outstanding 24 out of 24 rating from a Subject Review Panel from the Quality Assurance Agency – external assessors who review not only the quality but also the relevance of any course provision.

From 1992, Central's previously existing courses also went through changes. The BSc (Honours) Speech and Language Pathology became the BSc (Honours) in Clinical Communication Sciences and – for non-practitioners – in Applied Communication Sciences.

More controversially, the Acting Course became validated as a BA degree, becoming the first such degree offered to actors training in London. Other drama schools would soon follow suit, and most now offer a BA or a BA (Hons), but at the time, many feared that this would place academic requirements on what had always been a purely practical course. Nevertheless, the new degree qualification meant financial benefits to Central acting students and, for the first time, they became

YVETTE PIENNE STAGE '28

Yvette Pienne graduated from Central in 1928, and went on to considerable success as an actress. She was in an early BBC broadcast of George du Maurier's novel, *Trilby*, transmitted in February 1927, played Chloe in *Back to Methuselah* at the (Royal) Court Theatre (May, 1928), worked with Barry Jackson at both the Birmingham Repertory Theatre and his first season at the Malvern Festival in 1929, and appeared in the West End in, among others, *1066 and All That* at the Strand Theatre in 1935 and *Jane Eyre* at the Queen's Theatre in 1936. Pienne wrote *The Fame of Grace Darling*, Wendy Hiller's first television role, which took up the Alexandra Palace Television Society's entire evening's transmission (from 9:05 to 11:05 pm) on 9 July 1939. When Pienne passed away in 1991, she left her house on Lambolle Road to Central. After its sale in 1996, the School received £250,000 to be utilised in her name as an appropriate tribute.

eligible for mandatory rather than discretionary fee awards. Robert Fowler recalled the struggle for acceptance of the degree: 'The actors always thought they were the best, and it's true the reputation of the college rested on them, but in a sense they were always the most insecure, because they had all these people taking degrees in Speech Therapy – they had Teachers and so forth. So, I said they ought to get degrees like musicians get degrees. Well, you can imagine, there was a terrific storm about it with the Governors! I said, "Well, tell you what we'll do. We'll first of all see if we can get the course degree-worthy, but we won't make them have degrees. We'll give the students the option: 'Do you want the degree or do you just want the Central certificate, which says you've passed the course?'" So that's what we did. The course was validated as a BA, and every single student chose to accept the degree qualification… It was the *students* who had to teach the *Governors*.'

Achieving a degree qualification for the course did not mean writing a new and more academic syllabus. It meant describing the existing course and convincing the validation panel that the intellectual challenges it presented to students were equivalent to those of other degrees. As it happened, the panel took little convincing: as Fowler said, 'When the team actually came from outside to consider whether the course could be given a degree, they looked at it and said it was so good – the performance is so good, the assessments are so good, the staff are so good – we would actually be able to back-date the qualification, because the 'new' course would be no different from the course that students were already on. So we were able to offer the degree qualification to students who were already on the course at the time.'

· · ·

Central added courses and increased student numbers – and therefore its funding income – but it also had to get its expenditure under control. In 1987–8, the School was not only on course to be massively over budget, it had also spent most of its reserves. Cost-cutting measures were put in place, but money problems persisted. On Vesting Day, the School had not only received valuable land, it had also inherited the liability for pension costs from the now-defunct ILEA, and staff pay had to be raised to stay in line with Polytechnics and Colleges Employers Forum pay scales. In order to achieve a decrease in salary expenditure, the unpopular existing policy of compulsory retirement was enforced. The first of these compulsory retirements was executed within days of Fowler becoming Principal Designate, and although it conformed to the letter of the 'law', it was an alienating start to his tenure.

Peggy Brennan had long been secretary to the Principal, but shortly after Fowler became Principal, upon her return from a short holiday she was unexpectedly 'retired'. On 19 December 1986, eleven members of both the administrative and academic staff from all three departments wrote a letter of complaint that concluded, 'We think you can expect that, as more members of CSSD learn of this, they will share our disquiet, and we hope you are planning to explain the situation to the school.' Two days later, Audrey Laski followed this up with a personal letter, to explain the anxiety and indignation felt on behalf of Brennan. She concluded, 'Bob, I know that you have supported Central most strongly at DES and have come to us with many exciting ideas for development. It would be such a waste if staff were to begin to feel fear rather than respect for and enthusiasm to work with you at the very beginning of your time at Central.' There is no record of Fowler's reply, but Brennan remained 'retired'.

Another, more eccentric, complaint also emerged shortly after Fowler became Principal. Nickolas Grace recalls the 'Bathroom-gate' incident: 'I remember standing up at a Governors' Meeting and saying, "We've known about Watergate, well, now this is going to be Bathroom-gate." He [Fowler] had spent a lot of money on Thurbie's old office

– the Principal's office – putting in a sofa bed and a bathroom, so he could stay over. It angered me, and it angered a lot of the staff. I said, "If there is extra money, it should go on a student bursary or for improvements to a different part of the building." That was when I realised I was almost on my own.'

Negative attitude shifts may have occurred initially within the staff and widened to the student body, but unease inevitably spread to ex-staff and alumni, and it was not long before word went out that Central was undergoing unpleasant changes. With academic budget restraints and compulsory retirement, coupled with visible (and what some saw as frivolous) expenditures that were apparently unrelated to providing education for the students, there was a gradual collapse in positive public perception. Rumours spread. As with all hearsay, there were inconsistencies and fictions just as there were personal observations and truth, but management was unwilling, or unable, to calm concerns and complaints. Whatever the realities behind the rumours, and regardless of the political triumphs occurring behind closed doors, it is undeniable that some students during those years had an unsettling time. This was certainly true within the Acting Course.

• • •

In the spring of 1987, George Hall retired after 24 years as Head of the Acting Course. William Hemmingway, a friend of Fowler's, was hired to replace him: ' I brought Bill from Bretton Hall to Central. I wanted someone very upright, someone who could be looked up to, who was respectable as a person. I had a high opinion of him… He seemed just the kind of person to lead the department. Not necessarily to teach acting, that wasn't what was needed. What was needed was someone who could run a budget, write syllabuses and get them through, and who could run a team.'

Central actors, however, had been used to having a Head of Course who was a 'man of the theatre' – someone who not only understood actors and their craft, but also had a commitment to actor training. Hemmingway's appointment was not a success, and he left Central after only six weeks. This was the beginning of a long line of official, and unofficial, Course Leaders.

Stephen Hazell, Deputy Principal, became the 'Acting Head of the Theatre Department', that incorporated both Acting (Stage) and Stage Management (Technical), and Anthony Falkingham stepped in to become Acting Head of the Acting Course for one year.

Darren Lawrence (Stage '89) was at Central during the time that included Fowler's appointment as Principal, the changeover to the PCFC and Hall's retirement. In an interview in 2005, Lawrence spoke of some of the student unrest in Fowler's first years:

He seemed to typify what was happening in the world. We'd got a Tory leader, and it was all about saving money – nothing to do with training actors. It seemed he was out of touch with the heart of the school, and we felt abandoned. The School was in a lot of unrest; there was a great sense of unease – a feeling of the place changing into something we hadn't auditioned for. There'd been talk that Fowler was going to cut the number of shows for our third year, and we were trying to get meetings with him, just to get him to explain himself, but he only met us once, and it was very much like dealing with a politician. He didn't answer your questions directly, and when he left, we were none the wiser. People were very, very highly strung at the meeting, and after. I don't know if it was true or not, but we felt as if we were being shafted.

I don't think any of it impacted on our year in terms of work or what we're doing now, but we were unsettled. I've only been back in the building once. I didn't want to go back. I think the word on the street was that the reputation had taken a real nosedive after we left. There was a feeling in the business that it had lost its reputation. Now, it's a great place to go again.

Between 1986 and 1989, there were four Heads of the Acting Course, though not always under that title. In February 1990, a National Council for Drama Training report strongly recommended that, with minimum delay, permanent appointments be made to the posts of Head of Theatre Department and Head of the Acting Course. Fowler responded in a letter headed *without prejudice*: 'Until a satisfactory appointment can be made for the post of Chair of the Theatre Department, and until we are satisfied that the advice of the panel with regard to course provision has been acted upon sufficiently, the Deputy Principal will continue to hold this brief… To assist in solving the problem of securing the involvement of really distinguished professionals of national standing and repute who are not able (or do not wish) to commit themselves to full-time professional appointments with the additional responsibilities such posts carry, the possibility of Visiting Fellowships for distinguished practitioners who have expressed an interest in working at the School is now under discussion.'

Discussion came to fruition when Bill Alexander, Royal Shakespeare Company Associate Director, became the first Visiting Fellow to the Theatre Department. As Fowler recalls: 'I did that as a deliberate move to appoint someone straight out of the theatre. That's what distinguished places do.'

For the next seven years, there were a number of appointments to the position that was now known variously as Course Leader, Course Director, Artistic Director, or Head of Acting. Fowler's early attempts to find someone who could lead the course to its previous standing were creative, if unsuccessful. The position seemed difficult to fill, perhaps because it remained unclear what the position entailed. A Course Leader who could fulfil administrative requirements would have to possess exactly the qualities Fowler saw in William Hemmingway: the ability to run a budget, write successful syllabuses, and run a team. However, to run the course artistically, a successful Course Leader should also have experience in the theatre and a vision for actor training. In addition, if the course were to maintain its standing within the School, its Leader had to be able to 'do meetings' – willing not only to sit through them but also to manoeuvre politically for the very best facilities and budgets for his, or her, course. Successful applicants to the position, whatever it was called, did not always get the job for which they thought they were applying.

From the retirement of George Hall in April 1987 until Geoffrey Colman took over in 1998, nine different people – in a permanent or acting capacity – were engaged as Head of the Acting Course or under a different title in an equivalent, and even an unofficial, role: William Hemmingway, Anthony Falkingham, Mark Wing-Davey, Donna Soto-Morettini, Nick Phillips, David Carey, Anthony Castro, Pippa Ailion, and Nigel Rideout. The shortest time in the position was six weeks; the longest was three years.

As well as a quick turnaround in Course Leaders, there was also a shift in the course numbers. Instead of the traditional 28 to 30 acting students accepted each year, at the beginning of the 1990s a new total of 45 included students on a new Musical Theatre strand. This brought increased funding but only a minor increase in staff, so it limited the amount of time each student could directly interact with tutors – either in class or for tutorials. Perhaps more disturbing for the students, there were fewer chances in their final year of training to play larger roles in the public shows – their only means of attracting an agent and

ALISON GRAHAM STAGE '92

66 Coming to Central from the United States was a dream come true. I had always noticed in the Playbills on Broadway that the actors who interested me the most on stage had trained in England. I also had a few American friends in New York, who had graduated from Central and RADA, whose work I respected – especially in the classics. I thought it made sense to study in Shakespeare's native country where his words came naturally trippingly off the tongue. So, I auditioned for Mark Wing-Davey and Mark Dornford-May in New York. During the interview and call-backs, I knew these were two directors who would challenge me, and I chose Central over RADA. The 'two Marks', as we would come to call them, did not fail my expectations, nor did the rest of the staff that first year in 1989.

Sometime in the first week of the course, Mark Dornford-May said, 'You are all good actors and that is why you were selected. No one is going to be cut from this class. It is our job to make you better actors, and we have three years to do it.' Our three years with the 'two Marks' was, however, sadly cut short our first year. The discovery that Robert Fowler wanted to make great changes to the conservatory experience at Central and that Mark Wing-Davey was leaving was shocking to us all. To learn that Mark Dornford-May would leave as well added salt to the wound. The students in Stage '91 and Stage '92 decided to take action.

We met in the dingy canteen on the second floor, and after long and boisterous deliberation (the American contingent being the most vociferous), we decided to strike. And we did just that. We arrived at school with picket signs in our hands and marched in front of the entrance stairs shouting, demanding, and refusing to go to our scheduled classes until we got our way. But this was to no avail, and our cries fell on deaf ears. At the end of the year when we said to the Marks: 'What will do we do without you? Who will teach us?', they said: 'You have each other, and you will learn from each other'. **99** future employment. (The Musical Theatre strand gradually accepted fewer students, until the final three undergraduate students graduated in 1998 and the strand was phased out in favour of a new one-year Postgraduate Diploma in Musical Theatre.) Ironically, within the School some felt that Fowler focused his attentions on the Acting Course to the exclusion of others while, with the proliferation of courses and increased total enrolment, the external perception was that the standing of the Acting Course within Central was gradually being diminished.

In spite of this, there were a great number of successful third-year shows, many directed by prestigious professional guest directors. In 1989, Dame Judi Dench directed a sold-out production of *Macbeth*. In 1990, third-year students visited Romania for interviews and research, resulting in a new play by Caryl Churchill that was directed by Course Leader, Mark Wing-Davey. Students would perform *Mad Forest* not only in the Embassy Studio but also at the Royal Court Theatre. In 1995, the Theatre Department, now renamed the Performance Department, hosted a conference on 'Voice in British Actor and Performance Training', and that same year, a delegation of students was invited to the 40th Annual Student Drama Festival in Scarborough. Dedicated long-time tutors such as Sally Grace (voice), Debbie Green and Vanessa Ewan (movement), and Alan Dunnett (acting), successfully influenced the training and growth of actors throughout the 1990s, and the decade saw no diminishment of success for Central actors. In 1998, 83% of graduates were employed in the acting profession within seven months of leaving the course. In 1996, and again in 2001, the National Council for Drama Training (NCDT) gave full and unqualified accreditation to the Acting Course for the maximum of five years, and in 1998, the Quality Assurance Agency rated the Performance Department an impressive 23 out of 24.

• • •

Meanwhile, government educational policies continued to influence Central's future. Since the 1988 Education Reform Act, two different bodies had provided funding: one for universities and one for colleges and polytechnics. The 1992 Further Education Act created the Higher Education Funding Council for England (HEFCE) to provide funding for both groups and remove any elitism there might have been between the two. Most polytechnics became universities, and the old validating body that had served polytechnics and colleges – the CNAA – was abolished, with many of the new universities acquiring powers to bestow their own degrees. To protect themselves from dependence on larger organisations, smaller colleges would either have to form a liaison with a new validating institution or, as was Central's aim, seek their own Taught Degree-Awarding Powers (T-DAPs). It would take ten years for Central to fulfil the strict criteria to achieve these powers. In the meantime, arrangements were made to transfer course validation from the CNAA to the Open University Validation Services (OUVS). Robert Fowler:

'That was something which only people running colleges and their deputies knew about – people like Debbie Scully and Linda Cookson, those who had to drive to get the money and get the accreditations. You couldn't carry this too far down, you couldn't tell the students a lot about it...'

Central now had to meet the challenges presented by a new validation organisation. Since becoming Academic Registrar and Senior Tutor in 1987, Linda Cookson had worked behind the scenes to train staff in the writing of course documents. This staff training had already secured the successful validation by CNAA of the BA Acting, but even if a course did not earn external validation, she had insisted it at least merit internal validation from Central's Academic Board. Now, with these documents already

STUDENT FEES AND MANAGEMENT SALARIES

With changing government educational policies, there was a gradual deterioration of government funding for students, culminating in its total loss. By 1995, the Acting Course fees were £2880 per year and still paid by the funding body, but each student was also charged what was called an 'enhancement' fee, an additional sum owed directly to the School by the student, over and above their set tuition fee. Overseas student fees rose to £6250. By 1999–2000, student enhancement fees (now called 'top-up' fees) rose to £1200 for undergraduates (graduate students: £3500 to £4395), and overseas student fees rose to £7000 per year.

in hand, it proved a surprisingly easy journey to gain external degree status from the OUVS for a number of former Central Diploma or Certificate courses. Cookson had also instilled in staff the value of fair criteria for student grading and the importance of consistent management practices for any circumstance across all courses. In an on-going training programme, she kept the staff up to date with external agency guidelines (including those of the Quality Assurance Agency, following its formation in 1997) to ensure that students' work was properly assessed against national standards. Improved procedures for monitoring courses were established, and democratic systems were put in place to seek student opinion (and act on it).

From 1992 through to the end of the decade, Central re-accredited existing courses and created new ones with the OUVS. The School still worked closely with what was by then called the Queen Mary and Westfield College (within the University of London) in relation to the BA in Drama and a Language, and it worked with the University of Westminster (the old PCL) in relation to the BSc in Clinical Communication Sciences. The Advanced Diploma in Voice Studies was revalidated by the OUVS as a Postgraduate Diploma in Voice Studies, and later as an MA. The 'Sesame' (Drama and Movement Therapy) course followed the same route. New OUVS validations included a BA (Honours) in Theatre Studies (Design), a Diploma in Higher Education in Design Interpretation, and a part-time version of the existing MA in Stage Design. The BTEC in Stage Management and Technical Arts became a Higher Education Diploma, which later merged with Design

Interpretation to become a combined BA (Honours) in Theatre Practice, with strands in Set Design, Scenic Art, Scenic Construction, Technical Stage Management, Costume Design, Costume Construction, Prop-Making, Puppetry, Stage Management, Production Lighting, Lighting Design, Production Sound, and Sound Design.

Some existing courses also changed their names and/or their qualification routes. Although often confusing for the 'outsider', these changes were not whimsical but had a direct relationship to the evolving requirements in the larger world of education and employment. From 1990 to 1993, applications to the BEd Course had quadrupled, but in 1993, Drama was subsumed as part of English in the National Curriculum. A concurrent government consultative document proposed that drama now be viewed only as a medium for teaching other subjects, which obviously diminished the status of drama in the curriculum. The Government also announced proposals to curtail the role of teacher training within colleges and universities, placing greater emphasis on on-the-job training and requiring that 66% of training take place in schools. There was an acknowledged lack of skilled drama teachers in schools to undertake this training in the workplace, and the future of specialist drama teacher training courses looked grim. Central's Education Department had to change with the times.

In 1993–4, the four-year BEd (Hons) in Drama and Spoken Language was restructured into a three-year BA (Hons) in Drama and Education. This BA (Hons) did not give qualified teacher status, so a one-year Postgraduate Certificate in Education (PGCE) course was added for the approximately twenty percent of graduates who wanted to teach. Sally Mackey, Course Leader of the new BA, was positive about this new offering: 'The shift to the BA from the old BEd was not just as a result of keeping one step ahead of the government. There was a genuine desire to encompass a more relevant and broad area of drama – not just training teachers but also working with communities, alongside theatre education departments, and in other specialist areas.' In 1994, the traditional production held at the end of the first year of the old BEd was replaced by a week of performances at the cliff-top Minack Theatre in Cornwall, where BA students performed for adults in the evenings and children during the days. Now the shows at the Minack are an annual tradition. Simon Cooper retired as BEd Course Leader in 1996 when the last year of BEds at Central graduated.

● ● ●

Just as the 1988 and the 1992 Education Acts had intended, student numbers grew nationally. In 1987–8, full-time student enrolment at Central stood at 300. By 1991–2, this had risen to 490. By 1993–4 it stood at 600, and by 1994–5 there were 650 full-time students. In the wake of this expansion, Central urgently needed more space.

Between 1990 and 1994, Central received £2.4 million in grants from HEFCE. Phase Two of the Building Project was completed in the summer of 1993, and Central's

Patron, HRH Princess Alexandra, opened the Embassy Extension in the spring of 1994. By building on top of the Embassy Studio as well as the Phase One Embassy Extension, the School gained a new studio theatre, a lecture theatre, design studios and wardrobe facilities. Phase Three – to replace the John Davis Wing and the Stage Management Block with the East Block – was made possible by another £1.15 million grant from HEFCE, as well as a £1.15 million bank loan. To provide teaching space during this disrupting period of redevelopment, in 1993 Central acquired a lease on 1–5 St Pancras Way.

Before any building could begin at Swiss Cottage, Central had to be assured either of a long-term lease or the outright freehold purchase on the Embassy Theatre site. In 1995, Eton College finally agreed to sell the land, and in December HEFCE made a single payment of £1.05 million as full and final settlement. As soon as the contract was completed in March 1996, the John Davis Wing and the Stage Management Block were demolished, and

SALLY MACKEY

Sally Mackey received an English and Drama (Hons) degree from the University of Exeter, a PGCE from Goldsmiths, University of London, and an MA in Arts Education and Cultural Studies from the University of Warwick. In 1992, Mackey began as a lecturer on the B Ed degree at Central in what was then the Education Department, and in 1993 became Course Leader for the new BA in Drama and Education. She recalls her early years at Central as a positive experience:

66 Fowler gave the Departments scope to undertake, develop and initiate new courses, new ideas, networking and moving out to our relative industries. Whilst he may not have been physically present in the building some of the time, we were given a lot of range to develop... And of course at the time, we had Debbie Scully and Linda Cookson who were, and still are, just incredible – very strong, dynamic female role models – very intelligent, bright, with a huge range of talents for encouraging staff and ensuring quality. 99

in October 1997, HRH Princess Alexandra opened a magnificent new five-storey block that housed a library, computing and learning resource facilities, a student common room and bar, a student counselling and advisory services unit, administrative offices, a board room, and a staff room.

Central's management had artfully navigated the maze of government funding to achieve the first phases of the Building Strategy, but there was still more to do. Late in 1997, Central applied to the HEFCE Poor Estates Initiative for money to refurbish the Embassy Theatre and to build an Atrium link to achieve disabled access to all principal parts of the Embassy site. The following year, HEFCE approved a 50% contribution from Poor Estates Funding to go towards the estimated total cost of £5,072,000. Central would have to come up with the remaining 50%, either through additional funding by HEFCE, fundraising, loans, or use of reserve investment funds, but within months, HEFCE released a further £1.25 million and agreed an interest-free loan of up to £1.2 million, to be repaid over ten years. Phase Three construction was now brought forward, and Central began to plan for Phase Four development on the College Crescent Bank Site – the West Block.

This surge of growth created the perception that with Central's focus so firmly on additional building, its proliferation of new courses and the resulting increased enrolment, the School was not paying enough attention to its existing strengths. Seemingly, there was proof of this when the 'three-legged stool' of John Allen's day was irrevocably broken, and Central closed one of its most famous Courses: Speech and Language Therapy.

• • •

The Speech and Language Therapy Department had been through many changes since its creation in 1945, but throughout its history, the Royal College of Speech and Language Therapists (RCSLT) had always provided the course's accreditation. This was vital. Whatever the external degree validation arrangements for the course, a graduating student could not practise as a therapist without a Licence from the RCSLT. If the RCSLT felt there were problems to address in a course, they could demand an accreditation visit take place as often as every year. Likewise, they could accredit a course for a longer period if they believed that an institution was providing appropriate training.

The first major setback to Speech Therapy at Central occurred in 1991 when the government decided that, as requirements were becoming more and more medically-orientated in terms of equipment needs and expectations in curriculum, the course should be funded by the NHS and not through the PCFC. This effectively separated the course from other funding opportunities within the School. Next, for a couple of years the Department was unable to recruit to a number of vacant key posts, which led to increased pressure on existing staff. This was officially attributed to a national shortage of clinical staff, but some observers felt it was directly due to rumours in the profession that the Central course was in trouble. To address the RCSLT's ongoing requirement for more practical and clinical work, Central opened its first on-site clinic facility for BSc students on 11 December 1995, and the Principal's report noted: 'The clinic co-ordinator took up her post in September, and in the same month we appointed a new BSc leader from the University of Cape Town. We ran four training days for clinicians and thus strengthened and nurtured our vital relationship with the Speech and Language Therapy profession. Work is continuing in a difficult national environment to enhance the BSc provision.'

Enhancement of the BSc provision had complicated undercurrents not mentioned in the Principal's report. The 1995 RCSLT accreditation visit had noted a lack of medical experience provided by Central's BSc, which would have to be provided if the course were to retain its accreditation. Nevertheless, the RCSLT agreed (exceptionally) to place the course on a further, and final, one-year review period until December 1996, and an action plan was agreed.

When the RCSLT returned in December 1996, their two-day final review of the Department concluded that Central had still not met all of the conditions set and that accreditation should be withdrawn. Central appealed, and once more the RSCLT agreed (again, exceptionally) that the BSc could remain accredited for a further year, in the hope that the course could be restructured. Elaine Hodkinson, previous Head of the Department: 'The RCSLT didn't want to withdraw accreditation. The whole history of the profession started at Central, and they felt that the heart would be taken out of it.' In spite of this sentiment, the RCSLT was concerned over Central's lack of a medical science base, which was now deemed to be a requirement in the delivery of modern day training in speech and language therapy. The demands of the accrediting body were getting heavier and heavier in this respect. Other courses had access to medical schools and technical assets, and if Central were to retain its accreditation, major and expensive changes would have to be made.

While the RCSLT accredited the BSc, the Open University Validation Services (OUVS) validated it, and the course was due for Joint Review by both the RCSLT and the OUVS in the 1996–7 academic year. This was deferred until autumn 1997, while Central tried to address the RCSLT requirements.

Prior to this official external Joint Review, the Central Academic Board scheduled an internal review (involving external professionals) that would evaluate both the effectiveness of the BSc course provision over the previous six years and the appropriateness of its future plans. In November 1997, the

ADAM HUNTLEY
SPEECH THERAPY '98

❝ It happened so quickly. No sooner were our names called to enter the graduation queue than I was handed my degree with a smile and applause – the last person ever to be granted a speech therapy degree from the Central School of Speech and Drama.

Central was a different place then. It didn't have security doors. The library was stocked with books on stuttering, psycholinguistics and cognitive neuro-psychology journals. But there were books on dance or radical puppetry to satisfy our curiosity. Even the canteen was different. You could easily spot from the tables that the seriously minded were the theraps; the stunning, beautiful people were the actors and actresses and the raucous show-offs were the BEds. The shaven-headed hammer carriers had something to do with stage management. Together we saw free end of year plays from the actors, and I wondered how many of them I would see again in episodes of Soldier Soldier.

…Central had been uniquely an institution of art and science, and I hope that anyone who has the good fortune to be accepted to a full-time course there now will be made familiar with the School's founding principles. Apprentice actors should not forget that their training shares the same root as today's objectively minded therapists… Granted, in those early days fluency in communication was naively seen simply as a place on a spectrum. But it was called Speech and Drama because both are to do with expression and the exchange of feelings, views and insight. ❞

Academic Board panel concluded that it was unable to confirm that the BSc had met the baseline of a satisfactory overall operation. In the opinion of the panel, the course would succeed neither in re-accreditation by the RCSLT nor in revalidation with the OUVS. An Extraordinary Meeting of the Academic Board in December 1997 accepted the conclusions of the internal panel and, as a result, agreed there should not be a 1998 intake to the BSc Clinical and Communication Sciences Course. In March 1998, the Governors resolved to transfer continuing students to City University. After 43 years, the Speech and Language Therapy Department at the Central School of Speech and Drama ceased to exist on 31 August 1998.

Although it is not mentioned in any of the documents, according to Robert Fowler there was another consideration that influenced Central's decision. Central's senior management and Board of Governors had firmly set their sights on applying for Taught Degree-Awarding Powers. To make this application, Central would have to prove to future assessors that it had consistently and successfully exercised managerial responsibility for its courses. It also had to show an unblemished track record in securing and maintaining the validation and (where relevant) the professional accreditation of courses. If the RCSLT didn't accredit the Speech and Language Therapy Course, it was likely that Central would be ineligible to apply for Taught Degree-Awarding Powers. Central had been given a year to put its house in order, but when it became apparent the BSc would not be accredited without major restructuring and unsustainable extra expenditure, the course was sacrificed.

Speech and Language Therapy had gone through enormous changes since Elsie Fogerty, and as a small arts-based institution, Central was not ideally placed to satisfy the course's modern medical requirements. In spite of this, some will always maintain that the BSc at Central should never have been allowed to get to a state where it could not be accredited. Perhaps an earlier understanding of, and a respect for, this course might have prevented its demise. Nevertheless, by the mid-1990s the bottom line had really become 'the bottom line'. As expensive as it was to transfer the students to City University – and it was expensive – with the increased and increasing medical requirements for accreditation Central could not afford to maintain the Speech and Language Therapy Course over the long-term. Central had seen a small surplus (£202,000) in 1995–6, but by the end of July 1998, there was again a deficit of almost £500,000. By letting the Speech and Language Therapy Course go, Central could address how best to balance its budget – and keep open the possibility of achieving its Taught Degree-Awarding Powers. In spite of this, with the loss of its Speech and Language Therapy Department, Central undoubtedly and permanently forfeited an integral part of its personality and history.

• • •

Whatever Central's place had been in the past, it was now carving a unique position in its present. Throughout the 1990s, Central not only began to reflect the changes in theatre, but also helped shape its future. Presenting new courses in a number of emerging disciplines, the School took a lease on the Lion and Unicorn Pub Theatre to provide performance space for theatre companies nurtured at Central.

Early in the 1990s, two separate postgraduate diploma courses in Design and Creative Theatre were amalgamated into an MA Advanced Theatre Practice (MAATP), enabling performers (not just actors), dramaturges, set, light and sound designers, puppeteers, writers and creative producers to work together, form a company, devise, and present projects within the boundaries of a theme. Head of Undergraduate Studies, Ross Brown wrote in 2006: 'MAATP's groundbreaking work in the 1990s is perhaps best characterised by its site-specific productions, which happened in disused churches, factories, boat-houses, and – infamously – at the Oval cricket ground, where the finale, a mass "streak" across the pitch, ruffled a few feathers in the pavilion. Some of these were text-based and developed the role of the dramaturge as creative collaborator (*The Dog Beneath the Skin* in a disused warehouse which later became Central's St Pancras Way annexe, and *Ghetto* in a disused factory in Docklands), and then later, with the addition of the writing strand, they became collaboratively authored pieces. It can be claimed with some justification that the MA Advanced Theatre Practice course was ahead of its time. Influential, award winning site-specific theatre practitioners – such as Ben Harrison of Gridiron, and Shunt – were early graduates.'

In 1998, ten young MAATP students with diverse backgrounds and talents formed their highly acclaimed theatre company, Shunt. Having presented a Central project on medieval torture in a former railway arch in Bethnal Green, for the next five years they maintained this space as a home for their new company. By combining theatre with circus, dance and the audio-visual arts, Shunt continued to create distinctive, innovative and site-specific collaborative performances, and in 2003, the company moved to a new home in the London Bridge Vaults.

End of year events in the design department also began to add performances. Again, Ross Brown gives this perspective:

> The BA (Hons) Theatre Studies course, which began in 1993, brought theatre design to Central at undergraduate level for the first time. Unlike the traditional art school

JOAN HAINES

In 1998, Joan Haines was elected an Honorary Fellow of the Royal College of Speech and Language Therapists for her 'outstanding contribution to the profession in her role as Administrator to the Speech and Language Therapy Department at Central.' Haines worked for the Speech Therapy Course from 1974 to 1998, and in the Education Department until her retirement in 2001.

SPECIAL FUND ACCOUNTS FOR STUDENTS

In 1996, there were four Special Fund accounts: Student Hardship (£7856), Clive Brook (£4470), Syvia Strutt and Hilda Brettel Memorial (£748), and the Jane Cowell Memorial (£5859). That same year, the Gary Bond (Stage '62) Memorial Fund was started (£15,000), which would annually award £750 to an acting student. In 1999, a former student endowed the Milner Scholarship with £130,000.

design course – which tended to concentrate on 'dry' model-box design – Central's approach to design was, of course, thoroughly immersed in the 'wet' processes of collaboration and rehearsal. The course offered lighting, sound design and puppetry as well as set and costume, and worked in close collaboration with the Diploma courses in Stage Management and Design Interpretation (and of course, with the Acting Course). Rather than culminating in a degree show (as was the art school convention for theatre design courses), BA Theatre Studies, or BATS as it was affectionately known, pioneered a series of performance events to showcase the work of its final year students. Memorably these included, in 1996, a transformation of Central's impressive new scenic workshop into a beautiful, if death-defying, aerial performance that predated work by companies such as De La Guarda. For this show, the students elicited the help of an opera singer and students from The Circus Space. Other degree events that were decidedly 'ahead of their time' included a themed club performance entitled *The End* (at the End nightclub – co-ordinated by the recent Central graduate David Jubb, now Artistic Director of Battersea Arts Centre) and a site-specific themed party at the disused Aldwych Tube station under the Strand entitled 'Lost and Found', with sound and light installations, built sets, puppetry and interactive performance – all co-ordinated by the recent Central graduates Shunt. In 1997 the BATS course merged with the Stage Management and Design Interpretation Diplomas to become BA (Hons) Theatre Practice.

After the 1996 BATS collaboration with The Circus Space students, Central took this relationship further. In 1998–9, Central offered a one-year Certificate in Higher Education in Circus, which was later developed into a degree. The Circus Space had opened its doors in 1990, and in 1994 had taken over as its home a derelict electricity generating station in Hoxton. In The Circus Space's first collaborative year with Central, 72 people applied for 20 places on this new, accelerated course. Students trained for 45 weeks, and graduates formed the Ensemble Company that performed in the Millennium Dome in 2000.

• • •

One of the first drama schools to become part of the world of Higher Education, Central had grown into an institution far beyond anything its founder could have envisaged. The argument as to whether Central was on the correct path for a practical drama training

GRAHAM NORTON STAGE '89

66 Central auditions were kind of like a Drama X Factor – before there was X Factor. The first year I auditioned, I got a gazillion recalls. I was on the waiting list, and I was even called in during the summer. I don't know if they still do this, but then Central kept bringing you back and back and back, so even if you didn't want to go there, by the end you'd have cut off your grandmother's arm to get in. Very clever. When I auditioned the next year, I just got in. No recalls or anything. Then again, by that time we all knew each other so well.

Going to drama school is the safest, most indulgent thing you can do. It's great. You get up every morning and say, 'What am I going to do today? Hmmm. Okay, today I'm going to focus on me.' That's it. That's all you're going to do. Focus on you. 'My what a lovely hand I have.' I was lucky because I was a bit older. To go straight to drama school at 18 – that really has to mess with your head. It's all so emotionally charged. By the third year, you'd see slamming doors, and people running to the toilets to cry. You'd see people sobbing in the cafeteria. All I could say was, 'Get over it, you're not from Russia.' I don't know, what do you think? Maybe I didn't take it seriously enough.

I think the most valuable thing I took out of Central was what I couldn't do. I was bad at the serious stuff. And that gave me a direction. Up until drama school, I'd never valued my ability to make people laugh. It had always come so easy. I'd always try not to be funny in improvs, because it seemed to me like it was cheating. Some people are very good in improv. They have their moment of truth. I don't. I'm not serious; I'm just not being funny. I just stop. There's nothing. There's no light. It's just all gone. In the end, I'd give in, and people were glad I'd been funny – I'd have cheered up a very dreary improv. But then I saw that there were some very good serious actors who didn't know how to do comedy. They didn't understand the jokes. That grammar, that rhythm was instinctive to me. It was then I began to value it as a skill.

I think the oddest thing about drama school is that it trains you to be a star. It trains you to play lead roles and not to play the neighbour who comes in briefly with a note. But that is what you'll be. The vast majority of actors will be the neighbour with the note. I was 27 when I left Central and you'd think I'd have figured that out. It's only when you get into the profession and you find that you are playing some waiter that doesn't have a name, that maybe you realise, actually, I don't enjoy this very much. It's not about the money. It's about the work. You could hold out in penury if you thought the next job would be satisfying. But then, I don't think there's any way around it. You can't train people with only half a line: 'Here's your half a line – you get interrupted when a bus goes by.' You can't train people like that. They used to warn us, but nobody listened. And there was always, 'There are no small parts, just small actors.' No. That's not true. There are *reeeaallly* small parts. I played a dead person in a BT training film. Worse, I had to go and meet them to get the job. I didn't have to audition, but I did have to go and meet them. Imagine if I'd not got it! I mean, I was dead. Well, at least not moving. And I was face down on the ground. That's a small part.

I don't know how writing my own stuff came about. Maybe it was just desperation. I can't imagine the 'me' that had that much confidence to say, I'm going to write this, and say it out loud, and you'll all sit in rows and be delighted. I can't imagine I did that, but I must have. I did this Mother Theresa show, and that went to Edinburgh, and from that I did other shows. Then I started doing stand-up. Once you're doing stand-up, life becomes easier. You can make some money, because there are lots of clubs, and people know what you are. When I was doing the one-man shows, it was:

[*continued…*

'What is he? Is he an actor?' In fact I wasn't anything. I was in transition. I didn't want to be a stand-up, and it's very hard to let go of wanting to be an actor.

I did do a bit of acting last year. I was put in a film as a sort of 'stunt casting'. But, you know, they said I was okay in it! Which is pathetically needy of me. They liked me! But there you are. I do think the root buzz to all performers – and I think a lot of actors would like to not believe this – the buzz is people going hurrah, hurrah, and clapping. It is about acclaim, and the acclaim is about 'you've done a job well'. If a man came and painted my front door, he'd probably enjoy painting my front door a lot more if at the end of it the neighbours all gathered around and cheered and threw flowers at him. He'd like it more. Acting is doing something that the people in the audience can't do. It's a feat.

And I'd say still I will go to my grave a failed actor before a successful anything else. It's in you. That was my first love; that is what I wanted to do. All this other stuff? Great, I'm so pleased and I love doing it. But somehow, I know that this, weirdly, is a compromise. **"**

institution would continue, but by the time Robert Fowler stepped down as Principal, this was largely an intellectual debate. Central was committed to, and firmly planted within, Higher Education. The primary discussion for the 21st century could no longer be whether this had been the right decision, but rather how best to address and conquer the challenges presented by this new world.

During Fowler's 13 years as Principal, his position had become that of a Chief Executive Officer whose job it was not only to run an educational corporation but also to guide it through a maze of governmental and funding politics. Although Fowler was not always a popular Principal, under his leadership Central had acquired its own land and buildings, thereby gaining security for the future. The Speech and Language Therapy Course had been lost, but a highly respected Production, Art and Design Department had been created – a replacement leg to John Allen's 'three-legged stool'. Student numbers had increased nearly 250%, and this included over 200 students studying for postgraduate degrees – making it the largest 'Drama Department' in the country. All of Central's full-time courses offered degrees and provided qualifications for students who in the modern world would need not only an education but also the credentials to prove it.

In March 2000, the Governors announced Fowler's formal retirement on 31 August. Contractually entitled to a period of Sabbatical leave, Fowler carried out his 'agreed European/international responsibilities' until 31 March 2001.

In June 2000, Professor Gary Crossley was appointed Principal and Chief Executive Officer of the Central School, and he began his tenure on 1 October 2000.

• • •

ADDITIONAL CENTRAL FACTS

1987
- Douglas Cornelissen retires, and Karen Stone becomes new Stage Management Course Leader.
- David Terence, tutor on the Stage Course since 1964, takes early retirement.

1988
- Alan Allkins leaves Central after 17 years in the Teacher Department.

1989
- Lord Olivier dies. Dame Peggy Ashcroft becomes President of Central.

1991
- Brian Goodban, Manager of Coutts Bank, forms an external Audit Committee to achieve correct levels of funding from the HEFCE. In 1992, he joins the Board.
- Audrey Laski retires on 31 December.

1992
- Central Syllabus of Assessments is launched, to incorporate the Poetry Society Assessments. This remains at Central until 1999, when it is transferred to Guildhall.
- Dame Judi Dench becomes President of the School.
- Diana Cooper, Clare Jeffery, Jackie Masterson, Nigel Morgan and Claire Topping leave at end of summer term.

1993
- John Davis dies.
- Gwynneth Thurburn dies, and a Memorial is held at the Embassy Theatre to celebrate her life.

1995
- Paul Taiano, Chartered Accountant, is appointed to the Board of Governors and the Audit Committee.

1996
- Renee Hosking retires as Registrar, the last to hold this position as it had traditionally stood, and the second-longest to hold the position since Vera Sargent.

1997
- Dame Judi Dench resigns her position as President of Central in protest against School policies. The position remains unfilled for the next four years.
- Jocelyn Herbert becomes an Emeritus Fellow and gives her archive to Central in return for an annual payment of £10,000 for ten years. This rare and important collection of works is to be made available to the Royal Court Theatre and other bodies for research and exhibition purposes.
- Ex-Governor Joan Sutro donates her collection of first night programmes. She retires from the Board, and is appointed Emeritus Fellow in recognition of her long and loyal service to the School.

1998
- Central hosts NUS Conference.
- Friends of the British Theatre donate £750 to final Showcase and £250 to Student Hardship fund.

1999
- Brian Goodban replaces Laurence Harbottle as Chairman of the Board.

2000
- Central hosts an international symposium, 'The Artist in the Community', which draws representatives from 16 countries.
- Central launches the International Centre for Voice (ICV), and in association with the NCDT, holds its first conference at Central: 'Voice in British Actor Training – The Moment of Speech'.

17
2000–2006

GARY CROSSLEY was born in Portsmouth in 1946. After attending Portsmouth Grammar School on a scholarship, he studied sculpture and painting at Portsmouth Art College and completed postgraduate studies in film and new media at Hornsey College of Art. He exhibited at the ICA, the Young Contemporaries, the Milan Triennale and ICOGRADA, provided work for BBC Horizon and CBS news, and collaborated with the conceptual architecture group Archigram. Along with experience in theatre design, interior design and film-making, Crossley taught in a variety of art schools before committing to a full-time post at East Ham College of Technology in London and becoming, at 28, one of the youngest Heads of Department in the UK. In 1985, Crossley became Vice Principal of the West Surrey College of Art and Design at Farnham, a position he held throughout the changes brought about by the 1988 Education Reform Act. He remembers those years as a time of shift among senior staff 'away from practitioner scholars to corporate managers – producing variously resentment as well as excitement'.

In the last decade of the 20th century, Central had made its grand leap into Higher Education, but when Crossley became Principal in 2000, the School was still a small and vulnerable institution. Funding had increased with enrolment, and money had been allocated for new buildings, but having endured a decade of under-funding that was specific to colleges providing practical training and particular to those providing training for the professional theatre, Central's financial health was still far from robust. When in 1998 the Department for Education and Employment published funding figures for the 29 drama schools, it was revealed that the four HEFCE-funded institutions received less public resource per student than the private schools. After further investigations, in 2000 HEFCE began to award 'premium' funding for Central students, which is a 60% premium on top of the basic funding. Nevertheless, as some other institutions receive twice that amount, there is still a long way to go before Central achieves parity.

In the 1990s, all small Higher Education colleges had faced the same difficulties: fixed overheads, increased accountability, restricted full-time staffing levels, and governmental insistence on 'efficiency gains'. In spite of these obstacles, under strict financial management Central had cleared a large accumulated deficit by July 2000, and accounts even showed a surplus. However, it was obvious that this was merely a hiatus in Central's ongoing financial struggle. Crossley encouraged the Governors to draw up a stringent fiscal plan for the future, and he put restrictions on staff costs as well as limits on borrowing. To give a more accurate picture of the School's continuing financial health, 'carry forward' balances were no longer allowed in Central's financial accounting and, in future, surpluses would be placed in a reserve fund and not used to prop up future deficits.

In addition, a Remuneration Committee was formed to appoint, grade, suspend, dismiss and determine pay and conditions for senior positions within the School. The Committee's powers were limited, but its key responsibility was to ensure pay levels for senior post-holders, while remaining fair, would also giving due regard to public expenditure probity and the financial health of the School.

> **TIMES HIGHER EDUCATIONAL SUPPLEMENT PRINCIPALS' SALARIES**
>
> The *Times Higher Educational Supplement* reported that, not including pension contributions, for the following years the Principal of Central received:
>
> | | |
> |---|---|
> | 1993/94 | £80,000 |
> | 1994/95 | £95,000 |
> | 1995/96 | £98,000 |
> | 1996/97 | £101,000 |
> | 1997/98 | £108,000 |
> | 1998/99 | £117,000 |
> | 1999/2000 | £131,000 |
> | 2000/01 | £87,600 (Gary Crossley) |
> | 2002/03 | £108,000 |

• • •

At a fork in Central's history, the School took an unpopular route towards Higher Education. Intervening years have shown that the ultimate destination was perhaps inevitable, and most other drama schools now struggle with some of the same problems Central addressed a decade ago. In fact, the Conference of Drama Schools has recently established a Research Forum to help them on this journey. Nevertheless, when Crossley took over as Principal he became heir to a number of negative perceptions that had built up over many years of change: 'One of the first things I saw when I arrived was that everyone here at Central had received a real bashing, and there was a lack of self-belief. Central was suffering from the briefing against the School that had preoccupied much of the profession for more than a decade. As an example: "Is it right that you no longer teach RP [Received Pronunciation] on the Acting Course?" – Of course we do. Or: "Voice training is now a disaster at Central." – There are competitions out there, and often enough we still win them. We are as successful as the trajectory of our alumni, and we are at least as successful as anybody else, and in most cases more successful. As part of the public sector, we are included in League Tables, and Central comes at the top of the League Tables for employment for all of our students. The so-called evidence against us just doesn't stack up.'

2000 George W Bush declared winner of American presidency by 537 votes

2001 Map of the human genome completed

11 September: Al Qaida terrorist attacks on USA

Chechen rebels take 763 hostages in Moscow theatre

2003 Columbia Space Shuttle explodes, killing all seven astronauts

2004 Yasser Arafat dies in Paris

2005 7 July: Four bombs explode in London during morning rush hour

With a new Principal, Central's focus was on the future. It was the beginning of a new century, and the major challenge facing the School was how best to take advantage of the opportunities being presented to Higher Education Institutions. As Crossley wrote later, 'Central was in position. All it needed was a shove in the right direction.'

The Government's 1992 Further Education Act had pressed small colleges to merge, to form 'strategic alliances' or to become independent by achieving their own Taught Degree-Awarding Powers (T-DAPs). For Central to achieve the latter, it had to prove it was capable of taking full academic responsibility for both its courses and its students. The School would have to show that its organisational structure was able to sustain standards over time and guarantee quality for all courses, both old and new – and no matter what Principal was in power. Lines of accountability would have to assure responsible care for students on any course, should that course undergo changes to its qualification or its provision. In addition, frameworks needed to be put in place to support any course closure that might become necessary.

With Crossley's arrival, the move towards achieving these goals began in earnest. During his first two years as Principal, he wrote Central's first 'Corporate Strategy' document, which formally laid down a plan for the future and, most visibly, included a reorganisation of the School's academic structure and its administrative composition. In 2002, separate academic departments were abolished, and for the first time since the Speech Therapy Department was created in 1945, all of Central's courses were again configured as an institutional whole, divided simply into undergraduate and postgraduate.

In 1994, Ross Brown had joined Central as a Lecturer in Sound Design and Music for Performance, bringing to his students not only his practical skills, expertise and professional experience as a sound designer and composer, but also his intellectual understanding of both research and experimentation. Brown had trained for a year at West Surrey College of Art and Design, and received a BA (Hons) in Fine Art from Newcastle University. After eight years at Central as a lecturer, within the new structure, he was appointed Head of Undergraduate Studies.

Andrew Lavender had gained a BA (Hons) from Nottingham University and a PhD from Goldsmiths College. He had become Course Leader on the MA Advanced Theatre Practice in 2000. In 2002, he was designated Head of Postgraduate Studies.

Both Brown and Lavender reported to the new senior appointment, Director of Programmes, Simon Shepherd. Shepherd had received a BA, MA and MLitt from

VOICE CARE NETWORK

'The Teacher's Voice, Essential Part of the Personality', *Times*, 8 January 1938, reported an address by Gwynneth Thurburn to the Association of Teachers of Speech and Drama:

Miss Thurburn said teachers had to use their voices for long periods on end, and most classrooms were over-resonant; the teacher usually obeyed his natural instinct to 'speak up', and the louder he spoke the more noise and the less effect he made, until in the end he shouted himself hoarse. The necessity for continuing to use the voice after the first signs of fatigue were apparent and might produce some kind of muscular tension, so often the forerunner of loss of voice. If the teacher's personality was to have the fullest response his voice must be unhampered by tension of any kind. To attain this end the voice should be separately trained and considered an instrument of sound.

In 2006, Caroline Cornish (Teacher '53) wrote of The Voice Care Network:

The Voice Care Network grew over concern for the vocal health of classroom teachers, a disproportionate number of whom were seeking help in Voice Clinics. Discussing this in the early '90s, Roz Comins (nee Dorey, Central '44–7) had a brainwave – create a network of Voice teachers and Speech and Language therapists to share expertise and work together to address this situation. From the drawing board (aka the Comins' kitchen table) to its present status, the organisation has come a long way.

Officially launched in 1993 and becoming a registered charity in 1998, the VCN now has a membership of 260 teachers and therapists, in equal numbers. Over 100 of them are designated VCN tutors who deliver workshops in schools, colleges, universities and to other groups of professional voice-users. VCN publishes resource material, lobbies the government for better provision of voice training for teachers and has currently initiated The Year of the Teacher's Voice, conceived by member Lesley Hendy – trained at Central naturally!

With Cicely Berry as our Patron, the Network is becoming a powerful voice in the land. Roz has worked tirelessly for the past 13 years together with her wonderfully supportive husband, David; and she has turned her brainwave into a thriving reality. It is a remarkable achievement and one of which Central can be very proud.

Oxford and a PhD from Nottingham University. He had been Professor of Drama both at Nottingham University and Goldsmiths College, where he also had held the position as Head of Department for three years. Credited with many books, both as author and co-author, he has also written a number of essays and had numerous reviews and articles published in *New Theatre Quarterly, Modern Language Review, Renaissance Studies, Renaissance Quarterly, Journal of Gender Studies* and *Theatre Research International*. Ross, Lavender and Shepherd brought professional and practical talents, as well as academic experience and intellectual abilities to their new posts.

The university-like structure encouraged interaction between courses and across subjects, but also required a number of changes. With three highly qualified and capable new leaders in place, Central began its reorganisation. Academic planning and budgeting were redefined. Staff responsibilities were clarified regarding accountability and decision-making. Clear guidelines were set down to handle either the creation or the closure of any course, including the special care necessary for continuing students.

Central management was also restructured, and a more streamlined administration was put in place to address the burdensome proliferation of bureaucracy produced by the 1988 move into Higher Education. Three distinct lines of responsibility were created: Resources and Planning; Quality; and Programmes. Under this system, the Principal is the Chief Executive Officer of the entire institution. The Deputy Principal is in charge of Corporate Services' staff. The Director of Quality is in charge of Academic Support and Quality staff. As noted above, the Director of Programmes manages the Heads of Undergraduate Studies and Postgraduate Studies, academic staff and, from 2005, the Head of the Centre for Excellence in Teaching and Learning (CETL).

With its new academic and administrative structures in place, in July 2002 Central submitted its application for Taught Degree-Awarding Powers (T-DAPs) to the QAA. The application was quickly judged as one of a very few ready to progress directly to the next stage, and in October of the same year assessors appointed by the QAA began to visit Central to observe a range of meetings and activities. Between October 2002 and June 2003, assessors spent 14 days at the School. In addition to accessing 113 main files and over 1000 documents, they attended or presided over 47 meetings. They met 45 students, 60 members of staff and 19 visiting lecturers, as well as 16 Governors, eight employers, three external examiners and four external validation panel members. By June 2003, the panel's examination of the School was complete, and in April 2004 a panel from the QAA Committee made a final day-long visit that included more meetings with students, staff and Governors. Finally, in August 2004, management received formal notification from the Queen's Privy Council that from 1 September of that year the Central School of Speech and Drama would have undergraduate and postgraduate Taught Degree-Awarding Powers – external recognition of the quality of education provided at Central, and a first for any drama school in England. Central would no longer be dependent on outside validation of its courses. It had finally gained a solid base for an independent future.

One would assume Central would rest, at least for a while, to relish this achievement; but while management and staff were seeking T-DAPs, they were also in negotiations to become a federal member of the University of London. Again, the application was a success, and after more negotiations, meetings and consultations, Central was notified in May 2005 that from September it would become a member college – and eligible to award University of London degrees to all its graduates. Governors and staff were delighted. Although this meant that Central's hard-won degree awarding powers would not be exercised, T-DAPs are permanent and can be invoked at any time. In addition, the School's acquisition of these powers had been a major factor in convincing the University of Central's worthiness to become a member college. In 1921, Elsie Fogerty had applied to the University of London for affiliated status and been turned down. The wheel had come full circle.

Membership in the University of London in no way infringes on Central's autonomy, yet it entitles the School to participate in the University as an equal of such eminent institutions as UCL, King's, the London School of Economics, the Courtauld Institute, the School for Oriental and African Studies, the Royal Academy of Music and the Slade School of Art. Central is the first, and therefore probably the only, drama school member. As well as benefiting from the material advantages to the School in terms of shared administration and marketing, Central students now have access to the University's library, student residences and Student Union. Perhaps most importantly, as Crossley said: 'It provides a platform for us to work internationally, and it widens our connections within a research university.'

To aid and support Central's research trajectory, the School's designation in 2005 as a national Centre for Excellence in Teaching and Learning is invaluable.

CADISE

The Consortium of Arts and Design Institutions in Southern England (CADISE) was formed late in 1998 to create a voice for providers of specialist arts education. Members were all Higher Education Institutes in the South of England, and CADISE included: The Arts Institute at Bournemouth, The Central School of Speech and Drama, the Kent Institute of Art and Design, Ravensbourne College of Design and Communication, Rose Bruford College, The Surrey Institute of Art & Design University College, Trinity College of Music, and Wimbledon School of Art.

In 2000, Central led a HEFCE-funded project to explore the assessment of student group performances, with the aim of making assessments clearer and identifying all elements of performance: preparation, individual and team contribution, and post-performance critique. The study's findings were shared with fellow members of CADISE.

This successful alliance was eventually wound down in 2005, having achieved its key objectives.

• • •

Centres for Excellence in Teaching and Learning (CETLs) were first introduced in the 2003 White Paper, 'The Future of Higher Education'. This White Paper announced that there would be little new money available for 'teaching and learning', with most funds earmarked for selective research. To reward excellence in Teaching and Learning, Centres for Excellence would be created as individual subject focal points.

In anticipation of the resulting 2004 Act, Director of Quality Linda Cookson and the Academic Board began work on an application for the School to be named one of only 70 Centres for Excellence in the country. Central was one of a very few non-university bids and the only 'whole-institution' bid, and its application focused not only on the School's successful interaction with industry and vocational partners, but also on the quality of Central students' experience and their preparedness for work in a wide range of professional theatre settings. Cookson had worked closely with the Principal to secure success with both T-DAPs and membership of the University of London. Now the School waited to find out if she and Crossley could make it a hat-trick. They did, and in January 2005, Central was named the Centre for Excellence in Training for Theatre (CETT).

From 2005 to 2010, CETT work will focus on research, consultancy, training, performing, and innovation in all areas of theatre and theatre education, making it a 'national resource' in Higher Education vocational learning and training, as well as a forum for both HE institutions and professionals in the industry. Besides a grant of £4.5 million over five years, HEFCE awarded the School another £509,000 for building works and the purchase of additional equipment. This support has created both a new laboratory for multi-media performance and an object theatre laboratory. Existing music room facilities have been upgraded for sound recording and editing, and technical facilities for sound, lighting and digital media have been improved. Existing spaces have been refurbished, and the Design Studio has been altered to encompass interdisciplinary collaboration. CETT money will also fund research secondments for Central staff, as well as allowing staff from other institutes to spend time at Central. In 2006, Sophie Nield was appointed Head of the Centre. Having received a PhD from the University of Manchester, prior to her appointment to CETT, she held lectureships at the Universities of Roehampton and Glamorgan, and at Goldsmiths College, University of London. Her personal research encompasses space and theatricality; cultural theory and performance; theatrical 'magic' and stage-technology.

Elsie Fogerty had recognised co-operation and communication among experts and disciplines as vitally important for the advancement of any field, and to this end had organised national and international conferences to bring experts from both within and without these fields. CETT, too, will sponsor international conferences and research – as a means of sharing and disseminating ideas, innovations and scholarship. Students will directly benefit not only from Central's outstanding full-time staff, but also from its ability to attract a wide range of visiting professional practitioners from all areas of the theatre.

In less than a year, Central gained Taught Degree-Awarding Powers, became a constituent College of the University of London, and was designated as the Centre for Excellence in Training for Theatre. This external recognition, in triplicate, was an extraordinary achievement. Even more remarkable, perhaps, is that Central also has become financially solvent for one of the rare periods in its history. In spite of all this good news for Central, and while the School thrives, its students – like most other students in Higher Education – face mounting debt.

• • •

The fiscal brass ring seems always to have been just out of reach for drama students. The 1944 Education Act had established the idea of free education for everyone, but even though government grants were mandatory for most students, they remained discretionary for those training for the professional theatre. Just as acting courses began to earn mandatory awards for their students by becoming degrees, some students were asked to pay 'enhancement fees' to cover the difference between government funding and the actual cost of their course. Then the 1998 Higher Education Act made all HE students liable for a proportion of their tuition fees, and to add insult to injury, in 1999, student maintenance grants – awards for living expenses, with no expectation of repayment – were replaced by low interest student maintenance loans, with instalment repayments due once a graduate's income reached £10,000. The 2004 Higher Education Act allowed colleges and universities to increase 'top-up' fees to as much as £3000. Postgraduate drama students still had no entitlement to government help with their fees.

The 2004 Act was intended to encourage a greater number of young people to attend university – students from lower income families should now be better able to afford a university education should they so desire one – but no one knows what impact this will have on students from middle-income families. It also sets new problems specific to those students whose choice of subject means their future income will be uncertain. The prospect of owing a large sum of money upon graduation from a drama course could deter potential students who may be looking at a number of no- or low-income post-graduation years. To attract students, drama schools may again have to look for a market-driven solution and alter their course provision so that it promises more secure prospects. The future is uncertain, but higher fees always have an effect on students' lives.

In February 2004, the Central Student Union was active in the national demonstration against 'top-up' tuition fees. An article in the local *Ham & High* newspaper reported on a protest outside the Embassy Theatre, and Student Union President Alastair Laverty was quoted: 'We are dressing up as the living dead to show the government what students will look like in 2006 if they introduce top-up fees to this institution... Student life in London is extremely expensive. By introducing top-up fees, students will either look like the living dead or universities will only attract students who can afford their education.' Just so there were no hard feelings, the Central Student Union sent a letter to the management after the *Ham & High* article to clarify that students were 'at loggerheads with the Government... We are NOT at loggerheads with staff or management at the CSSD.'

As a generous counterpoint to the government's tightened purse strings, over the years Central alumni and friends of the theatre have donated funds, bursaries and scholarships for students in need of financial help. Besides the Student Hardship Fund, a number of other awards have been created for students in need: the Jane Cowell Memorial, the Gary Bond Memorial, the Clive Brook Memorial, the Syvia Strutt and Hilda Brettel Memorial, the Diana Wade Memorial Award and the Milner Bursary. All provide temporary financial aid for needy students, but they go only a small way towards providing the necessary ongoing support for today's students, and many more will need financial assistance in the future.

All the same, no matter how impoverished students at Central have been or how much worse their penury may become, they always have and always will find a room or a flat or a garden for a party. (After one such event, the portrait of Elsie Fogerty spent a night in a nearby living room – no doubt enjoying the attention lavished upon her by two handsome, and hungover, young actors.) For over half a century, the Central Student Union has organised student mixers, parties, dances, Summer Balls, Winter Balls, Fresher Balls and Fairs, cabarets, speeches and workshops. In the last few years it has become more active in other areas as well. Students have developed their own website and introduced a range of merchandising. They have negotiated special discounts for Central students, celebrated Black History month, established a Theatre Practitioners Forum, and inaugurated Student Union charity events. In a return to Fogerty's admonishment to always work for a good cause, the Student Union has raised money for Red Nose Day, Breast Cancer Awareness and Children in Need – and, oh yes, it negotiated the daytime use of the student bar facility.

• • •

In the 1990s, there had been extensive building, expansion and renovation of Central's facilities, but by the turn of the century, the Embassy Theatre was no longer able to survive on mere repairs. In 2000–01, in line with Phase Three of the Building Strategy, it was fully refurbished. An Atrium link was created between the Embassy and the new library, disabled access was added, and the 228-seat Embassy Theatre officially re-opened in April 2002 with a Gala Evening. Third-year actors and postgraduate musical theatre students presented a production of Sondheim's *Sweeney Todd* that took full advantage of the new stage, fly-tower, lighting and sound system, under-stage access and orchestra pit. With this refurbished theatre, production values of third-year shows continue to grow.

In 2002, the balance remaining from Embassy refurbishment was used to renovate the foyer and to refurbish the theatre façade. Controversially, this work included the carving of alumni names into the front steps. With Central students facing economic hardship and course provision constantly under budgetary constraints, there were murmurs that surplus funds should not have been spent on what some considered a distasteful elitism. Responses to this criticism are twofold. First, as has been the case with all governmental capital grants, the funding could only be used for what it had been awarded – in this case, improvements to the Embassy Theatre – and could not legally have been diverted elsewhere. Secondly, and more germane to Crossley's decision, the Principal had consciously chosen to promote unashamedly the names of Central's graduates, and thereby their School: 'When I came to Central, I knew one of my first tasks was to get the Funding Council to understand who we were. HEFCE thought Central was a former teacher-training college struggling around in the world of drama. I thought, "What we have to do is get some faith and arrogance back into the school. We have to be proud of its graduates, let everyone know how big a name Central is." You've got to recognise that people who are not part of the industry won't know who our famous alumni are unless we tell them.'

• • •

Shortly after the Embassy Gala, Central gained outline planning permission from Camden for Phase Four of its Building Project: mixed development of the 'Bank Site'. An original proposal had called for the inclusion of storefronts and residential flats, but later

HONORARY FELLOWS AND HONORARY PHDS

At the graduation ceremony in 2001, Central's first Honorary Fellowship was awarded to George Hall for 'outstanding achievements in the training of a generation of actors'. Since then, Fellowships have also been awarded to Jocelyn Herbert, Diana Cooper, Nickolas Grace, Declan Donnellan, Richard Schechner, Yvonne Brewster and Jude Kelly. Cicely Berry, OBE and former Governor, Sir Ken Robinson, have received Honorary Doctorates of the Open University.

West Block plans were amended in favour of a glass and zinc building to house rehearsal rooms, workshops and performance spaces. The new educational building would be four storeys high internally but, taking into account the height of the rooms, Camden classified it as seven storeys externally. It was given final planning permission in January 2004, and construction began in April of that year.

Unsurprisingly for any large building works, and de rigueur it seems for Central, the £6.26 million construction project suffered a number of obstacles, ranging from (predictably) bad weather to (unpredictably) hidden underground gas pipes. Anticipated completion for August 2005 was delayed and delayed again, but though late for the start of the autumn term, the West Block finally opened for classes in October 2005. First outlined when Central became a Higher Education Institution in 1989, the Four Phase Building Strategy was finally complete. The annexe at the Oval, leased in 2000 to replace the St Pancras site, was finally relinquished in January 2006, and all Central students were finally brought together at Swiss Cottage.

As a result of this Building Strategy, Central's accommodation and facilities are now second to none. Performance and rehearsal facilities include not only the refurbished Embassy Theatre and the Embassy Studio, but also a New Studio with sprung floor, bleacher seating, a control box and fixed lighting grid. Studio One West has fixed lighting and moveable seating, and Studio Two West is a small black box suitable for installations and puppetry. There are also two large movement studios with sprung floors, as well as one large, three medium, and three small spaces for rehearsals, performances or lectures. However, this is not the end of Central's development, and there are plans for another building in the future – to house both another new studio and a café theatre.

• • •

Throughout all of the building work and its accompanying disruptions, the quality of Central's courses has remained exceptionally high. In 2000–01, the last of Central's three Quality Assurance Agency Subject Review visits took place, with the Subject Review Panel for Education awarding the School a score of 23 out of 24. With Art and Design previously having received a 24, and with Performance having received a 23, Central's aggregate Review score was 23.3, the highest in the sector for an institution being assessed in more than one discipline.

Since Crossley became Principal in 2000, the curriculum at Central has not grown and changed at the same frantic pace as in the 1990s, but neither has it remained static. In 2001, there were some changes to the MA Advanced Theatre Practice, and in 2002, the Acting BA was validated as an Honours degree. In the same year, Central's solitary Foundation Course, the BTEC Foundation Studies in Art and Design, was recognised as out-of-step with the School's Higher Education mission, and was, therefore, brought to a close. In October 2003, with only 20% of its graduates working in the traditional field of teaching, the BA (Hons) Drama and Education course was renamed the BA (Hons) Drama, Applied Theatre and Education and restructured to address changing employment requirements. Also in 2003, The Circus Space gave notice of its intention to withdraw from Central. In a move away from degree requirements, it wanted to refocus its course on physical training and, after five years of collaboration, from 1 August 2004 Central and The Circus Space no longer offered a BA (Hons) Theatre Practice (Circus). The Circus Space is now a constituent College of the Conservatoire for Dance and Drama.

During 2003–4, Central continued to expand its postgraduate courses, offering new MAs in Classical Acting, Movement Studies (for actor movement education), Acting Musical Theatre, Drama in the Community & Drama Education, Theatre Studies (Theatre in London), and Performance Practices and Research. Validation for MAs in Actor Training and Coaching, Acting for Screen, and Writing for Stage and Broadcast Media followed in 2004–5. PGCEs, in both Drama and Media Studies, as well as Postgraduate Certificates in Directing Text with Young People and in Learning and Teaching in Higher Education, are also part of what has now become the largest postgraduate school of drama in Europe.

Alongside full-time undergraduate and postgraduate programmes, Central's current curriculum also encompasses a wide range of short courses, bespoke courses for businesses and individuals, weekend workshops and summer schools. STEP-UP became known as Continuing Education and offered a wide range of part-time courses in Physical Theatre, Clowning, Life Drawing, Puppetry, Writing, Design and Theatre Crafts. In 2000, it developed Short Business Courses for Equity. Continuing Education is now known as the School of Professional and Community Development, and offers an even wider variety of short courses in: Combat and Stage Fighting, Masks, Devising, Musical Theatre, Historical

Dance, Singing, Acting, Text, Movement, Scenes, Dialects, Shakespeare and, of course, Voice.

In 2001, as part of a HEFCE programme for gifted young people, Central also presented its first 21st century summer school. For one week, forty 16- and 17-year-olds, and for two weeks, sixty 11-year-olds, are offered voice, text, speech, and stage fighting workshops. This ongoing programme completed its fifth summer school in 2005, having attracted 120 students.

Budgetary restrictions still dictate staffing constraints, but in a reinstitution of the practice initiated in the 'old days', increasingly staff teach across a range of both undergraduate and postgraduate courses. A majority of the School's courses remain vocational and professional,

CONSERVATOIRE FOR DANCE AND DRAMA

The Conservatoire of Dance and Drama is a Higher Education federation of: the Royal Academy of Dramatic Art, the London School of Contemporary Dance, Central School of Ballet, Rambert School of Ballet and Contemporary Dance, Northern School of Contemporary Dance (the Dance and Drama Conservatoire), the Bristol Old Vic School, London Academy of Music and Dramatic Art and The Circus Space.

continuing to provide students with experiences of contemporary professional practices in all areas of theatre, Central maintains a high number of visiting professional staff to the undergraduate, postgraduate, short and part-time courses.

• • •

Course offerings at Central have expanded beyond anything Fogerty could have envisaged in 1906, and there has been great concern during the last two decades – both within and without – that Central might have forgotten its roots. Crossley recalls his first meeting with staff: 'My opening statement was, "Right at the heart of this institution is Acting. You'll see me polishing Elsie Fogerty's picture, and you'll see evidence that we need to make sure that we are first and foremost an acting school and everything else comes out of that. That doesn't mean everything else is not of value – it is of immense value – but acting is the soul of the School, and we've got to build on that idea."'

In spite of the sentiment, during the early years of Crossley's tenure any efforts towards its becoming the 'first and foremost' were hampered by an increase in enrolment on the Acting Course. Nevertheless, the will was there. In an affirmation of the course's centrality, the BA (Hons) Acting was revalidated in 2004–5 to allow for expansion, and although this seems like a dichotomy, the creation of two new and separate pathways within the Acting Course – Musical Theatre and Collaborative and Devised Theatre – has meant a *decrease* in numbers to the traditional route: Acting for Stage. The BA (Hons) Acting now accepts 60 students each year. Thirty students are equally split between the two new strands, and the remaining 30 students make up Acting for Stage – one of the smallest professional acting courses in England. These two new strands to the course offer more

CENTRAL ENROLMENT
2000–06

2000–01	586
2001–02	623
2002–03	662
2003–04	715
2004–05	723
2005–06	870

than just a reduction of student numbers on the traditional pathway. According to Head of Acting, Geoffrey Colman: 'The changes directly address the fact that the acting paradigms of the conservatoire have done little to engage the recent changing stylistic modes of the playwright and performer. Young actors are predominantly conditioned by old performance methods and ideologies. Traditionally, the dominant consideration of the actor in training is how to achieve (exclusively) a seamless psychological pretence. Training actors for the industry has long been about teaching a form of cultural/political passivity – the traditional commercial hierarchies offer little time for questioning beyond that of the rehearsal context. I believe that the current course addresses this anomaly.'

Colman has been Head of the Acting Course since 1998, coming to the job from both the professional and the academic world. In 2006, he wrote: 'The training we offer hasn't fundamentally changed, but there are undoubtedly changes that might seem, on a cursory glance, quite significant. Clearly the move to Honours a few years ago was a significant milestone in the history of the course. However, I so firmly believe that acting is an Honours-worthy discipline. The constant drip feed question from many alumni has been "but do they write essays? – actors don't write essays". The course does have written elements in it – but these are relevant and appropriate. Character studies, vocal profiling, phonetics, professional development planning all require a pen or laptop, but the rehearsal room and practical classroom are still the dominant modes of teaching on the course. In addition to the Honours validation, I think that the key changes might lay in the sense of the actor being much more a pluralistic practitioner in a diverse performance field. Students are exposed to a vast portfolio of practitioners and theories – there is no dogma or creed.'

In spite of changes to the course, the traditional Acting for Stage pathway has a structure recognisable to anyone who trained under George Hall. The first year includes plays and extracts focusing on character development, with a final term devoted to a Shakespeare comedy. The second year begins with an American realist play, goes on to Restoration and ends with a Greek tragedy (different from the old training) and a Shakespearean tragedy. The biggest change seems to be in the choice of plays for the third-year public shows, with an emphasis on new writing and living playwrights. In the first term of the third year, there is a training course for television, and in the second term training for radio. Both media courses were previously taught in the second half of the second year. As was the case traditionally, however, training is scaled down in the last term of the third year, and students may only be required for rehearsals and performances.

Central still plays an active role in helping its actors find agents. The Agents' Showcase attracts approximately 180 agents, and over the five performances of each of the public shows, twenty to twenty-five agents will attend. Between 75 and 90 percent of actors will have agents by the time they leave and almost all will have had their first job by the winter after they have graduated. Perhaps the biggest difference in employment is that over 85% of first jobs are now in television.

Even though the three strands on the Acting Course remain separate but equal, there is a significant organisational challenge to provide third-year students' showcases for a much larger number of students on three separate degree pathways. To address this problem, outside theatres and the new performance spaces in the West Block will be utilised.

• • •

CENTENARY EVENT

In 2006, Central's Centenary Celebration was held at the Old Vic Theatre. Organised by Chairman of the Alumni Committee, Nickolas Grace, and hosted by Central graduates Lynda Bellingham (Stage '69) and Graham Norton (Stage '89), the show featured contributions by a host of graduates and staff from all courses, both past and present. Contributors included: Jae Alexander, Jay Benedict, Cicely Berry, Michael Chance, Wendy Craig, Amanda Donohoe, Helen Dorward, Martyn Ellis, Serena Evans, Jerome Flynn, Tanveer Ghani, Nickolas Grace, Lionel Guyett, George Hall, Carol Harvey, Elaine Hodkinson, Wayne Jackman, Sara Kestelman, Cheri Lunghi, James Nesbitt, Neil Pearson, Adam Price, Jennifer Saunders, Rufus Sewell, Sukie Smith, Neil Stuke, Lolly Susi, Catherine Tate, Harriet Thorpe, Hilary Tones and Emma Watson.

In addition to the two new pathways on the Acting Course, for two years – starting in 2005 – Central is also training a group of students who spent the first year of their training at Webber Douglas Academy of Dramatic Art.

Central's initial move towards negotiations with Webber Douglas Academy was both selfish – an immediate gain of sixty funded student 'numbers' from HEFCE – and altruistic: Central could help in the winding down of one of England's oldest and most respected drama schools.

Webber Douglas Academy of Dramatic Art was originally founded in Paris in 1906 by the world famous Polish operatic tenor, Jean de Reszke. De Reszke began teaching in Paris in 1902, and after his retirement from the stage in 1904, focused his talents on a growing number of students, officially opening his School two years later. After De Reszke's death in 1925, Amherst Webber and Walter Johnstone Douglas brought De Reszke's School to London, where it became known as the Webber Douglas School of Singing and Dramatic Art. In 1965, Raphael Jago was appointed Principal, bringing both a new name – the Webber Douglas Academy of Dramatic Art – and a modern approach to the training. Webber Douglas has produced a legion of fine actors over the years, including some of its most famous graduates: Dulcie Gray CBE, Angela Lansbury, Terence Stamp, Sue Johnston,

Anita Dobson, Hugh Bonneville, Julia Ormond and Minnie Driver. Alumni Antony Sher and Donald Sinden have both been knighted for their services to the theatre, and Julian Fellowes was awarded an Oscar for his screenplay of *Gosford Park*.

Central's connection to Webber Douglas began in 2003 when the Dance and Drama Awards (DADA) scheme for students in colleges of Further Education was discontinued. To maintain funding for their students, many private drama schools, including Webber Douglas, had to explore academic collaboration, relationships, or mergers with Higher Education Institutions. This coincided with the impending retirement of Principal Raphael Jago, and meetings were initiated between Central and Webber Douglas Academy of Dramatic Art to discuss how best to provide ongoing course content for continuing Webber Douglas students without interrupting their training. Initially a possible merger was considered, but this was soon seen as unworkable. Instead, in autumn 2005, Webber Douglas students were transferred to continue their training under the auspices of Central. Upon graduation, successful graduates will receive Central's University of London BA (Hons) in Acting. In return, Central has secured additional HEFCE-funded student places, which will be retained after the Webber Douglas students graduate.

· · ·

Central is the brainchild of Elsie Fogerty, a gifted and dedicated teacher who for years kept her little School alive solely by her sacrifice, her generosity and her extraordinary ability to enthuse others with her dream. As Central 'grew up', her School experienced both gradual and (occasionally) catastrophic changes, but it also produced thousands of graduates whose abilities, talents, curiosity and commitment regularly placed them at the forefront of their chosen fields. Central's history may have been peppered with near-death experiences, alterations and altercations but this has always been balanced by the dedication of the School's Governors, its staff and students. It is due to them that Fogerty's Central School, started in one room at the Royal Albert Hall a hundred years ago, has now achieved an international reputation for outstanding academic and practical training in all areas of drama and the professional theatre. It has been an extraordinary 100 years, and there is more to come. As Gary Crossley says: 'We now have a future that is certain. – And for the first time we don't have to worry about turning off the lights.'

· · ·

ADDITIONAL CENTRAL FACTS

2000 • Three Shakespeare Master classes recorded for Radio Three, with group leaders Cicely Berry, Fiona Shaw and Mike Alfreds.

2001 • Peter Mandelson becomes President of Central, filling a position vacant since Dame Judi Dench's resignation in 1997.

• International Centre for Voice hosts a week of workshops on Roy Hart Theatre.

2002 • The Central catering contract is awarded to H & S Catering.

2003 • Eton Avenue is designated for street-trading purposes.

• Margaret McCully, long time administrator to the Stage Course, receives an MBE for her service to Central and its students.

2005 • Brian Goodban comes to the end of his Chairmanship and retires from the Board after his allowed two three-year terms.

• Paul Taiano is elected Chairman of the Board of Governors.

• Simon Quy, Course Leader of PGCE and PGCert Learning and Teaching in Higher Education, is awarded a 'Rising Star' National Teaching Fellowship by the Higher Education Academy.

SELECT BIBLIOGRAPHY

Albert Hall Prospectus (1901)

Altick, Richard D, *The Shows of London* (Harvard Press, 1978)

Banham, Martin, *The Cambridge Guide to Theatre* (Cambridge University Press, 1995)

Beaton, Cecil, *It Gives Me Great Pleasure* (London, Weidenfeld and Nicolson, 1955)

Billington, Michael, *Peggy Ashcroft* (John Murray Ltd., 1988)

Burnie, Colin, *The Riverside Players*, 2001

Chronicle of the 20th Century (London, Chronicle Communications, 1988)

Cole, Marion, *Fogie, The Life of Elsie Fogerty, CBE* (London, Peter Davis, 1967)

Coleman, Terry, *Olivier: The Authorised Biography* (London, Bloomsbury, 2005)

Devlin, Anne, *A Speaking Part* (London, Hodder and Stoughton, 1982)

Encore, Central Student Magazine (March, 1954)

Fogerty, Elsie, *Rhythm* (London, George Allen and Unwin, 1937)

Fogerty, Elsie, *The Speaking of English Verse* (London, J M Dent, 1923)

Fogerty, Elsie, *Stammering* (New York, E P Dutton & Co, 1930)

Fogerty, Elsie, 'The History of Central', Programme for Twenty-first Birthday Matinée at Scala Theatre (1927)

Fogerty, Elsie, translation and introduction of Coquelin's *L'Art du Comedien* (*The Art of the Actor*) (George Allen and Unwin, Ltd, 1932)

Hibbert, Christopher, *The Illustrated London News, Social History of Victorian Britain* (Angus Robertson Publishers (UK) Ltd, in conjunction with Sphere Books, 1975)

Hume, Elizabeth, *A Laboratory Theatre, The History of the Embassy* (A Central School of Speech and Drama Publication, 2002)

Kiernan, Thomas, *Olivier, The Life of Laurence Olivier* (Sidgwick & Jackson, 1981)

Leon, Ruth and Morley, Sheridan, *A Century of Theatre* (London, Oberon Books Ltd, 2000)

Mann, William J, *Edge of Midnight: The Life of John Schlesinger* (Hutchinson, 2004)

McCall, Margaret, *My Drama School* (London, Robson Books, 1978)

McCarthy, Lillah, *Myself and My Friends* (Thornton Butterworth, Ltd, 1933)

Mirodan, Vladimir, 'The Way of Transformation (The Laban-Malmgren System of Character Analysis)', PhD Thesis, London University, 1997.

O'Connor, Gary (ed) *Olivier, In Celebration* (Hodder and Stoughton, 1987)

BIBLIOGRAPHY 241

Olivier, Laurence, *Confessions of an Actor* (George Weidenfeld and Nicolson Ltd, 1982)

Powell, Kerry (ed) *The Cambridge Companion to Victorian and Edwardian Theatre* (Cambridge University Press, 2004)

Prompt, Magazine of Students' Association Committee of the Central School of Speech-Training and Dramatic Art (February 1949 and January 1950)

The Queen, 'The Spoken Word', 27 January 1954

Robertson, Sandra, Kershner, Myra & Davis, Shirley (eds) *A History of the College 1945–95* (Royal College of Speech and Language Therapists, 1995)

Saint-Denis, Michel *Training for the Theatre* (ed Suria Saint-Denis) (New York, Theatre Arts Books, Heinemann Educational Books, 1982)

Sanderson, Michael, *From Irving to Olivier* (London, The Athlone Press, University Press, Cambridge, 1984)

Seaman, L C B, *Life in Britain Between the Wars* (Norwich, Jarrold and Sons Ltd, 1970)

Selingo, Jeffrey, 'What College Presidents Think: Leaders' Views About Higher Education, Their Jobs, and Their Lives', *Chronicle of Higher Education*, 4 November 2005

Thurburn, Gwynneth, 'The Elsie Fogerty I Knew' (private papers, 1966)

Thurburn, Gwynneth, *Elsie Fogerty and Central* (1967)

Thurburn, Gwynneth, *Elsie Fogerty Memorial Lecture* (1978)

Thurburn, Gwynneth and Sargent, Vera, *History of Central* (1967)

Thurburn, Gwynneth, 'Training the Actor', *Theatre Today* (1947)

The Times, 'The Teacher's Voice, Essential Part of the Personality', 8 January 1938

The Times, Gwynneth Thurburn Obituary, 26 March 1993

Viva Voce, Pivot Magazine for the Central School of Speech-Training and Dramatic Art, 1914 to July 1948

Woman and Home, 'My Life with Many Voices', December 1958, January to May 1959

Woman's Illustrated, 'School for Stars', 8 August 1953

Extracts of Elsie Fogerty's writings are from her personal memoirs, the *Viva Voce* and *Fogie*.

INDEX